The Asante

The Asante

M. D. McLeod

Published for the Trustees of the British Museum
by British Museum Publications Ltd

British Library Cataloguing in Publication Data

McLeod, Malcolm D
  The Asante
  I. Ashantis
  I. Title
  966.7   DT507

ISBN 0-7141-1564-9 (cased)
ISBN 0-7141-1563-0 (limp)

© 1981 The Trustees of the British Museum

Reprinted 1984.
Published by British Museum Publications Ltd
46 Bloomsbury Street, London WC1B 3QQ

Designed by James Shurmer

Set in Monophoto Baskerville and printed in
Great Britain by Jolly & Barber Ltd, Rugby

Frontispiece: A senior Asante chief and his officers,
c. 1897.

Cover: The Akyempemhene of Kumase seated on
a *hwẹdom* chair with officials holding gold-handled
swords.

Contents

Preface

This book has been published to accompany and complement the exhibition 'Asante, Kingdom of Gold' held at the Museum of Mankind in 1981. It has been written for the general reader and attempts to show something of the complexity of Asante society and culture. Inevitably certain areas of Asante life cannot be examined in such a work: it has not been possible to discuss the elaborate and beautiful music of the Asante, nor their songs and poetry, in which some of their highest art is to be found. Attention has been confined to material culture and especially to the items used in political display in the last century. Then Asante power was at its greatest, and the Asante empire controlled most of the territory which is now the state of Ghana and in places extended beyond that modern state's boundaries. In recent years there has been an explosion of publications on the history and culture of the Asante, one of the most complex and fascinating of all African peoples, and the interested reader is urged to seek out some of the other publications listed in the bibliography at the end of this book, publications which cover in great detail subjects only touched upon here.

I should like to acknowledge the help I have received in writing this book and preparing the exhibition it accompanies. I am grateful to many Asante friends, too numerous to mention individually, for their kindness and hospitality, but especially to Bishop Peter Sarpong for first introducing me to his people, to Nana Wiafe Akenten, Omanhene of Offinso, in whose state I first lived, and to Paul Atta Asante who worked with me. I am also grateful to the late Dr A.A.Y. Kyerematen for all his help. Ivor Wilks, Edmund Collins, Tom McCaskie, Meyer Fortes, Marion Johnson and Doran Ross have freely shared their knowledge of Asante with me. The staff of the Foreign and Commonwealth Library have been most helpful in locating nineteenth-century photographs of Asante, Henry Brewer, Nigel Killey, Kate Janes and Neil Bicknell have patiently photographed items in the British Museum's collections, and Iris Walsh has tirelessly and impeccably typed and retyped from my manuscript. I should also like to express my gratitude to the Wenner-Gren Foundation, the Ankoh Foundation and the Emslie Horniman Fund for supporting my research in Ghana.

Note: Open 'o' and open 'e' sounds, roughly equivalent to the sounds in 'pot' and 'let', are indicated throughout by ϱ and e; n is sounded like 'ng' in 'sing'.

M.D. McLeod, Keeper of the Museum of Mankind
February 1981

A senior Asante official in 1884: the King's spokesman Boakye Tenten (seated right).

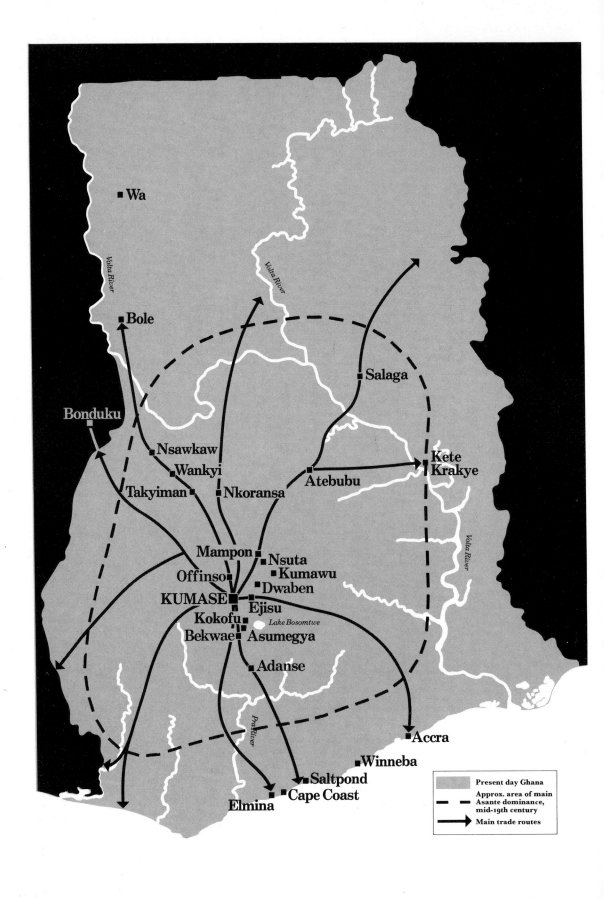

Wa

Volta River

Bole

Bonduku

Nsawkaw

Wankyi

Takyiman   Nkoransa

Salaga

Kete
Krakye

Atebubu

Mampon   Nsuta
                  Kumawu
Offinso   Dwaben
KUMASE   Ejisu
Kokofu   Lake Bosomtwe
Bekwae   Asumegya
              Adanse

Volta River

Prah River

Accra

Winneba

Saltpond
Cape Coast
Elmina

	Present day Ghana
	Approx. area of main Asante dominance, mid-19th century
	Main trade routes

1 Introduction: the Asante background

In May 1817 a group of Britons was making its slow way towards Kumase, the capital of the West African kingdom of Asante. As they entered the city they were immediately overwhelmed:

Our observations [had] taught us to conceive a spectacle exceeding our original expectations; but they had not prepared us for the extent and display of the scene which here burst upon us: an area nearly a mile in circumference was crowded with magnificence and novelty. . . . The sun was reflected, with a glare scarcely more supportable than the heat, from the massy gold ornaments, which glistened in every direction. More than a hundred bands burst at once on our arrival, with the peculiar airs of their several chiefs; . . . At least a hundred large umbrellas, or canopies, which could shelter thirty persons, were sprung up and down by the bearers with brilliant effect. The caboceers [chiefs] as did their superior captains and attendants, wore Ashantee cloths of extravagant price. . . . They were of incredible size and weight, and thrown over the shoulder exactly like a Roman toga; a small silk fillet generally encircled their temples, and massy gold necklaces, intricately wrought; suspended Moorish charms . . . a band of gold and beads encircled the knee, from which several strings of the same depended; small circles of gold like guineas, rings, and casts of animals, were strung round their ancles [sic]; their sandals were of green, red and delicate white leather; manillas and rude lumps of rock gold hung from their left wrists, which were so heavily laden as to be supported on the head of one of their handsomest boys. Gold and silver pipes, and canes dazzled the eye in every direction. Wolves and rams heads as large as life, cast in gold, were suspended from their gold handled swords.[1]

These are the words of T.E. Bowdich, the first Englishman to leave a written account of the court of the King of Asante. They express one side of Asante life: the splendours and wealth of its rulers and their servants. Such power and display was, however, only the most obvious aspect of a complex society. This chapter attempts to give the background to the rise of Asante, to the peak of power it enjoyed in the early nineteenth century.

The people of the great kingdom of Asante, fiercely proud of their past and confident of their own innate superiority, inhabit most of what is now central and southern Ghana, a region they have long dominated. The area is green and fertile: from the surf-pounded Atlantic coast, after a coastal plain around Accra, the land rises steadily, crossed by ridges or scarps running from north-west to south-east. Most of Asante is between 150 and 300 m above sea-level, but in places hills may rise 700 m or more. Until recently much of Asante was dense tropical rain forest, a few large trees growing to 60 m or more, standing above the leafy canopy formed at about 30 m by the majority of trees, with smaller trees and bushes densely occupying the zone below. No traveller in Asante can escape the overpowering presence of the forest and the cool and humid gloom beneath it. Even today, after much of it has been cut for timber,

anyone flying over Asante sees mainly large stretches of forest dotted with villages in scattered clearings.

The Asante see their history very much in terms of wars and victories up to the terrible moment in 1896 when British forces seized the Asantehene, or King, Prempe I, and many of his most senior chiefs and advisers, took them to the coast and from there into long exile in the Seychelles. Looking back they recall how, until the last quarter of the nineteenth century, they controlled an ever-increasing area which at its peak stretched over 550 km into the interior and encompassed many distinctive groups and regions. Asante armies were powerful and well-organised, equipped with imported firearms scarcely available to poorer and more isolated northern groups. The porcupine (*kɔtɔkɔ*) with its many quills came to stand for these armies and the Asante nation as a whole; a saying emphasises their almost limitless numbers and bravery: '*Asante Kɔtɔkɔ* kill thousands and thousands more will come'.

The region occupied by the Asante is little more than 5° north of the Equator, and temperatures are high for most of the year: the annual mean maximum at Kumase, the capital, is about 27°C. At noon the sun is almost vertically overhead, beating down fiercely from a cloudless blue sky during most of the year and producing intense colours and hard shadows. Day and night are of almost equal length varying little with the seasons. Dawn comes quickly at about six o'clock and the air soon warms up; at around six in the evening there is a sudden brief dusk.

The tropical forest zone is damp as well as hot: at times the humidity may

10

The reception mounted at Kumase for the British Embassy, 1817. The illustration is taken from T.E. Bowdich, *Mission from Cape Coast Castle to Ashantee*, London, 1819.

reach 90 per cent; only in December and January, when a hot dry wind blows south from the Sahara, does the air become dry and dust-filled. Small amounts of rain fall throughout the year, and the total annual rainfall is around 127–178 cm with two distinctive rainy seasons in May–June and September–October. In these periods several centimetres may fall in a single day. The rain normally begins before dawn and is continuous to mid-morning; people sleep late, wake cold and stay indoors as long as they can. It begins again in the late afternoon and may continue into the hours of darkness: there is mud everywhere, and moving even short distances becomes difficult.

Almost the whole of Asante is seamed by innumerable streams and rivulets feeding the few large rivers such as the Tano, Pra, Offin and Volta. In the forest no village is very far from water. About 35 km south-east of Kumase is the country's only natural lake, Bosomtwe, from which fish were once sent daily for the King of Asante. Two visual impressions predominate: the luxuriance of the forest, damp and gloomy, and the bright red-brown of the underlying lateritic soils showing where paths have been trod and colouring the clay walls of village houses. The rain forest is the heartland of Asante: only in the drier north does the high forest begin to thin until the land becomes more open and is covered by orchard-like trees.

It is difficult to trace the early history of the Asante: little forest archaeology has been carried out, Asante oral traditions are complex, sometimes contradictory, and no visitor before 1816 left useful accounts.[2] Nevertheless, the Asante first came to the attention of Europeans on the coast at the end of the seventeenth century. Then it became apparent that the gold-supplying interior kingdom of Denkyira had been displaced or weakened by a group further from the coast. This group was to emerge as the Asante, rulers of a new and expanding kingdom.

The ruler of Asante at the start of the seventeenth century was Osei Tutu, today honoured as the founder of the nation and its first great leader. He became the overall King (or Asantehene) of a group of allied towns or states centred around Kumase. According to Asante traditions he followed earlier rulers, the almost mythical twins Twum and Antwi, then Oti Akenten and Obiri Yeboa, his predecessor, slain in war. Traditions indicate that the kingdom's founders spread out from an early settlement in Adanse to settle at Kumase, near the earlier trading town of Tafo. They conquered groups already settled in the area and were joined by other bands of immigrants from earlier states to the south, attracted by the opportunities the new area offered. The new kingdom included the towns of Bekwae, Kokofu, Mampon, Nsuta, Dwaben and Edweso and was apparently organised on principles evolved in earlier, more southerly kingdoms like Denkyira and Akwamu. The founding *amantoɔ* states each had its 'paramount chief' or *Omanhene*.

It is today recounted that Osei Tutu, helped by Anokye, the legendary priest (*ɔkɔmfoɔ*), gave the new kingdom a symbolic unity: the existing stools of the leaders of local groups, their marks of authority, were buried and a new stool, *Sika Dwa Kofi* ('the Golden Stool created on a Friday'), was fetched down from heaven to serve as the symbol and to contain the *sunsum*, or spirit, of the whole nation. The start of the state, therefore, is today visualised in terms of the creation of a new, dominating item of regalia, supposedly more important than the individual rulers entrusted with it during their reigns.

Cast-gold sword ornament in the form of a porcupine. Offinso state regalia.

Lake Bosomtwe, c.1890.

The foundations for the new kingdom must have been laid long before Osei Tutu helped give it its political form. We do not know when and how the ancestors of Asante entered the forest zone, but it seems clear that some essential changes in the population and economy of the area provided a springboard for the emergence of Asante and helped fuel its rapid conquest of surrounding groups.

There is ample evidence for the early occupation of the forest: fragments of ground stone axes or adzes, '*Nyame akuma* ('God's axes'), believed to be thunderbolts, continually wash out of the forest soil, and other stone and pottery artefacts are occasionally found. Probably small groups settled in the forest long before Asante evolved and lived by hunting, gathering and yam cultivation. Some time in the first millennium AD ironworking was introduced into this area, almost certainly from the north, and metal must have increased the efficiency of hunting and cultivating.

Asante oral traditions are contradictory about their own earliest existence. Some indicate that they entered the forest from the savannah to the north. Other accounts tell how the founding ancestresses or ancestors of particular clans came from the sky or from caves and holes in the ground.[3] The latter traditions or myths seem to assert that the Asante had always inhabited the central area.

13

The Asante, however, are only the most successful of a number of people in southern Ghana, with offshoots in the Ivory Coast, who are closely related and probably have a single origin. To the south are groups like the Fante, Akwamu and Akyem, speaking virtually identical tonal languages (sometimes called Twi, or Akan) of the Kwa family and with whom the Asante share many elements of culture. Among these groups, for example, there are traces of the great matrilineal clans (*abusua kese*) formerly recognised in Asante, the practice of naming children according to the day of birth (for example, Kofi, a Friday-born male; Abena, a Tuesday-born girl), and many closely similar religious ideas and rituals. Some of these groups also retain traditions of a move to the south from the open areas north of the forest.

The exact pattern of early migration may never be firmly established, but traditions indicate that the area has seen constant movement and change in the last 400–500 years. It follows that there is no such thing as Asante or the Asante kingdom in any simple sense: there is only a succession of groups whose actions and resources gave shape to a continuously and rapidly evolving state in which innovation was often essential for survival. The history of Asante is largely a history of change and incorporation.

Several factors seem to have interacted to help Asante expansion after 1700. One of the most important was that parts of the region contained large gold deposits. These attracted outsiders from two directions and introduced two conflicting interests. Earliest to come were Manding-speakers who settled in towns like Begho on the edge of the forest in the middle of the fifteenth century or earlier. Their trade routes stretched northwards, eventually across the Sahara, and in trading for gold they probably introduced new metalworking techniques, especially brass-casting, and metal goods and cloth into the proto-Akan zone. Possibly they also traded captives from the north and so helped the forest's increasing exploitation. Europeans reached the coast by sea towards the end of the fifteenth century and also began to trade for gold. Like the Manding-speakers they offered mainly metalware, cloth, and slaves, fetched from Benin and elsewhere on the West African coast. This early demand for slaves suggests a need for labour in the forest, either to mine or pan gold or to clear the forest for cultivation.[4]

The forest zone also supplied resources obtained by hunting and gathering. Game was formerly abundant: monkeys, wild pig and the delicious grass-cutter rodent, and in the more open areas various sorts of antelope, elephants and baboons. These were trapped or shot by Asante men, the meat eaten fresh or preserved by smoking. Giant forest snails are still collected by women and children and eaten in stews or pushed on to lengths of cane and preserved by smoking. They were probably an important source of protein. River fish which were caught in basketry traps, by poisoning or by damming a section of river, and freshwater crabs made a welcome ingredient of stews and sauces.

The forest also provided wild yam, edible fungi, the red and black oil-palm fruit, used to produce a rich red oil from the outer parts and a clear oil from the kernel, and the delicious sap of the *Raphia vinifera*. This grows by many streams and in swampy areas: if a hole is drilled near the top and a hollow reed inserted, large quantities of frothy white sap, which has a high sugar content and quickly ferments to produce a pale, fizzy, alcoholic drink, are exuded. This was used both for refreshment and for libations to ancestral spirits and gods. Until recently much of the Asante diet was obtained from hunting, fishing and gathering.

But the basis of Asante expansion seems to have lain in cultivation, and from about the sixteenth century it is probable that cultivation became more productive than before. Several factors were responsible: iron now became available in quantity by sea from Europe. (Possibly local production had been increasing steadily.) Secondly, Europeans introduced new crops: maize, cassava, one or more sorts of coco-yam, ground-nuts, oranges, avocados, tomatoes and pineapples. It seems that the forest was a yam-growing zone long before the introduction of these new crops, and yams may have first been domesticated in West Africa. They have gradually been displaced by plantain (green banana) and maize in the forest zone. Thirdly, imported firearms may have made hunting more productive, at least for an initial period, and perhaps also helped keep down animals which preyed on new crops.

It is probable that the overall productivity of the forest zone increased throughout this period as it was exploited by a growing population able to trade gold, and later slaves, to Europeans on the coast in return for metal, cloth, firearms, liquor and luxury goods. In addition, kola nuts were traded to the north where they were used to suppress thirst. Cotton, leather and metal goods were received in exchange.

The Asante form of shifting agriculture made good use of the shallow forest soils which become exhausted after a few seasons' cultivation. As the dry season approached, small bushes and plants were cut down and piled on the ground to dry. They were then burned, usually in December and January. The fire helped destroy smaller trees, but larger ones were rarely felled. The wood ash fertilised the soil, and the fire uncovered the surface. The farmer carefully probed to find the best places for planting his crops. Plots were usually run on a cycle of three to four years. Maize (which could produce two crops a year) gave quick results, as did yams. If plantain and coco-yam were planted in the first year, their broad leaves sheltered other growing crops from the sun and heavy rainfall, and they were harvested in following years. Cooked, fermented maize, parcelled up in leaves, was used to make various sorts of 'kenkey', a food often eaten on journeys or when cooking was impossible. Yams could also be stored for considerable periods: most other crops were eaten soon after they were gathered, although cassava was cut up and dried for storing.

After a few seasons' cropping, the farm was shifted and the land allowed to lie fallow. Cassava was usually planted when the soil was becoming exhausted, producing large tubers but making it unsuitable for reuse until it had lain fallow for ten to fifteen years. Each family group had a right to a parcel of land around its village. This was usually divided into two main areas: one under cultivation and one lying fallow. A group retained some rather vague rights in land it had once used but which was reverting to thick forest, a process that could take more than seventy years.

15

During the nineteenth century family-based farming was modified in some areas to meet the food needs of the capital and a few other large towns. Large tracts of forest were cleared to set up 'plantations', some of which, producing primarily for market, were manned by unfree labourers.

The exact relationship between population, productivity and prosperity in Asante is still unclear. However, it seems a considerable amount of food could be produced from a relatively small farm, provided the land was allowed enough time to lie fallow after a few years' cropping. Where there was insufficient land, groups were forced to settle new areas, a process which has continued down to the present day.

The peaceful advance of the Asante through the dense forest plays little part in their traditions: these tend to concentrate upon their more sudden and violent military successes and movements from place to place for which few

An exotic gift for the Asantehene, a carriage presented by the Methodist missionary T.B. Freeman, on its way to Kumase in 1841. The illustration is taken from T.B. Freeman's *Journal of Various Visits to the Kingdom of Ashanti, Aku and Dahomi in Western Africa*, London, 1844.

reasons are usually given. In a series of campaigns the new Asante confederation defeated a number of established states and also gained dominance over other groups which were never fully incorporated into the Asante political system but which provided tribute in men and materials. Many of the defeated states such as Denkyira (1701), Wankyi (1711–12), Takyiman (1722–3) and Akyem (1742) contributed skilled personnel as well as portable wealth to the growing confederation, and gave the Asante access to more resources and trading opportunities.

The vast area brought under Asante control by force or threat of arms could not be governed unless new methods of controlling it were developed. From the 1760s, beginning under Asantehene Osei Kwadwo, various steps were taken to bring the control of outlying areas directly under Kumase.[5] Senior office-holders in Kumase were placed in charge of particular areas of the administration, controlling considerable numbers of lesser officials. Some supervised the trade in ivory and kola, while others oversaw the gold-producing regions which now fell within the borders of Asante. A form of treasury partly staffed by literate Muslims was created. Groups within the capital began to build up expertise in particular areas of administration and to concentrate on this as a way to power and wealth. Careers began to open for those with intelligence, negotiating skill and a steady nerve.

As the power of Kumase over the outer dominions increased, so the rulers reduced the powers of the early founding states (*aman*). Kumase became the absolute centre of the political structure. A system of spying, constant checking and reporting back to the King developed. But the system remained largely non-literate, based on directly issued verbal orders and upon the reliability of

those commanded. Many of the splendid objects used around the court – swords, staffs, gold pectorals – were used to identify and facilitate the work of these royal servants in a largely non-literate governmental system.

During the nineteenth century the ruling group began to participate more directly, and advantageously, in trade. The Kings of Asante demanded that European groups on the coast seeking alliance should give them special rates when they bought guns or powder or other goods like cloth and liquor. They also expected, and got, many gifts – silver vessels, clothing, flags, gold-topped canes, elaborate hats – all items to raise them above their subjects. Occasionally these included odd items like wheeled carriages (pulled by men as no suitable horses were available),[6] magic lanterns, lathes, leather shoes and other objects the donors thought might beguile minds whose sophistication they seriously underestimated. In Kumase the Batahene controlled a large number of traders financed from the palace. Some had priority in carrying the year's kola-nut crop to northern markets. As they did not have to pay levies along the road, they were thus assured of high prices and low costs.

Despite the splendours of the capital, most Asante lived in villages and probably kept as far from the court and its ruthless politics as they could. The basis of Asante social organisation at the village level was and is the localised matrilineage (*abusua*). This is a group of people who trace their relationship to each other in the female line (that is, initially through their mothers) and see themselves as descended from a common, named forebear who lived some time between six and eleven generations previously. The *abusua* is supposed to be

18

united by having a common blood (*mogya*) which is passed from women to their children but not, however, from fathers to sons. *Abusua* members tend to live fairly close to each other in a village and they are headed by a senior man, or elder (*abusua panin*), and a senior woman (*obaa panin*). The group may hold rights in particular village offices and in local land. As a group it ideally works together to acquire resources and to help its members; property and leadership are passed down from maternal uncle to sister's son.

This system of matrilineal inheritance is a dominant feature of Asante society, but some important state offices were also passed down in the male line, or to people who had links through both their mothers and fathers with previous office-holders. These different systems seem to have arisen in situations where a group had responsibility for a particular skill or resource, especially as the bureaucracy developed in the late eighteenth and early nineteenth centuries.

The Asante also believed in a form of patrilineally inherited, non-physical link: this *ntoro* was a kind of spiritual influence which entailed certain dietary and behavioural prohibitions. The exact operation of *ntoro* rites is rather obscure – today few ordinary people know about them – and the picture is further complicated by the frequent substitution of *ntoro* or *nton* as a term for *abusua*. *Ntoro* groups seem to have played some part in military organisation, providing a potential patrilineal grouping.

The power of the Kumase court fluctuated during the nineteenth century. At its height the capital was large and prosperous, the centre of a radiating web of roads leading to all the main areas under Asante control and influence. But centralised rule could collapse with dramatic suddenness. In the second part of the century two rival policies were propounded: a continued reliance on war and conquest to keep the machine of government fuelled and to provide profit and power; alternatively, a demand for concentration upon peaceful development and trade. British interference increased and internal splits could no longer be avoided. In 1874 a British force invaded Asante, destroyed part of Kumase, and then left quickly. In 1896 the King and many of his chiefs were forcibly removed by the British: independent Asante was at an end. In 1924 the Asantehene was allowed to return from exile, and in 1935 the Asante confederacy was restored under Prempe II who was succeeded a few years ago by the present Asantehene, Opoku Ware II.

The nation ruled by Opoku Ware II is, in many ways, very different from that depicted in this book. In the last eighty years great changes have occurred in Ghana; many were brought about by the efforts and initiative of the Asante. Cocoa and other cash crops, commercial mining, the timber trade, the growth of schools and universities, new roads and motor transport have all altered Asante life. Yet despite such changes the Asante proudly retain many of their customs, display the subtlety, wit and sophistication which pervades their culture, and act always with a consciousness of their great past.

2 Forest and settlement

The contrast between the luxuriant and almost trackless forest and the ordered existence of the town or village recurs constantly in Asante thought and is basic to the Asante conception of the cosmos. Most Asante lived in small, neat settlements encircled by tall forest trees: these and a few major towns formed the setting for virtually all social activities. Narrow twisting paths ran through the forest from village to village, and from them even narrower and fainter tracks led to hunting areas, or to patches of bush cleared for farming. The main bush paths of some villages ran directly to the great roads (*akwankese* or *akwan tempon*) which, radiating from Kumase, carried the bulk of the kingdom's long-distance trade, and along which royal officials and messengers made their slow way on state business.[1] Villages away from the main roads had indirect access to them by paths which first passed through many other settlements.

The inescapable contrast between forest and village struck most nineteenth-century European visitors. Nearly all were oppressed by the forest's luxuriance and apparent impenetrability. Their earlier experiences and the traditions of European art had accustomed them to wide vistas, long views and the line of the horizon as essential elements for orienting themselves. All were lacking in the Asante forest. Vision was restricted to a metre or so on either side and a dozen metres in front, and the paths rose and fell and twisted and turned as they followed the hidden contours of the land or swerved around fallen trees or other obstructions. 'Few people, who have not experienced it, can understand the loathing with which one regards the endless monotony of the forest, through the dense dank vegetation of which one moves on day after day, as if between two lofty walls of foliage, without seeing a single glade or break in the sameness.'[2]

Travel was slow: even the best routes kept clear at royal command became mires in the rainy season, and were soon overgrown if neglected in times of civil disturbance or when closed by war or a trading blockade. 'The path was a labyrinth of the most capricious windings, the roots of the cotton trees obstructing it continually, and our progress was generally by stepping and jumping up and down, rather than walking; . . . Immense trunks of fallen trees presented constant barriers to our progress, . . . The path was still of the same rugged nature, and the gloom unvaried. A strong fragrance was emitted from the decaying plants and trees of the mimosa kind, whilst others in the same incipient state of putrefaction were very offensive.'[3] Thus Bowdich wrote of the slow journey towards Kumase in 1817 when it took his party four weeks to cover about 230 km. Many of the whites who came after him agreed that the bush was a most unpleasant and threatening place. Austin Freeman, travelling through Adanse in the late 1880s, noted the paths there had become almost completely overgrown through disuse: 'Underfoot a network of roots rendered

A path through the
Akan forest.

walking most painful, while the interlacing branches of great lianas that
blocked the way had to be hacked through with cutlasses before the loads and
hammocks could be dragged through. Every few minutes a fallen tree was
encountered lying across the track.'[4] It was all so difficult that many Europeans found it easier to get down out of their hammocks and walk.

By contrast Europeans were favourably impressed by Asante villages and
towns; many noted how villages became neater and more prosperous in
Asante. 'At Attobiasi one sees the first Ashanti hut and marks the improvement
of the architecture. The walls are solidly built of wattle, no brick, the flooring is
raised two feet, carefully smoothed and painted red. The outer wall, also
painted up to a certain height, is stuccoed in deep panels, circles and other
devices',[5] wrote one of the British invaders in 1874.

Visitors also remarked upon the cleanliness of Asante settlements. Dupuis
noted that in 1820 the streets of Kumase had been cleaned at the royal
command and how the markets and main streets of many, perhaps most, towns
were kept clean of dirt and litter (although the side-streets and back alleys
were less attractive in some places).[6] The British governor Winniet, who

visited Kumase in 1848, praised the width and cleanness of the Kumase streets. Even the hostile reporters and soldiers with the 1874 British invasion forces admitted this, although some claimed the stench of 'human sacrifice' filled the city. 'Clean', 'attractive', 'neat' are epithets which occur again and again in reference to Asante settlements.

It was the best sort of houses which most impressed visitors as, of course, they were intended to impress members of local society. Situated each side of straight, clean streets, perhaps 50 or 60 m wide, these houses, covered in red and white low-relief decoration, were a pleasing and striking sight. This decoration was restricted to temples of major gods (*atano*, *abosom*), to palaces and houses of those high in the political hierarchy. 'Houses consist of various classes, from the rectangular buildings to the common bamboo hut. The white clay washed walls generally distinguish the habitations of the wealthy; but they are not numerous.'[7] Others noted the clear contrasts between the palaces and impressive houses (some of two storeys at Kumase) which lined the main streets and the smaller, less permanent-looking houses of villagers and the urban poor. Writing in the 1870s of Abankro on their road to Kumase, the captured missionaries Ramseyer and Kuhne found it 'a well built place, having a large street which resembles a square, laid out with shady trees; a contrast to the poorer quarters, where the huts are pitched about anyhow'.[8]

The difference in houses and settlements must be understood in relation to

The outskirts of a 19th-century village, with plantain or banana plants growing in the foreground.

the development or decay of the occupying groups. Towns were continually changing; houses, so different in size and complexity, indicated the rise or fall of particular groups. Asante houses, being made of wood and clay, and usually roofed with leaves, were quick to build but decayed quickly if not carefully maintained. War, disease, the movement of trade or failure of local resources, and torrential annual rains could cause an established house or village almost to disappear in a few years. Equally, a new village could spring up almost overnight if conditions were favourable.

The capital itself was subject to this rapid cycle of building and decay. In 1817 the King planned improvements: older buildings were to be replaced and small houses pulled down to improve the road to near-by Bantama where the royal mausoleum was situated. The city gave the impression of prosperity. A few years later Dupuis found it less impressive with dilapidated houses and deserted streets: the expense of wars since Bowdich's visit and the absence of many senior chiefs from the capital had led to decay. The city soon recovered but it was again in decline in 1874 following military and political problems. In the 1880s the whole kingdom was torn between rival candidates for the Golden Stool and shaken by the destruction caused by the British invasion of 1874: much of Kumase was in disrepair, and grass grew in the almost empty streets.

To understand the sequences involved in the growth of houses and settlements it is necessary to start with the simplest house. This is a single-roomed rectangular building made from canes or lengths of branch, or large palm-frond ribs, set vertically in the ground and tied together by lengths of interwoven bark or creeper. These huts (*ọsese*) are still made by farmers who, with their wives and children, or with one or two matrilineal kinsfolk, stay at their bush farm for weeks on end. Palm fronds make a simple roof, the walls are unplastered, and sometimes no door is fitted. The inhabitants will sleep inside on a mat, wrapping themselves from head to toe in cloths (*ntoma*). Three pots or stones in a triangle in front of the hut serve as a hearth, and food is obtained by hunting or trapping, from the farm or wild plants. Life is slow, quiet and peaceful, a welcome escape from the noise and disputes of the village where everyone knows everyone else's business and where malice and gossip can become unendurable.

In the past these rapidly built shelters for farming and hunting were also used by the Asante army. British forces came across 'little huts with low sloping roofs, thatched with green broad leaves of the plantain. Each hut or lean-to had a couple of bamboo bedsteads on posts. . . . They had also taken the pains to make comfortable settees with backs'.[9] Indeed, Sir Garnet Wolseley was so impressed with the camp-beds that he urged his troops to copy them.

Such basic huts provided the first dwellings in a new area, or the first for a developing social group. Reinforced and covered with puddled clay, and linked with similar units, they formed the unit from which larger houses, even palaces, developed. Asante settlements originated and evolved in a variety of ways; perhaps the most common began with movement into a new area and the building of temporary cane huts of the sort described above.

The origins of every village are recalled in traditions passed down verbally

among the most senior men and women of the village and among family elders. Traditions often tell how the village site was discovered by a hunter who returned to his home village and fetched matrilineal kinsfolk to set up a temporary camp in the new area. These stereotyped traditions may record actual events or, perhaps, are myths in which the role of the hunter, venturing into the wild, expresses the start of the complex process by which the bush was brought under human control by the creation of a village. Nevertheless, these traditions express the basic sequence of discovery, temporary encampment and then increasingly permanent settlement. Thus initially a small group would set up temporary shelters while they lived away from their established home village. Such a temporary collection of huts is an *akuraa*, an impermanent place which lacks (and has no need of) any system of formal political authority.

At the end of each hunting or farming season the inhabitants of an *akuraa* would return to their own villages. As time passed, the temporary settlement could be occupied for longer and longer periods, and its buildings made more weather resistant by adding a plaster of puddled clay to their frame or by making an inner and outer frame and filling this with clay and plastering the outer surfaces. At some stage a number of the temporary inhabitants would make a break with their home village and spend the greater part of the year at the new site. There could be many reasons for this: disputes within their home lineage over inheritance or other matters, the shortage or exhaustion of farm-

24

The outskirts of a 19th-century settlement.

land around the older settlement, problems caused by wars or invasions, or the overwhelming advantages of the new area. Not all such temporary, seasonal settlements developed into permanent villages; many lacked the resources to support even small populations throughout the year. However, much of Asante was settled by this hiving-off process.

Thus an *akuraa* might, in favourable circumstances, develop into a village proper (*okrom*), with its own name and chief or *odekuro* and a clearly defined position in the kingdom's political and military framework. This change in status usually occurred gradually and only after the place became the primary residence of many of those using it.

A village proper is distinguished from less permanent settlements as much by social complexity as by sheer size. Nearly all established villages are occupied by a number of distinct matrilineal groups, perhaps as many as five or six. This allows local intermarriage and permits the local burial of the dead, for in most areas the task of digging the grave and performing essential parts of the funeral is done by people from a different lineage. Today the final break between a sub-lineage and its parent lineage and village of origin is usually signalled by a decision not to bury its dead there or to participate in, and contribute to, funerals there. Birth is also important. Women prefer to return to their mothers' houses to have their children; children tend to identify with the towns of their mothers' matrilineal kin. The establishment of a core of women in a

25

village, who have children there, and whose daughters there give birth to other daughters who will continue the matrilineage, marks that settlement's existence as an independent and viable unit. Marriage, birth and death, as much as sheer numbers, mark the distinction between a well-established village and a settlement of less certain status.

Each established village has a headman or village chief (*odekuro*), usually chosen from the eligible males in the lineage which first settled the place. In the past it was his job to judge disputes arising between members of different lineages within the *okrom*, or to see serious cases were reported promptly to the Omanhene ('state chief') above him. He was also responsible for collecting levies and taxes and perhaps deciding, in consultation with lineage elders, who should be sent to meet the military allocation of the area. As village headmen and lineage heads died, stools were blackened to them (see Chapter 7), and their successors had the duty to sacrifice to these stools for the good of all the people they represented. Each of the other village lineages was represented in local affairs by one of its senior men, chosen by its mature members, and he also arbitrated in disputes between his kinsfolk so long as these did not affect the welfare of the whole village. Senior women were also important, offering advice and guidance, while at the level of the *oman* ('state') and the kingdom as a whole the role of queen mother (*ohemaa*) was one of great prestige and considerable power.

Many, perhaps the majority, of Asante villages grew up gradually in the way outlined above. Settlement took place within the established political framework, and most incomers had to seek permission to use previously unexploited land from chiefs who claimed jurisdiction over it. To flourish a settlement needed access to a reliable water supply and cultivable land near by. A new road, the nearness of an easy river crossing, the growth of a market, or the local presence of a god who attracted supplicants were all factors which could draw settlers or cause a village to move nearer to a potential source of benefit. In the nineteenth century, and probably before, specialist craft villages grew up near the necessary sources of supply.

In some cases people of unfree status were deliberately settled in particular places for economic and strategic reasons. The claims of the Kings of Asante in this field were put most blatantly by one king who offered to relocate the whole Fante population of Cape Coast (numbering several thousands) to end a perennial source of trouble in Asante-British relations. Other groups were also resettled in central Asante: traditions relate how one group of Ewe went to Kumase to be rewarded for helping the Asante forces and were forced to settle near by to provide farm labour. Other groups were given into the custody of chiefs or priests as rewards for services in war.

Some of the Kumase goldsmiths were brought to Asante in the eighteenth century following the defeat of earlier kingdoms. Special settlements were also set up to house those employed in mining gold or providing other services for the ruling group. At the village of Bare, a few miles north-west of the capital, many of the makers of medicines and fetishes for the King were installed and placed under the control of the Nsumankwahene ('Chief of the Mystical

The main street of a 19th-century village.

Specialists'). No women were allowed to reside in the village, and the buildings were unusually linked together: an English observer noted a man could travel the length of the village without once going into the street.

Livestock was kept in most Asante villages: chickens, more rarely ducks and turkeys, and sheep and goats, although the latter, 'hot' animals were not permitted in places like Bare where there were powerful fetishes or in settlements housing gods (*abosom*). The eggs produced by chickens were used mainly to make offerings to gods or the Supreme God, or eaten, boiled, in ritual meals with mashed yam (*eto*). Sheep were also used sacrificially and rarely, if ever, killed simply for their meat. In some areas cows, imported from the north, were kept; dogs were used in hunting. A few people, including the Kings of Asante, had cats.

In nineteenth-century Asante the pattern of political control over land and people was extremely complex. Some major administrative offices controlled areas of land (and the use of it) but were not served by those who lived on the land. In other areas the same offices might control the people but not the land, or elsewhere again a mixture of the two. Holdings of both people and land by major chiefs and officials were often fragmented and scattered over wide areas, a useful feature when crops failed or when a chief had to flee the capital. At times groups of people were transferred from the authority of one office-holder or 'stool' to another, or villages under one chief ('stool') had outsider groups serving another stool added to them. In achieving political success a delicate process of balancing resources was necessary: at times the service of people, at times the exploitation of land, at times trade and profits from office would bring the best return or ensure long-term survival. Attempts to achieve the optimum combination of resources resulted in forced movements of population, the creation of new villages, or additions to the populations of established villages.

Yet despite the fact that the social and political make-up of any Asante village might vary greatly, most established villages showed the same general

27

A village street with a shade tree, 19th century.

structure, and their physical layout, so far as the lie of the land permitted, had a number of common features. The majority of towns and villages were built along a broad main street (*abɔntεn*), in many cases intersected at right angles by another narrower one. Other lesser streets or lanes ran between these so the settlement was divided up into blocks. The main street of even a small village could be 50–100 m wide and often had slight ditches on each side to help drain the torrential seasonal rains, when some villagers walked on elevated wooden sandals to keep their feet dry. Beyond these ditches was a strip of cleared ground on to which the first row of houses fronted. The strip of ground between was left uncleared or occasionally planted with peppers, ground-nuts or medicinal herbs, its green growth contrasting with the red of the street.

The street formed the principal parade and display area and was the scene of many important rituals involving the whole village or major parts of its population. Here were held parts of the *bragoro* rites following a girl's first menstruation by which her new potential was publicly acknowledged and symbolically controlled and directed. Here too were celebrated the funerals (*ayi*) of adults, with villagers, friends and family gathering to mourn and to listen to the dirges sung by the women of the deceased's matrilineage. The street was also the place where women performed the *mmumue* rite to protect their husbands while they were away at war. Almost naked, they marched backwards and forwards along the main street for several hours each morning, singing and chanting and imitating male behaviour as if at war themselves.

The main street was usually kept spotlessly clean, swept each morning and

Odumase in the 19th century; the unplastered framework of a house can be seen on the right.

evening by women and children, or slaves. It was also swept as part of the *mmusuoyiede* ritual when all the town's dirt was taken to its outskirts and placed across the main paths to remove mystical danger and to prevent disease or death from entering the settlement.

Main streets could indicate a settlement's age and something of its history. The number of houses, their size, complexity and state of repair naturally gave an indication of population size and prosperity, but far more indicative were the spreading shade trees (*gyannua*) which, in an old town, lined each side of the main street. These large-leaved trees, of the *Ficus* family, throw out many almost horizontal branches producing wide pools of shade. In this shade were placed stools, logs and large stones so that adults could gather there to gossip, discuss village disputes, or play the board-game *oware*.

These trees were planted not merely to provide shade in a land where the fierce sun is almost vertically overhead for the middle part of the day; they were also connected with the concept of chiefship and with the spiritual 'coolness' (*dwo*) or peace of the whole town. In major towns they were associated with the continuity of chiefly rule and with proper succession. On his accession a chief was expected to plant a new shade tree, the trees of his predecessors were decorated with white cloth, and before them he swore an oath to rule well and guard his people.[10]

Trees and monarchy were related in many ways. The tree planted in a new town was believed to be the potential dwelling-place for the spirit of the chief who planted it. Before going to war a chief swore that he would not permit the

29

enemy to cut down the tree; and the heads of defeated lesser chiefs brought back from war were buried under it. A new tree was planted after each war fought by a community. The shade of a chief's state umbrellas was likened to the shade these trees gave to his people. An enemy aimed to destroy a town's shade trees to show they had destroyed the rule and order manifested through its chief's reign. The tree was part of the town's moral state. If, for example, a couple committed incest, which could pollute and bring disaster to the community, part of their fine was used to buy white cloth, a sign of freedom from pollution, to adorn the *gyannua*. On installation a new chief was shown all the shade trees of a town as he was shown other things of power, like local gods, which could be harmed by mystical pollution.[11]

The spiritual state of the whole town was thus connected with these trees. Tree and King were sometimes synonymous: a circumspect way of talking of the King was to talk of the shade tree,[12] and 'to tear the leaves of the shade tree' was a guarded way of saying 'to curse the King'. Interfering with shade trees could be dangerous. In 1839 one of those with the Methodist missionary Freeman accidentally plucked a few leaves of a tree which brushed his face on the Bantama to Kumase road, and was told he had committed a serious offence.[13] Shade trees provided a clear reminder of the chief's power and an indication of the town's age: as Freeman was told, each indicated a reign. The tree was treated as if it had a quasi-human existence, and if it fell down a brief form of funeral was performed for it. When the chief died, the *wirempefo*, responsible for the care of the regalia during the interregnum, would tear the branches of the tree – an act, otherwise forbidden on pain of a heavy fine, which served as a sign of the disorder which had come upon the world with the chief's death.[14]

The provision of trees indicated a degree of chiefly control over a village's appearance. A few villages, more regular in plan than others, may also have been formally laid out under chiefly direction, perhaps when the whole village was shifted a short distance from an earlier site. Some of these regularly patterned villages were probably entirely new creations in the nineteenth century.

The layout and architecture of the village was, of course, strongly influenced by the status and prosperity of the groups occupying it. By and large the form of each house (*efie*) related directly to the stage of development reached by the social group using it. The basic building unit was the simple rectangular hut, measuring perhaps 3–4 m by 2–3 m at most. Such houses were used by the poor, but they also formed the first stage of more elaborate dwellings.

The social system of Asante, to a large extent based on the matrilineal group, produced a variety of residential patterns. These constantly shifted and altered. Any house or any room might contain a different combination and number of people every week of the year. Early in a marriage man and wife might co-habit, but the wife could also spend a great deal of time elsewhere – with her mother and sisters in her matrilineal house, travelling to trade, or with her husband on their farm. Children might live a while with their fathers and then stay with their mothers' brothers from whom they could eventually

A 19th-century village.

inherit property, rights and duties. A woman, after marriage, might stay in her matrilineal house, visiting her husband by day or night and sending over his meals by one of the children of the house. Strangers would seek lodging with people in the same great clan, and people would leave their villages to farm, hunt, trade, to seek opportunities at court, to visit relatives in other areas, to supplicate to distant gods, or to seek mystical protection in far-off areas. Richer families owned slaves, or people of varying degrees of unfree status, and these, when not farming or on trading expeditions, were sheltered in or near the family house. By looking at a house it was impossible to predict the number of people using it and their relationship with each other.

Beneath this ever-varying system, however, there were constant elements which were reflected in the physical structures of houses. The basic rectangular hut could provide shelter for a single man, a man and his wife, a pair of sisters lacking brothers to support them, or a single man living with his sister. Houses became more elaborate as those using them extended their social links and influence, had children and acquired relatives, servants or clients. A house was developed by adding units of the basic type, that is, by constructing one or more rectangular huts next to it, usually so that they would eventually enclose a central courtyard. Thus the first extra unit was added at right angles to the

31

original house, the two units abutting directly or linked by a short fence, and the next additional unit added opposite it to make a three-sided block, a fence or, in due course, a fourth unit closing its open end. Access was by a door in a corner between two units or, in some cases, by a doorway through the centre of one of the units.

The various stages in this development of complex dwelling-units from simple huts can still be seen in many Asante villages. Some basic units were walled only on three sides to create an open room or 'verandah' (*pato, adampan*), as white visitors sometimes called it. These open rooms were employed for several purposes: sleeping, sitting and talking, or, in chiefs' houses and temples, for the storage of drums, regalia and other items. Visitors had experience of all types of rooms and houses. Writing of Agogo in the early 1870s, Ramseyer and Kuhne noted: 'The house in this place mostly consisted of only one room open in front, the entrance being formed by a few steps, being polished daily with an oily red earth. We were taken into a small yard surrounded by four of these apartments, each of them about 5 feet by 6, so that we barely found space to lie down in the one allotted to us.'[15] Dupuis, about fifty years earlier lodged in 'one of the best houses the place contained. This was a small enclosure, with four thatched rooms'. He noted the mixture of house types at Amoafo: '. . . some of the houses are tolerably well constructed; but still the clay and bamboo hovels predominate, perhaps, here, in the proportion of 12 to 1 in the main street.'[16] (Probably many of these poorer huts had been erected to shelter some of the 7,000 prisoners of war then in the place.)

The house proper, therefore, was formed by a number of units, subdivided into rooms, arranged around a central court. In most cases the exterior walls were unbreached by windows or doors, and the only access to the court (*gyaase*) was by a door in one of the corners. With the door closed, as it was every night, the inhabitants were completely secluded from the rest of the village.

Larger, more complex houses were generally built and inhabited only by developed social units, that is, lineages of two or three generations and with some dependants and servants. Rooms had their own wooden doors and sometimes small square wooden shutters looking on to the yard which could be opened to let in light and air. Some rooms had ceilings of barkcloth (*kyenkyen*) fixed to rafters, but most had no ceilings at all, and light and air entered through the gaps between the tops of their walls and the overhanging roofs.

The huts and rooms which were intended to be permanent were built with floors about 30 cm above ground level and were entered up a step or over a sill (*apunwa*). This raised them above the mud and water of the rainy season and the dust and dirt of the street or court during the rest of the year. When a central court was created, this too was filled in so that it stood 30–60 cm above the natural ground level. Roofs overhung the walls by 30–60 cm to protect them from the direct force of the rain. In each rainy season the road outside the house was eroded away, so the house walls, sheltered and periodically re-plastered, increasingly stood on a platform, whose top represented the original land surface.

The interior of a house, with children pounding grain.

Most houses thus tended, with time, to be in the form of a rectangular compound entered by a single door. When further expansion was necessary, units to make extra courts were added so that a palace or the house of a well-established family might, over the decades, grow into a series of courts each connected by lockable doorways. The extended matrilineal group living in such a house might eventually begin to split internally and one part break away to build elsewhere. Sometimes this internal segmentation was visualised in terms of the doors or entrances which separated the courtyards occupied by the different groups: *ye kye no aboboǫno* ('we split [the lineage] between the entrances').

A house could also reflect a decline in a group's size and fortune: as people moved away or died, rooms were left empty and neglected, the roofs fell in, and the unprotected walls crumbled. Often unoccupied rooms were used to store pots, firewood or other household goods, or provided a roosting-place for the compound's chickens. Unfinished or broken rooms (*adan tutuom*) seem to have been a constant feature of Asante villages, an indication of the great variability of the residential group and perhaps a source of the well-known saying that 'it is better for the occupant to be bad than for a dwelling to be deserted'.

The furnishings of most rooms were simple and mainly of local manufacture. Most people slept on vegetable-fibre mats laid directly on the floor, but a few had beds made by stretching and interweaving strips of hide over a rectangular frame, or of slats of wood or cane laid on a frame. A room might contain a person's own stool, but this might also be kept outside in one of the open rooms

or in a corner of the yard. Valuables were wrapped in a length of cloth and hidden among the rafters and thatch of the roof. More wealthy and senior people probably had a trunk or box (*adaka*) to store valuables, securing it by a lock. Most rooms contained a locally made water pot in a corner and one or more shallow bowls from which the water could be drunk in the night. Light was provided by a pottery or brass lamp in which palm-oil or shea-butter was burned. A few rooms contained items of exotic origin – the guns of hunters and warriors and the occasional imported brass basin or bowl.

Closed rooms were primarily used for sleeping: most activity occurred in the central yard or open rooms. This and its hearth were the centre of women's lives: here they prepared the food which was eaten on the open clay platform (*pato*) or, in cold or wet weather, inside the rooms, each sex eating separately. The hearth (*bukyia*) was made of three inverted pots, each with a hole in the bottom so it could be lifted and moved, arranged in a triangle on the ground, or of three mounds moulded in clay and joined together by shallow walls. It is still the almost universal practice to colour the hearth bright red with *ntwuma* clay and to renew and polish this periodically. Hearths of priests (*akɔmfo*) and those used for cooking food for offering to gods and ancestors were coloured white. The hearth was also used to heat water for bathing and occasionally to heat medicinal herbs in a crock to reduce them to dust for rubbing into small incisions or to make into an ointment. The great majority of these hearths were inside the house and, indeed, the word for court or yard, *gyaase* ('under the

A shrine to a god or major fetish outside a village, *c.*1890. Ramseyer and Kuhne in 1874 described a similar 'Fetish house, inside of which a globe shaped mound of white earth marks the burial place of a python snake . . . a carved human figure with a cloth cap and sword in hand keeps watch in front'.

fire'), is sometimes said to take its name from the hearth. A woman who made a separate hearth, or had one built away from the house, was declaring her independence or, more likely, showing that she was being ostracised by the other women of the compound.

A number of houses, usually the original dwellings of local matrilineal groups, had rooms in which the blackened ancestral stools were kept. These usually had a clay platform (*pato* or *ase*) along one of the walls away from the door, and on this the stools were placed on their sides. Water vessels and food pots were put in front of them to receive offerings. It was the duty of the head of the lineage to sacrifice to the ancestors at these stools on behalf of the whole group for which he was responsible. Some stool rooms also contained the brass basins which served as the shrines of gods (*abosom*), if these were not housed in a separate room or building. The doors of these rooms were usually festooned with a sheet of white cloth or coated with white clay to indicate the powers they housed and remind menstruating women to keep well clear.

The houses in a village were usually grouped into 'quarters' (*abrono*), named areas, usually identified according to some particular natural feature. Some quarters might contain only a few houses, others a score or more, and each quarter was usually associated with the group which had settled there first and was numerically predominant. As population grew, the village expanded outwards, for all buildings, except in Kumase and a few state capitals, were single-storey ones. The newer, outer areas of villages might, therefore, be filled with clusters of small huts, creating new quarters, perhaps eventually leading to the physical merging of two near-by villages, which nevertheless kept their political distinctiveness.

In many towns and villages the chief and his advisers imported mystically powerful objects or medicines to protect the village and help it prosper. Some were buried at the town centre, others at the edge where the main paths entered and left it. Ramseyer and Kuhne saw 'Elevated on four poles at the end of the village . . . a Fetish house, inside of which a globe shaped mound of white earth marks the burial place of a python snake, to which offerings of palm wine are presented, being poured into a hollow at the top of the grave. A carved human figure with a cloth cap and sword in hand keeps watch in front'.[17]

These fringe areas (*kurotia*) were of importance. Here were built the huts occupied by menstruating women. Menstruation was the centre of a complex of beliefs and prohibitions: it was 'hot' and dangerous, and menstruating women were confined to certain locations and excluded from many activities. Menstruation was a prohibition (*akyiwadie*) to gods and black stools, and even to some fetishes (*asuman*) and medicines (*aduro*). It is said that if a menstruating woman entered a stool room she was slain, for her state would drive away the spirit (*sunsum*) of the ancestors. Both Dupuis and Bonnat record tales of how the wives of an Asantehene tried to harm him by rushing up to him while they were menstruating – a crime for which they were killed.[18] Menstruating women were not supposed to touch or handle tools used to make things or to change one sort of thing into another: if the tools of a potter, weaver or carver were so handled, or a menstruous woman approached a man who was using them, they would break or slip and harm him, and what he was making would be ruined.

Menstruating women could not, of course, cook or come near to a senior chief or be present when important cases were being tried. Menstruation was also associated with night, and in ordinary conversation it was referred to in an oblique way only. A disobedient young girl was threatened: 'you will menstruate for the first time in the day'; and even now girls always pretend they have first menstruated in the night or at dawn.[19] It was therefore the custom for menstruating women to remove completely from their houses and to occupy either a small unplastered hut a little way from their house, or to move to one of a number of simple menstruation huts (*bradan, brafie*) built at the edge of the village, hard against the bush.

In the same fringe zone were a number of other places which had to do with intermediary or special conditions and entities: the graveyards, middens, some temples of gods and the village latrines.

The midden (*sumina*) was the dumping ground for all the dirt, scraps and peelings produced in running a house. These were swept up, normally in the morning and in the late afternoon, carried in a basket or balanced on a large leaf, and tipped on the midden. This was the task of women or children, who kept the inside of their compound scrupulously clean. The size and position of the midden depended on the size and age of the village. Large villages sometimes had two or more middens, and the middens of old villages often grew into small hills. As a town grew, its midden might be abandoned and another made nearer its new edge. Sometimes the old midden would be built upon or, because middens produced fertile black soil, used for growing such small-scale domestic crops as red peppers or ground-nuts.

Many nineteenth-century middens, detectable by the colour of the soil, reveal pieces of broken pots and clay pipes mixed among decayed organic material; a few also contain animal and human bones. The latter indicate the place these sites held in Asante thought. To understand this it is necessary to touch upon Asante ideas of dirt. It was important for the Asante to keep their homes and villages free of dirt (*efi*). Even today the *mmusuoyiede* ritual (see p.29) is performed to protect a village from danger or to relieve it of a major affliction, such as the outbreak of a disease. All the women and children collect dirty and broken objects and dump them in a line across the roads into the village. As they move from one end of the village to the other, they sing and stop to make sweeping gestures with the brooms or switches which they carry: 'Where are we sweeping to? We sweep to the village end, the death of old men, the death of children, the death of young men, the death of unmarried women.' As the women sing, they swing their skirts with a sweeping gesture. In 1874, for example, the ritual was performed by the women of the villages in the line of the British advance, and there are several accounts of dirt and broken pots spread across the path to keep away the British forces. This was seen by other visitors: 'Near the entrance to each village we noticed jars, sticks, corn and eggs heaped up as an offering to the Fetish.'[20]

In the past the midden was also used as the burial place for certain classes of

A 19th-century village; a small menstruation hut can be seen in the right foreground.

people (hence the human bones). These were babies and those who died before puberty, those who had shown themselves to be sterile, those slain (by man or god) because they were witches, executed criminals, and those who met inauspicious deaths (by snake-bite, lightning, drowning, falling trees, or by wild beasts in the bush). The defining characteristic of all these people is that they were, in some sense, damaged or incomplete beings.

Children, however much desired and loved by the Asante, were not accepted as full persons until adolescence and, in the case of girls, they had undergone the *bragoro* rite after their first menstruation. Young children, not yet fully human, were buried in the midden without full funeral rites. Those who lived to a good age but who had no children were clearly deficient in what made for the most basic of human purposes. Sterile men and women were buried in shallow graves in the midden, sometimes lined with thorny branches, and their corpses mutilated, verbally abused and their spirits told not to return to the world in the same sterile state. Witches (*abayifo*) were creatures who had perverted their lives and life's basic purpose by mystically killing their own children, or by making themselves abort or be sterile, or by destroying the fertility of matrilineal kin. Those slain as criminals by the royal power were forbidden proper burial, and the funeral rites for them could be held only at the time of the annual Odwira festival when, briefly, the ordinary rules of behaviour were turned upside down. Those who met inauspicious deaths (*atofo*), including those who killed themselves, showed by the manner of their deaths that they were guilty of some hidden offence (and a suicide could be tried after death).

Thus all such bodies were consigned to the midden, the place of the dirty and broken, to be buried there and not in the part of the cemetery reserved for their lineage. The midden was also believed to be the place where witches washed their children to make them into witches – a further overturning of the natural order and an evil parody of the normal washing by which dirt was removed.

Also in the same general fringe area were the latrines (*yaane*). Each village had at least one for each sex, positioned a little away from the main paths and often, in the case of the women's latrine, concealed behind a bank of trees. Each consisted of a trench with poles laid across it, surrounded by a concealing low clay wall and with a palm-front roof supported on poles. Today the walls of such latrines, which are still used in some rural villages, are almost the sole structures still to be plastered with the bright red clay formerly used for decorating the lower parts of all major buildings. Latrines were used for defecation by all except very small children, but it was the custom of both sexes to urinate discreetly behind houses or in odd corners, passers-by politely pretending not to notice.

The sanitary arrangements of Asante villages impressed many visitors favourably, although Dupuis, always ready to see the worst, complained: 'The favourable impression of Ashantee cleanliness, was checked by the exposure of nuisances in bye streets, in the environs of the town, and the backs of houses, where it becomes difficult to select a footway free of excrement and filth.'[21]

Temples of gods (*bosom'dan, bosom'fie*) were also often situated towards the edges of the village, although some were built well away from human habitation, usually on the banks of rivers or streams (from which gods were thought to come). In their simplest form the temples were small rectangular buildings, entered by steps, the outer surfaces decorated with low reliefs and covered with red and white clay. More usually they consisted of a number of units around a court. Here male priests would periodically carry the god's shrine on their heads, becoming possessed and showing their powers to see, say and do things beyond the abilities of ordinary mortals.

A few villages seem to have grown up around the temples of major gods to shelter supplicants and to house the drummers, cooks and other people who served the god and its priest. The social make-up of such villages was unusual for they contained men and women from many different areas who had come, perhaps with one or two kinsfolk, to seek the aid of the god. Such villages probably provided long-term refuges for people afraid that their relatives were causing them mystical harm.

Beyond these structures lay the bush and the farmlands. At the very edge of the intermediary zone between the human world of the town and the forest proper were two areas connected with death: the burial ground (*asiee*) and the grove of the ancestral ghosts (*asamanpow*) or 'place of pots'. Usually there was only one burial ground in most villages, although it is said that when only two lineages occupied a village each would have its own burial place, one each side of the main path into the village. The graveyard is usually to the left of, and a few metres away from, one of the main paths from the village. A small area is cleared of trees and bushes to serve as the burial place, and often each lineage has an area to itself within this.

Most corpses are now buried in wooden coffins but formerly were buried rolled in mats. In the mid-eighteenth century Asantehene Opoku Ware I had a glazed coffin sent from the Netherlands. Very poor people, those without family or who were once slaves, may still be buried without coffins, perhaps carried to their graves on doors. Many graveyards are surrounded by shrubs of the croton family which have leaves of dark green, dark red and brown, the colours of mourning. The burial places of important people are sometimes marked by the planting of a particularly symmetrical, green and flourishing type of palm-tree. In the old days a few people were buried beneath the floors of houses or temples. Some *akɔmfo* of exceptional power, as well as some of the most respected lineage heads or village chiefs, are said to have been buried in this way. It is also said that those who had gold-dust buried secretly with them were often interred within their houses so their graves could not be looted by outsiders.

The second area connected with mortuary rites is usually further from the village than the cemetery. This is the 'place of pots' (*asensie*), where various pots used in funeral rituals are finally placed and, in some areas, terracotta effigies (*akua'mma*) of important people (chiefs, queen mothers, family heads) and their servants. The place where such objects are deposited (and practices varied from area to area) was also sometimes known as the grove of ghosts (*asamanpow*), and was conceived as an intermediate zone where the dead lingered for a while (forty days in the Akan calendar) before finally parting from the world of the living.

The grouping of buildings and areas described above was not haphazard. The village and the bush were strongly opposed in Asante thought. It was believed that all essentially human activities, and especially birth, copulation and death, should always take place in the town. The town was ideally a place of peace and quiet, or 'coolness' (*dwo*). Ideally, a person should be born and die in the town, in the latter case with matrilineal kinsfolk near to give the final drink of water for the journey to the world of the dead, to listen to any last wishes, and to wash the corpse and carry out the essential funeral rites to separate the deceased's soul from the world of the living. Copulation in the bush was considered dangerous, polluting the Earth (*Asase Yaa*), subject to ridicule and heavy fines and, according to some accounts, even enslavement. No child should be born in the bush, and it was only those who had copulated before the woman's nubility rite had been performed, a major crime which endangered the whole community, who were driven forth to bear their child away from the town. To die alone in the bush, killed by wild beasts, by snake-bite, by falling trees or by lightning was considered both horrific and shameful.

The bush, as opposed to the town, was an area of disorder, potential power and danger. Besides being the place of wild beasts, it was the home of such superhuman beings as *sasabonsam* and *mmoatia*. *Sasabonsam* was believed to be a great hairy red beast which lived in the tallest trees. A combination of creatures from several realms with legs like snakes, wings like those of a bat, an ape-like body and a carnivore's head and teeth, it was believed to catch hunters with its long dangling legs and then devour them. It was the ally of witches. Its hairiness and redness, with its other characteristics, mark it out as something especially foul in Asante eyes, for the redness indicates heat and danger, while the hairiness is seen as being both dirty and uncontrolled to a people obsessive about preserving clear margins to their own bodies and to the world about them. *Mmoatia* (literally, 'short creatures' or 'little beasts') were envisaged as small and totally unpredictable goblin-like beings, red, white or black, with backward-pointing feet, who either attacked or succoured hunters or others who became lost in the bush.

The bush, then, was considered a realm set apart from that of man. It contained fierce beasts, *sasabonsam*, *mmoatia* and some of the great gods. Into it men went at their peril. Many, like hunters, who sought their living there were careful to obtain talismans and medicines to protect themselves against its dangers. The bush was also an area of potential power, a place where medicines could be learned, and where gods might reveal themselves to men and women whom they 'seized' and drove deep into the forest, or where strange objects with great powers might be found, or given by *mmoatia*. Even today people become disoriented and lost in the bush. Search parties are organised and the chief's drums taken into the forest and beaten, not only to act as a signal but also, it appears, to impose some sort of regularity and order on the disorder of the wild. Equally, the dangerous and disruptive is driven out into the bush and away from the order of the town. In the past witches and those who committed grossly polluting offences, if they were not executed, were driven into the bush, sometimes with a burning brand in their hand to warn others of their dangerous, 'hot' condition.

The structure of Asante settlements reflects this town/bush opposition. To-wards the edges of the settlements are the areas concerned with the removal of the dirt and decayed materials of the village, its excrement and its corpses, and the temples for the controlled entry of supernatural beings originating from outside (the rivers, the sky and the bush). Here also is the 'place of pots' where, temporarily, the spirits of the dead linger before they are reincorporated into human society as ancestral spirits (when their wooden stools are blackened) or finally quit it for the world of the dead. Thus town and forest, the realm of the dwelling (*efie*) and the bush (*wura'm*), are separated by the edges of the village (*kurotia*), a symbolic as well as a physically distinct zone. In the past this distinction between the two worlds was given formal physical expression: a small barrier or low stile made of a few thin logs was placed across the end of the village. This barrier (*pampim*) was not intended to prevent the entrance or egress of people or beasts – it was too low for that; it was intended instead as a mystical protection for the village against the dangers and powers which dwelled in the bush, and as such it represented the end of the village, the realm of man, and the beginning of the wild. As we shall see, this fundamental distinction reappears in an important area of Asante art.

3 Kumase

Kumase for most of the eighteenth and nineteenth centuries was a noisy, crowded, bustling place, the seat of the central government and a focus of trade routes that reached eventually across the Sahara to the centres of Islamic learning and business, south to the coast and, from there, to Europe and the Americas. At times the city presented an image of prosperity and power, its wide streets lined with ornate buildings, some two storeys high, with dazzling white and deep red plasterwork. Through the streets rushed officials, messengers and servants, bearing their distinctive regalia, linking the affairs of the King with those of the major chiefs and functionaries who kept great houses near to the palace. Visitors and traders from all over the realm and from outside thronged the streets. In the markets and courtyards dozens of different tongues and dialects could be heard, and the origin of each group was indicated by its distinctive forms of dress, hair-styles and facial scarification.

Periodically the King would venture from the sprawl of buildings which constituted the palace, perhaps to be carried in his palanquin to the mausoleum of his ancestors at Bantama, a couple of miles or so away, or to sit in state on one of a number of special platforms positioned through the city. There, surrounded by chiefs and court officials, he would ritually drink palm wine, greet visitors to the capital and hand out doles of gold-dust. At times the capital would also erupt into violence and bloodshed: convicted criminals would be publicly tortured and executed, or people suddenly cut down in the streets following the death of an important person, or killed during funeral rites. And at times the city emptied as people fled to their farms and villages or left because they could no longer afford to live there. Then the city and its buildings soon decayed, and its wide streets became overgrown.

Kumase was always an exciting and dangerous place. The great officers of the kingdom, even the King himself, were subject to rapid changes of fortune. Their patronage was a way to power and wealth, attracting supplicants and followers, but patterns of alliance were ever-shifting, and a prosperous group might quickly find itself in difficulties. Around the King and court men manœuvred, calculated, spied on each other and were spied upon. Alliances by marriage, trade or favour were made and broken. A large number of supporters showed a man's power; they also cost him money.

The need to provide food for a teeming city of 20,000 or more people required numerous farms and plantations around it, but food supplies were erratic and could quickly be cut off, prices could rocket, and the mass of ordinary people could burst into violence when things went wrong. In times of dispute and disorder even the palace could be invaded by armed men. Serious fires, particularly dangerous in a thatched city where small huts were huddled together and flames leaped from one to the next, occurred throughout the

nineteenth century; and the King had to be present to see the fires were dealt with properly. At night the corps of the King's *adumfo* patrolled the streets and controlled egress from and entrance to the city. At posts around the main roads royal officials checked those leaving and entering the capital, detaining those travelling without authority, as several Europeans, exasperated at the court's slow pace, learned when they tried to leave without royal consent.

The town itself grew up near the earlier trading centre of Tafo in or before the time of Osei Tutu. Traditions explain its name by the fact that it began under (*ase*) a *kum* tree. The lesser importance of the town of Kumawu is explained by the fact that there a similar tree did not flourish – *kum a wu* ('the *kum* tree which died'). Recourse to verbal formulations to explain material phenomena is a basic feature of Asante thought, and such formulations need not contain any historical truth. What is certain, however, is that by the start of the nineteenth century Kumase was thoroughly established as a trading and governmental centre, and the fame of the King's wealth and the richness of his palace had spread to the coast.[1]

The city was situated on a hill overlooking the Subin river and by 1817 contained twenty-seven major streets, the greatest of which, used for major receptions and parades, was over 100 m wide: '. . . four of the principal streets are half a mile long, from 50 to 100 yards wide. The streets are all named, and a superior captain in charge of each; ours for instance was Aperremso, big gun or cannon street, because those taken when Dankara was taken were placed on a mound at the top of it.'[2] Traditionally Kumase in the latter part of the last

42

Royal drums in the entrance way to the Asantehene's palace, c.1890. The skulls and bones are of defeated enemies.

century was divided into seventy-seven named quarters or *abrono* (this seems an idealised figure). Many of those who served the court were located in particular wards: Bowdich noted the areas occupied by the blacksmiths and umbrella makers; today some goldsmiths still occupy their traditional section; and in Adum lived the head of the executioners and those who patrolled the city after curfew (*abrafo*, *adumfo*).

The palace was the largest building, or rather group of inter-linked buildings, in the city. It was not only the primary residence of the Kings, some of their wives and many of their servants, but part of it also served as the forum in which the council of the realm decided on important matters. It seems to have grown in size and complexity until the final quarter of the nineteenth century, and its appearance at any one time was broadly indicative of the state of royal power. In the mid-1840s it was estimated that the palace covered an area of about 2 ha. At the front it was enclosed by a wall which created a sort of passage way, what Bowdich called a 'piazza', about 200 m long and with rooms off it used by some of the King's servants, those nearest the palace being the most elaborately decorated and used by 'the superior captains'.[3] Above these was a small gallery. Indications of power and status were shown along the 'piazza'. 'Piles of skulls, and drums ornamented with them' were displayed in the open rooms looking on to this, and on their walls were hung guns, ammunition belts and gold-handled swords.[4] The Great Court (*Pramakeseso*) was reached from the passage; here those involved in major policy decisions came together to meet and debate, sometimes daily. The court measured about 30–5 m by 14–15 m in Bowdich's time; galleries seem to have been added later. Like other, connected courts it was decorated with numerous designs in low relief: '. . . two rows of stakes and wattle work placed at a distance equal to the intended thickness of the wall . . . The interval was then filled up with a gravelly clay, mixed with water, with which the outward surface of the frame or stake work was also thickly plastered, so as to impose the appearance of an entire thick mud wall.'[5] The tiered gabled roofs were made of palm leaves laid over a framework of bamboo, which was 'painted black and polished' on the interior.

Pillars, used to support the roof over open-fronted rooms, were made from a central pole or poles covered with clay. They were decorated with twisted designs made by binding cane or creepers around the central support. 'I saw a few pillars, (after they had been squared with the plaster) with numerous slips of cane pressed perpendicularly on to the wet surface, which being covered again with a very thin coat of plaster, closely resembled fluting. When they formed a large arch, they inserted one end of a thick piece of cane in the wet clay of the floor or base, and bending the other over, inserted it in the same manner; the entablature was filled up with wattle work plastered over.'[6]

Room doors and those between courts were made of 'an entire piece of cotton wood, cut with great labour out of the stems or buttresses of that tree; battens variously cut and painted were afterwards nailed across'.[7] Many had locks which could delay the advance of enemies so that the Asantehene could escape through the buildings at the rear which backed on to a swamp.

Part of an interior court of the palace, c.1890.

Freeman noted such arrangements: because of 'the despotic nature of the Government under which this people live . . . all Ashanti Chiefs, Captains etc build their houses in such a manner, that they can readily escape at one door, the moment a person enters another'.[8] Secure entrances were also useful to others in the teeming city: 'When at last I reached my house, I immediately closed the door and freed myself of the importunities of the public', wrote the Dutch emissary Huydecoper.[9] Such security could work both ways, for Dupuis coming at night upon a drunken party held by his servants vainly waited at the street gate to catch the miscreants, who escaped through a gap they had cut in the reed fence surrounding part of his dwelling.[10]

Locks, of course, are machines of importance in the development of any society, for their existence indicates the evolution of private property, the desire to control it and its unequal distribution. The Asante had two sorts of locks available to them: those made in Europe and those manufactured by African, and especially by Hausa, metalworkers. The latter were used for locking treasure bags and boxes, for which their long hasps were particularly suitable, and possibly for securing doors.

The Hausa lock demonstrates one orientation of Asante culture and politics, namely, to the Muslim north; but the local eagerness for European-made locks indicates Akan involvement with the trade and politics of the Christian white world. Locks and lockable sea-chests were early trade goods. A king of one of the early coastal kingdoms sought from the Portuguese in 1513 a leather-covered trunk in which to keep his gold safe. Towards the end of the same century an English visitor noted caustically: 'If any of them has gotten a sailor's old chest, he passed for a great man.' When the British sacked Kumase in 1874, one observer said such lockable chests were 'numberless'.[11]

The primary function of locks was, of course, to secure valuables from the free access of others. From this use there derived at an early date the practice of displaying keys as a sign of wealth and eminence. In the eighteenth century Loyer noted that women on the coast 'tie to their waist large bunches of copper, brass and iron keys, by way of adornment, though', he added, 'perhaps they have but one box at home'.[12] Massive bunches of keys were carried by one of the Asantehene's officers to demonstrate the almost infinite wealth of the monarch, and most Amanhene seem also to have possessed large bunches of keys, carried in parade with other regalia. Some of these keys were cast in silver in a highly stylised form.

The small windows of the palace were exceptional: 'The windows were open wood work, carved in fanciful figures and intricate patterns, and painted red; the frames were frequently cased in gold, about as thick as cartridge paper.'[13] The number of these windows is probably exaggerated, but their fame had spread as far as the coast for Huydecoper wrote: 'At Elmina I have heard it said that the King of the Ashantis has gold and silver doors. This is not true, though he does possess a small window, one and a half feet by one foot, which has its beams overlaid with gold.'[14]

The palace contained areas for cooking, a room where the King could eat, another where he bathed, resting his feet on elephant tusks so that they might

An area of the palace, *c*.1890, possibly the place used by the Asantehene for bathing; the floor is paved.

never touch the earth, sleeping quarters, places for his wives and servants, and rooms for public or private discussion and for the storage of valuables. These rooms probably numbered several dozen in total. Behind the palace, towards the swamp, additional housing was provided for some of the King's wives and their servants. Nearly all visitors were impressed: 'The apartments of the Royal premises are of the same order and style as those of the native dwellings . . . but the Royal apartments are of much larger dimensions than those of the people, and are kept exquisitely clean. The King's residence in Kumasi with its numerous attached buildings covers a space of ground, not less perhaps than 5 acres.'[15] Even the hostile Sir Garnet Wolseley, having led the 1874 invasion, commented: 'I visited the royal palace and was surprised to find it though not imposing in character yet well laid out, clean and fairly well kept. Some of its buildings were of substantial masonry [he presumably means the nearby 'Stone Palace'], and most of it was solidly constructed and admirably roofed in.'[16]

The palace and other important buildings had internal lavatories 'generally situated under a small arch way in the most retired angle of the building, but not infrequently upstairs, within a separate room like a small closet, where the large hollow pillar also assists to support the upper storey: the holes are of a small circumference, but dug to a surprising depth, and boiling water is daily poured down, which effectually presents the least offence'.[17] The cleanliness of Kumase impressed most visitors. The red and white clay of the buildings was frequently renewed and polished during peaceful times, and the streets were

swept and cleared at the King's order before important visitors were permitted to enter the city.[18]

The buildings along the main streets belonged to important functionaries and to major chiefs from outside who had periodically to visit Kumase on political business or to attend the annual Odwira festival. Each house would shelter an ever-changing collection of dependants, servants, relatives and friends, and some of those young men who, as Bonnat noted, made their way to Kumase to seek their fortunes by attaching themselves to important men, even to the King, the first step to high office and wealth, or to disgrace, banishment or death. The majority of these houses had open rooms (*adampan*) overlooking the street: 'The houses looking into the streets are all public rooms on the ground floor, varying [in] dimensions from about 24′ by 12 to 15′ by 9. They are entirely open to the street in front; but raised above its level from one to six feet, by an elevated floor consisting of clay polished with red ochre. They are entered from the street by steps made of clay, and polished like the floor. . . . Each of these open rooms is connected with a number of rooms behind it, quite concealed from public view, which constitute the dwellings of the people; and these may be connected with each public room in the manner above described, from 50 to 250 inmates.'[19]

Office-holders transacted their formal business in these open rooms over-looking the street: to them came petitioners, clients and others. It is possible that they were used in this way in order to diminish suspicion that the office-holder was secretly plotting against others: the *adampan* allowed at least some

47

public businesses to be conducted publicly. In 1872 some of the Kumase offices were reorganised and new *adampan* were built for the new arrangements. The King took a special interest in these, inspecting them to see that they were properly refurbished for the Odwira festival.[20]

A 19th-century royal building.

The decorations of each of the major buildings in Kumase and elsewhere showed a considerable amount of variation within the same general style. The invention shown in this way contributed to the attraction of the city and gave the populace evidence of the ingenuity of the craftsmen employed. Of course, not all outsiders were impressed by these buildings. One British soldier wrote: 'Absolutely they have no idea of pictorial design, the rude scroll-work which ornaments some of their houses representing no animate or inanimate object.'[21]

Only a few houses and temples, all outside the capital, are still decorated in the old way, and the meanings of many of the traditional patterns have now been lost. However, a little can still be learned from surviving buildings. A few have low reliefs in representational form: for example, a crocodile grasping a mudfish in its mouth decorates one of the walls of an old temple at Dwenease. Several proverbs are associated with this image, one often used in connection with gods. One saying states that 'only a bad crocodile eats the creature which shares the same hole in the river bed', while another indicates that 'if the mudfish gets anything it will ultimately go to the crocodile'. Both, therefore, are concerned with ideas of co-operation or exploitation between the weak and

48

An interior court of the royal mausoleum at Bantama. Two English ewers dating from the reign of Richard II can be seen in the foreground.

strong. At the village of Saaman two images of the upper part of a figure holding a gun or stick in each raised hand flank the main entrance door to a temple. It is possible these are meant to suggest the power of the priest and his god. A similar image at another shrine is said to represent the priest beating an iron bell (*dawuro*) to call up the god. A figure of a man with gunpowder is said to indicate the god is ready for war, and other low-relief decorations show the backward-facing *sankofa* bird with the meaning that one should not fear to turn back to sort out a difficult situation.[22]

Besides images which are easily recognisable, there are a large number of designs which nowadays are sometimes interpreted by Asante as representational and sometimes seen as purely abstract cursive (*kyimkyim*) or rectilinear patterns with no clear meanings. One such design is a curved form which some informants claim represents a kola leaf and hence the proverb 'it takes a wise child to separate the leaves of (bitter) wild and cultivated kola'. Another design is thought for obvious reasons to represent a heart and hence, among other interpretations, the saying 'if you have (a strong) heart you will overcome all difficulties'. A lozenge shape is sometimes interpreted as a mirror and interlacing cursive designs as the holes in a tree used by nesting birds. Curved shapes, like loops hanging beneath horizontal bars, are said to be jaw-bones (of slain enemies) and chevron patterns, climbing snakes.

It is clear that although the surviving traditional buildings show great skill and command of design and materials the significance of much of their decoration has now been lost. How far this significance was generally known in the past is also debatable. It is possible that most Asante, apart from members of the court and those involved in their creation, did not know very much about these designs. It is also possible that if questioned they would have done as they do now and look for recognisable representational forms and from these move into verbal elaboration. We have no knowledge of when this style of decoration developed, although it was well-established by the first decades of the last century. It is just possible that the low-relief decorations on major buildings ultimately derived from Islamic inscriptions, either on imported metal vessels or those produced on wood, paper and cloth by travelling Muslim teachers who visited Asante; such writings were thought to give protection. The distinctive feature of Kumase building was the open rooms of major officials' houses looking directly on to the street. The whole history of this form of Asante architecture and decoration needs further investigation, for it is quite unlike that practised by any other groups in the area. The many pillars used are strongly reminiscent of the forms used in stone buildings, yet this, with a single exception, was restricted to European-inspired buildings on the coast; while the open-work screens in some houses seem more reminiscent of North African building.

The Asante kings took a close interest in their capital. According to Bowdich Osei Bonsu 'meditated great improvements and embellishments in his capital, on his return from the war, when it was intended that every captain should be presented with an extraordinary sum out of the treasury for adorning or enlarging his house. The ruined streets between Asafoo and Bantama were to be rebuilt, and the 6 or 7 small crooms [villages] between Kumasi and Baramang [the King's country residence] were to be pulled down and the inhabitants to occupy a wide street to extend from the city to that croom. This was the darling design of the King; he had already made a sound, broad and almost direct road, and numerous labourers were continuing to bring it as near as possible to a direct line.'[23]

The King was behind a far more revolutionary change in the capital – the erection of the extraordinary 'Stone Palace' or *Aban* completed in 1822 and modelled on the European-derived stone buildings on the coast. The King claimed that the idea came from the earlier Asantehene, Osei Kwadwo. The Stone Palace, the King said, was 'for his own immediate residence, roofed with brass pans beaten into flat surfaces, and laid over an ivory framework appearing within. The windows and doors to be cased in gold, and the door posts and pillars of ivory . . . the King dwelt ardently on the intention, and by their frequent conversations on the subject, his chiefs appeared scarcely less anxious for the execution than himself'.[24] A few years later Dupuis saw the work proceeding: the craftsmen and stone used had been sent up from the coast – some, at least, by the Dutch governor Daendels. The King reiterated: 'That building you see is to be made very grand. The inside shall be gold, ivory and brass-pan.' He asked Dupuis to help provide sacrifices to ensure it was well-founded and diplomatically offered to name his new 'fort' after King George IV of England.[25]

The *Aban* does not seem to have been used regularly as a royal residence; possibly it was too small to hold the hordes of attendant minor officials. It does not seem to have influenced political life in any major way except in so far as it demonstrated the King's power and willingness to innovate and to impress European missions which were received there. Freeman visited it in 1841 and noted thirty-one gold-handled swords and several gold-decorated calabashes displayed in one room, while in another room the King and some of his senior councillors were sitting, surrounded by various items of glass and other exotic valuables. One function of the place was as a treasure storehouse, and especially for those exotic items which were not absorbed into the established system of regalia or used for display.

Several soldiers and war-correspondents visited the *Aban* in 1874 and left their impressions: 'The exterior was surrounded, as were all the buildings of the palace, with a tall fence of reeds, closely bound together. It had a courtyard, under the sheds of which the King kept his cellar of palm wine – of champagne and brandy too, they say – his umbrellas new and old, his chairs and man-baskets of state, covered with scarlet cloth and leopard skin.' Horns and drums were also kept here, while on the upper floors were 'the art treasures of the monarchy'.[26] These upper rooms reminded one English visitor of the junk shops of Wardour Street because of the mixture of apparently unrelated items which filled them – books in various languages, paintings, copies of old newspapers, carpets, glass items, clocks and old furniture. The British seized some of these, and the building was later blown up. The pieces taken included a Queen Anne silver tankard, other items of plate, 'a fine old coffee pot', 'the King's collection of engravings, some of them fine old prints', and some lithographs of women in national dress.[27] This royal taste for new forms of building was re-expressed by Kofi Kakari in 1874 a few weeks before the

The Asantehene's Stone Palace, 1874.

British entered Kumase: he instructed the captive missionaries Ramseyer and Kuhne to build him a European house a little way out of the capital.[28]

Asantehene Kwaku Dua II receiving a British official, 1884.

Near the palace was the great market-place which had other functions besides the daily sale of goods (although so much business was transacted there that the King's servants sometimes scavenged for dropped gold-dust). As the largest open space within the city, it was used for major parades and some of the receptions for important visitors. Here, for example, the great general Adu Bofo paraded with 20,000 troops in 1871. The market was not a secular place; it contained special mystically powerful objects. There was a large brass basin, a great *suman* or even a *bosom*, which was somehow connected with the continued success of the market. A stone was thrown into this after each campaign to indicate the number of wars fought by the kingdom, and a captive was dedicated to it and fed free from the market. There was also a sacred tree of great age whose fall in early 1874 was seen as an omen of defeat.[29] The royal horn-blowers went into the market every night, as near to midnight as they could estimate, and blew a phrase which indicated one day had ceased and another was beginning.[30] The market was also used by armies returning from the field: here they paraded their captives, with soldiers carrying sticks to indicate the number slain in each unit.

The King attended some receptions in the market, but when he appeared in public he normally sat in state, surrounded by officials, on one of the circular, stepped platforms scattered throughout the city. These clay *sumpene* were burnished with a coat of red clay (*ntwuma*). In appearance they were rather like a stack of concentric discs of diminishing size. The *sumpene* of the capital seem to have had three to five steps with the top platform about 2–3 m in diameter, each step being about 30 cm in height. Similar, but smaller, platforms were usually positioned in the street near the palaces of chiefs of major states such as Dwaben, where Freeman noted 'a small mound, which was kept in proper form, and polished with red ochre, on which Boatin [the King of Dwaben] sat under his large umbrellas to keep the *adai* custom'.[31]

The life of the King, like that of others, was given form and rhythm by the Asante forty-two-day calendar. This determined on which days men and women could work and travel and on which days they had to stay in or near their houses, sacrifice to their ancestors or participate in the worship of the gods. In the case of the Asantehene the structure of time laid down by the calendar, as much as the needs of state, produced periods in which the King appeared in public as well as times when he remained secluded in his palace. On the former, public occasions the *sumpene* were used primarily, perhaps only, on or shortly before the two *adae* days. On these the King first made offerings to his ancestors at their blackened stools (see Chapter 7). Then he returned to his own quarters, bathed and dressed in rich cloth and ornaments, and with his temples and upper arms decorated with patterns in white clay he proceeded to one of the *sumpene*. 'At the commencement of the *adae* custom all strangers are expected to go and pay their respects to the King, by way of congratulation on his continued good health.'[32]

A gold-decorated calabash used by the Asantehene for drinking palm wine. Diam. 17.9 cm.

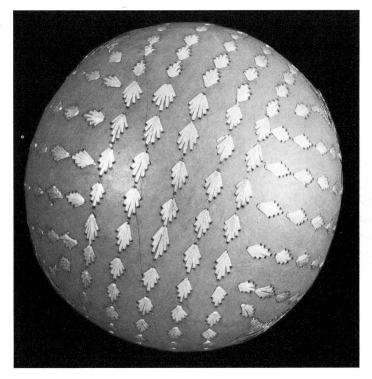

53

There the King sat in state on one of the royal leather and wood chairs, members of his entourage seated beneath and in front of him. To this *sumpene* would come all important visitors to his capital, to greet him and, in many cases, to receive from him gifts of gold-dust. At the same time he would drink palm wine with his followers and those he wished to influence. The wine was drunk from bowls made from half a globular gourd, extensively decorated with thin strips of gold and silver, woven in and out of holes drilled through it. The gourds leaked but that was immaterial, for the King also deliberately allowed the wine to spill from his mouth and run through his beard. Seated beneath one of his state umbrellas, the King's ritual drinking and giving combined public display with a more archaic symbolism. Bonnat saw many of these public drinkings during his captivity at the capital: 'The day of the great fetish, which precedes the big adae and which is always a Monday, the King quits his palace and goes solemnly to sit on one of the many stands of red stone which are placed here and there at different points in the town. There, surrounded by all the officers of his household and all the great ones of the Kingdom present in Kumasi, he drinks in two separate draughts a cup refilled with palm-wine.' After the King drank, the wine was shared with the chiefs and strangers. While the King was actually drinking, 'the large drums were played, and seven arrows were shot from the bow, to let the people know he was still holding the calabash to his mouth'.[33]

All at the capital had to keep strict behavioural rules. All Asante settlements had their own *akyiwadie*, that is, things hated and prohibited. The range of these was considerable and could include, for example, carrying in pineapples with the tops attached, or bundles of firewood, as well as excluding certain animals such as goats or black dogs, or certain humans such as albinos, hunchbacks, and so on. Such prohibitions are usually explained as having been imposed in the past by gods to end an affliction affecting the village; some are ascribed to the legendary priest Anokye. Those who break such prohibitions are thought to put themselves and the community in danger. In the past they were usually fined and ordered to make sacrifices to the stools or gods of the town. Such prohibitions gave an individuality to each settlement and provided its members with certain peculiar sets of knowledge and behaviour.

The Kumase prohibitions seem to have been exceptionally numerous and the penalties for breaking them, wittingly or unwittingly, particularly heavy as these were enforced by the King's officers. Bowdich noted that during his stay a man was beheaded 'for transgressing the law by picking up gold which he dropped in the public market place, where all that falls is allowed to accumulate until the soil is washed on state emergencies'.[34] The exact status of this particular rule is unclear, but visitors were also told of prohibitions of less directly economic importance. Ramseyer and Kuhne listed those in force in the 1870s, 'the breach of which was occasionally punished by death': nothing was to be planted there, no palm-oil was to be spilled in the street, no egg was to be allowed to fall and break, and no one with sandals made of horse hide was to enter the palace. No one was to whistle in Kumase, nor smoke a European pipe in the streets or carry such a pipe with a burden, and no burden packed

with green palm branches was to be carried in the town. In addition, people
were to hide themselves when the King's eunuchs called (probably as a
warning of the approach of the royal wives), and nobody was to work a farm on
Thursdays (the day of the Earth goddess *Asase Yaa*). The two missionaries also
narrate how a woman in whose market basket a vulture became entangled was
taken for execution. Grass roofs were forbidden in the capital, perhaps as a
precaution against the fires which constantly threatened the capital.[35] Bonnat,
their fellow captive, was also informed that anyone who spilled a drop of palm-
oil or an egg was immediately decapitated. He recorded a rule that whoever
did not use a pad of banana leaves under a head load when entering Kumase

A court of the
Asantehene's palace,
c.1880.

was put to death, that sneezing in the streets, and especially near the palace,
was punished by death, as was calling a chief by the wrong name.[36]

The exact rationale of the Kumase rules cannot now be recovered. Nevertheless, it is clear that many of them relate to the Asante concern to maintain
clear distinctions between different areas of their cosmos: items should not be
spilled, the wild should not be brought into the town, chiefs should be known
only by their correct names. In practice they most probably served to make life
in the capital a matter of constant fear and attention and to emphasise the
powers over life and death of the monarch and his officials. Possibly they also
provided the excuse for removing those who could not otherwise be eliminated.
Life in Kumase was never completely secure, and as nearly all its inhabitants
were involved, one way or another, with the court and the government of the
realm, violence and the sudden overthrow of fortune were never far from the
surface.

4 Gods and lesser powers

This chapter attempts to give an outline of nineteenth-century Asante religion. The evidence is poor and thin, for early European visitors were prejudiced against local beliefs, condemning without inquiring. Major rites were held on certain special days (*nnabone*) and were not easily seen by outsiders. Practices seem to have varied in different places and over time. Many religious activities were, by definition, mysterious and secret. Most Asante did not expect to know much about their gods; to those who did knowledge was power.

It is, nevertheless, possible to obtain a broad idea of Asante beliefs and practices. The Asante believed in a supreme creator, Onyame (or 'Nyame), who created the world but played little further part in men's lives. Beneath Onyame were large numbers of lesser powers. The chief of these were usually referred to as *atano*, after the river Tano, and were often associated with major rivers. Of lesser power, but with broadly similar characteristics, were the *abosom*, superhuman beings which, like the *atano*, came into contact with mankind by possessing individuals to serve as media. At a still lower level of power were the 'fetishes' (*asuman*), conglomerations or conjunctions of materials believed to be powerful, and initially activated by having offerings made over them. The Asante see their gods in a hierarchy beneath Onyame. In religion, as in political life, there are always superior and inferior powers; as the proverb says, 'There is somebody seated on somebody else' (*Obi-te-obi-so*).

Virtually all Asante firmly believe in the existence of the creator, Onyame. 'Nyame is known by a number of names of which Onyankopon and Otweadu-ampon are the most common. These are often scanned by the Asante as expressing some of God's major attributes; for example, Rattray was told that Onyame derived from *onya*, 'to get', and *mee*, 'to be full'. The Asante believe that 'Nyame responds to direct prayers and supplications, but for the rest he is almost unknowable by definition. 'Nyame is a typical West African 'withdrawn' god. The Asante version of a widespread African myth explains the split between man and God. In the Asante myth 'Nyame becomes annoyed by the noise of a woman making *fu-fu*, the Asante food *par excellence*, made by pounding boiled plantain or cassava in a wooden mortar. Separation between God and man is thus caused by a quintessential activity in Asante life: for man to live in the ordinary world there must be a division between him and God. Despite this man can still seek God's help through direct prayers. According to Rattray, there were formerly priests who served 'Nyame and temples to him in secluded parts of old palaces, but there is no other record of them.[1] Today virtually all prayers and libations start with a humble and pious request to 'Nyame for his aid and attention.

Formerly shrines to God were set up inside most houses. A brass bowl, clay pot or calabash was placed in the forks of a branch of the *Alstonia gongensis* tree set vertically in the ground. In times of need and trouble eggs or fowls were offered at this with a prayer. As the missionary Freeman noted, 'they keep [hens] for the sake of the eggs, abundance of which they offer to Fetish'.[2] This term 'fetish', from the Portuguese *feitiço* ('something made'), was used by Europeans to refer to virtually any thing, act or belief which local people seemed to treat as important. By definition things which were 'fetish' were irrational, and therefore further inquiry could not explain them. Anything Europeans could not understand was labelled 'fetish' and therefore put beyond explanation. The term had a long and useful life in helping whites maintain a grossly simplified view of local society and local ideas.

Sacrifices of an egg or a fowl at a *'Nyame'dua* are depicted in many goldweights. (Altars of this sort are erected to lesser gods today.) 'Nyame is mentioned in many sayings which emphasise his role as the ultimate power behind the events of life and the final source of justice. *'Nyame nkrabea nni kwatibea* ('The destiny the Supreme Being has assigned to you cannot be avoided') and *Onyankopon nkum wo na'dasani kum wo, wun wu* ('If the Supreme Being does not kill you but a human kills you, you do not die').[3]

Today the Asante paint sayings about 'Nyame on lorries or over doorways, or take them as pseudonyms or the names of businesses, declaring publicly their dependence on God and warning the envious of this protection. Although 'Nyame is used to explain such perennially vexing questions as differences in character, or the source of life in procreation, particular events and especially misfortune are usually ascribed to other causes, for example, the anger of ancestors or gods or to fetishes whose rules have been broken.

Beneath 'Nyame are the *atano* and *abosom*, 'gods' or 'powers' who possess men and women to serve as mediumistic priests (*akomfo*) and can provide guidance and aid. Each god has its own character, revealed by the movements and speech of the possessed priest, although the latter cannot recall what occurs when he is seized by the god.

Atano, the major powers, are believed to come from the Tano and other great rivers. Many have their main, possibly original, shrines in the Wankyi and Takyiman areas, although they are now spread throughout Asante. They are sometimes conceived as the 'children' of 'Nyame.

Atano and *abosom* have physical manifestations, such as *akomfo*, shrines or temples, and entering into transactions with mankind that are given a material expression. Formerly each area and state (*oman*) contained a large number of *atano* and *abosom*. Some would be active, having *akomfo* who periodically danced and became possessed, and some would be quiescent, because their medium had died or because the god had somehow 'left' him or her. People would come to worship active gods, seeking advice and healing, and fetching sacrificial thanks-offerings (*aseda*), usually sheep. While some gods enjoyed only local prestige, others attracted supplicants from afar; consequently some were poor, while others had land and servants given them by rulers of states they had helped. Southern Akan groups settling in Asante brought the shrines of gods with them; others were fetched from the Wankyi or Takyiman areas; new gods were continually making themselves known.

58

Gods still reveal themselves, perhaps most commonly by 'seizing' persons, making them behave as if they were becoming mad (*abondamfo*).[4] The person becomes disoriented (sometimes running wildly into the bush and becoming lost), speaks incoherently and hears voices. He or she may cease to eat and become withdrawn. Herbalists (*dunsinfo*) and priests will be consulted until the cause has been identified. Sometimes the priests will decide, while possessed by their own gods, that a new or an established god wishes the afflicted person to become its priest. The situation of the first seizing may suggest this: for example, if a person is possessed at a priest's funeral, it will be assumed that the dead priest's god is seeking a successor.

Once this was established, training followed. Traditionally this lasted seven years, the trainee living with an established priest and learning to control his possession (so that the god could speak through him) and to dance the *akom* dance in order to become possessed under controlled circumstances. The trainee was taught herbal lore and to treat illnesses. During this period he or

Wooden carving of a priest (*okomfoo*) wearing a palm-fibre skirt (*doso*) and with a headband of protective talismans. Ht 47 cm.

she was supposed to refrain from sexual intercourse and to keep the dietary and behavioural prohibitions of the god.

After training, the new *ọkọmfoọ* was tested at a ritual attended by his teacher and all local priests. At this he was expected to become possessed, with the god's help to answer riddles or questions set by the other priests, and to divine successfully using items fished out of a pot of water and herbs (*nsuoyowa*).[5] Today this training is usually paid for by the priest's matrilineal kin, and large thanks-offerings may be made to the instructing priest. The family will expect to profit later from the money the god brings.

When an entirely new god revealed itself for the first time and chose a suitable medium, a shrine had to be made. This was a container in which were placed objects and pieces of animal and vegetable matter which helped in 'holding' the god, so that the god entered the shrine and through it his priest or priestess. A seventeenth-century account of one of these shrines is given by Bosman: 'Each Priest or Feticheer has his peculiar Idol, prepared and adjusted in a particular and different manner, but most of them like the following Description. They have a great Wooden Pipe [cask] filled with Earth, Oil, Blood, and the bones of dead Men and Beasts, Feathers, Hair, and to be short, all sorts of Excrementitious and filthy Trash, which they do not endeavour to mould into any Shape, but lay it into a confused heap in the Pipe.'[6] At present the great majority of these shrines are brass basins (*yowa*). The earliest such imports from North Africa or Egypt, via the trans-Saharan routes, were costly items of great prestige, suitable receptacles for superhuman powers.

Bosman's derisive account indicates the underlying European contempt for many aspects of local life which were treated with a ruthless literalism. The contents of the barrel, 'Excrementitious and filthy Trash', were taken at face value and denied a symbolic dimension. To use such materials, whites assumed, indicated intellectual inferiority in the users. Local sculpture was judged in a similar way and esteemed according to its closeness to literal representation. This literalness, this inability to understand that indigenous peoples might think, act and speak symbolically or metaphorically, also hampered for years diplomatic relations between Asante and European powers. The highly subtle, verbal character of Asante court art and the allusiveness of Asante speech-making and negotiating were totally overlooked by the Europeans, who thereby grossly miscalculated Asante intentions.

These shrines (*yowa*) are of crucial importance in Asante religion. Each was usually kept in a special room inside a compound, a white cloth draped over the door to warn menstruating women away. Some of the most successful gods were kept in a separate temple (*bosom'dan* or *bosom'fie*). The shrine was placed upon the head of a male priest on 'bad' days (*nnabone*) in the forty-two-day cycle (see p.53), and the priest became possessed, usually inside the shrine room, where supplicants consulted him. Later in the day he would sometimes dance with the god on his head to the music of the god's drums and the songs of women devotees. Numbers of gold-weights depict this dance. Occasionally a priest would display his prowess by dancing with the heavy pan resting on his shoulders and the nape of his neck, his head pushed forward. The shrines were,

A small temple
(*bosom'dan*, *bosom'fie*),
late 19th century.

apparently, never carried by female priests but by specially chosen male carriers (*bosom soafo*).

It was the role of gods and priests to advise on obscure areas of existence, to trace the causes of sickness and misfortune, and help alleviate or remove these. The gods helped to make sense of the ways in which the lives of individuals and the community departed from the expected. Answers to supplicants' inquiries were often phrased in allusive and ambiguous terms.

Offerings and prayers are still made over shrines. Sometimes the blood of sacrificed chickens is dripped on them, but more usually raw eggs are rubbed on to 'wash' (*dware*) them. Over a period of time the brass bowls become filled by this and an accretion builds up at the top. At this point the full brass bowl is sometimes placed inside a larger bowl and the process continued. Alternatively, some of the contents of the old bowl can be put in a new vessel. Because of the former practice, it is possible that many nineteenth-century European brass bowls seen today may contain far earlier bowls within them.

Major rituals for *abosom* were held yearly, sometimes coinciding with the readiness of the new yam crop, and were attended by those who had been helped during the year, bringing their promised thanks-offerings of money, liquor or animals. Other priests would also attend, and sacrifices of sheep might be offered.

61

In general *abosom* were associated with the bush and the wild; and they are still believed to come from the areas outside human society – the rivers and the forest and, sometimes, from the sky. Thus Bonnat noted a belief that *atano*, '*les plus méchants*'[7] of spiritual beings, lived in the forest. Their temples were often situated at the edges of villages, between human society and the wild, or isolated on river banks. Gods were conceived as dangerous and unpredictable, and constantly seeking sacrifices to satisfy their greed: *Ọbosom a ọye nnam na odi aboade* ('The fetish [god] that is sharp is the one that has offerings vowed to it') and *Ọbosomfo ka ne nkonim, na ọnka ne nkogu* ('The priest tells of his victories but not his defeats').[8] Today the shrine of the god is often placed upon a stool, the favoured type depicting a crocodile with a mudfish in its mouth. This image has a range of proverbial meanings which turn upon problems of weak and strong living together. For gods the image is doubly appropriate: the power of god to man is likened to that of crocodile to mudfish, while the god's power to exist independently but also to enter partially the world of man is paralleled by the crocodile's amphibious abilities.

Powerful priests are believed to be aided by creatures from the wild – *mmoatia* (literally, 'short' or 'little beasts'), a term usually translated as 'dwarfs'. These are described as being about 30–60 cm in height, more or less of human form except that their feet point backwards. There are three sorts: red, black and white, the three basic colour groups of the Asante spectrum. Dwarfs are unpredictable: they may either attack or befriend those lost in the bush. A person befriended is miraculously sustained with eggs touched to the mouth. Dwarfs also teach the powers of herbs to lost people who help others when they return from the bush. They communicate by whistling, the pattern of tones reproducing those of ordinary speech.

Some *akọmfo* are believed to have troops of dwarfs who help them, bringing information or beating enemies. At some temples one can hear whistling and scampering from inside closed rooms or behind curtains hung to divide shrine rooms; it is claimed these noises are made by *mmoatia*. Priests claim dwarfs are greedy for sugar and the schnapps brought to pour libations, and that if not adequately rewarded they will beat the priest before returning to the bush. A few carvings are known which represent *mmoatia* with their backward-turned feet.

Mmoatia express the ambiguous feelings Asante have about the bush, at once a dangerous and unstructured area where humans may easily become disoriented and a source of certain types of power. It is risky for humans to use these and they can never by depended upon fully. Asante also accept that knowledge is unevenly distributed within society and often success is achieved only with some secret, mysterious help such as dwarfs.

A few gods come directly from the wild where hunters or farmers find mysterious stones or lumps of material (*dufa*) which they take home with them. Later, when people become sick or possessed, it is diagnosed that these items come from a god which wishes sacrifices to be made to it.

Formerly priests and priestesses lived somewhat outside normal society and were feared by ordinary people. Their primary function was to control the

A modern priest in front of a restored temple at Bawjwiase.

intrusion of supernatural beings into human life and they conversed with powers unknown and invisible to most humans. It is said priests and priestesses did not marry, and Bowdich claimed priestesses were highly promiscuous, that is they disregarded normal sexual rules. Appearance emphasised *akomfo's* difference. Their costume was a raffia skirt (*doso*) and when possessed they went barefoot – the antithesis of chiefs whose feet were supposed never to touch the earth. Priests' hair was allowed to grow into long, matted locks in the style known as *mpesempese* (a term sometimes translated as 'I don't like it'). Uncut hair is usually associated with dangerous behaviour: madmen let their locks grow, and the same hair-style was worn by royal executioners.

The relationship of priests to the system of chiefly rule is obscure, and it is unclear how far *akomfo* acted together, apart from training new members. Missionaries suspected that priests passed information to impress and trick ordinary people, but such charges are impossible to substantiate, and in any case it is hard to accept that the whole religious system was founded on trickery and self-delusion.

Many priests seem to have achieved an unusual degree of independence. This and their self-confidence struck several nineteenth-century observers favourably. Ramseyer and Kuhne, for example, testified to the kindness of one priest who sent them food and drink and to the way in which other priests visited them, apparently feeling that they and the Christians were engaged on the same type of work.[9]

There is evidence that chiefs tried to exercise a degree of control over priests. In several states (*oman*) it is claimed that new gods could not be introduced without the approval of the Omanhene and his council, although it is impossible to say how far this operated in practice. There also exist numerous traditions telling how rulers laid traps to see which priests could prophesy or divine accurately. The Asantehene had a god called Diakomfo ('eat priests'), and it is said priests adjudged false were killed over his shrine. Certain gods were classed as state gods and were thought to have a particularly close relationship to the state's success and prosperity. Many of these seem to have been brought by the first settlers in the area or to have been 'found' by them in the new land. Other gods seem to have been captured in war and, with their priests, to have been brought back to help the victorious group. Bonnat noted a tradition that the priests with a defeated army were not slain.[10]

War was one of the most important, and at times most profitable, activities of the Asante state. Before a war senior servants of the Asantehene visited the shrines of major gods with gifts, to ask for guidance and support, and to promise rewards for success. They may also, of course, have received knowledge obtained by the webs of communication centred on the shrine. After successful campaigns, gods were rewarded with land and captives, large umbrellas and *asipim* chairs, and their priests given gold or silver crescent-shaped pendants to wear. Some priests and gods accompanied the armies, or missions, as in the case of the three priests in the retinue of General Akyeampon when he returned to the capital after negotiating in the south in the early 1870s.[11] They also accompanied important diplomats. In 1881 an embassy arrived at Cape Coast 'consisting of a linguist, a sword-bearer, three court criers, and an old fetish priestess, the latter of whom threatened to destroy both the English and Fantis if they did not at once abandon any intention they might have of making war on Ashanti'.[12] Numerous sacrifices, provided by the rulers, were made to gods when armies met with reversals, as happened in 1873.[13]

Each god had a group who acted for it as trustees under the *bosom'wura*, a term which can be translated as 'master of the god', although this may give a wrong impression of human control. The *bosom'wura* was responsible for the maintenance of the god's room or temple, and the proper service of cooks, drummers and others who served the god. Offerings to the god were divided between him and those he represented, the priest and, usually, the village chief. The Omanhene was considered to be the *bosom'wura* of a state god; for lesser gods the head of the lineage which had brought the god or which provided the first priest was usually the *bosom'wura*.

The priesthood's political power is difficult to estimate, and in any case the situation was never static. Early in the nineteenth century some senior Asante appear to have considered that Islam could provide a firmer support for the state, but little came of this.[14] Later, the disruptive potential of Christianity was recognised, and its missionaries were given little chance of preaching either within or outside the capital until the British seized control. At the time of Bowdich's visit the cult of the royal ancestors, incorporated in the great annual Odwira new yam festival, may have been emphasised to counterbalance the priesthood. Towards the end of Asante independence the priesthood, or at least the idiom of priesthood, was used to counter royal power. In the troubles of the 1880s some of those opposed to Asantehene Mensa Bonsu claimed to be reincarnations of the famous priest Anokye and other long-dead priests. They tried to assassinate the King, and many were taken and executed.[15] The incident is obscure, but it appears that those involved were declaring their complete separation from the usual political process and appealing to a different view of the Asante state. The use of the names of famous priests for this purpose seems, therefore, to indicate a pre-existing tension between state and priesthood.

Today the Asante believe the priest Anokye helped Asantehene Osei Tutu (*fl.* 1700–10) to found Asante by various magical acts and especially by bringing from the sky the Golden Stool. This seems a recent myth: earlier traditions of the kingdom's origin make little or no mention of Anokye and are couched in terms of the powers of monarchs.[16] It seems that as real political power has been eroded the myth of priestly power has grown. However, if priests had formed in any sense a secret, unofficial network, they signally failed to act in any concerted way once the political regime which had opposed or used them was destroyed by the British in 1896.

Asante religion was never static. New gods revealed themselves and established ones 'withdrew' when their priests died or ceased to become possessed. The prestige and wealth of individual gods fluctuated. Some great *atano* in the Wankyi-Takyiman area seem to have been pre-eminent for long periods, while

others enjoyed briefer popularity. Their prestige depended greatly on the personality of their priests and their power to advise and prophesy correctly. Supplicants would travel about until they found a god to solve their problems. Each god therefore had a shifting congregation as well as a central core of local people owing a more enduring allegiance. In some cases *asuman* may have begun to be given the attributes of *abosom* after their power was widely accepted.

Change was also inherent in the underlying structure of Asante belief. Supernatural power was seen as originating beyond society. New, exotic powers were actively sought. Nineteenth-century rulers consulted gods beyond the kingdom's boundaries. Ordinary men were willing to travel far to obtain new *asuman* and medicines. The great god Dente, from Kete Krakye, the most northerly navigable point on the Volta River, was introduced into some parts of Asante in the late nineteenth century, as were many lesser fetishes and medicines.

In broad terms the Asante used their *abosom* and *asuman* as ways of dealing with unclear or unusual situations. As far as can be established, images were never shaped to represent the *abosom* and *atano*: these were spiritual powers, insubstantial like the wind (*mframa*) to which they are sometimes likened. Nevertheless, the shrines of some deities contained images. Dolls carved to help women become fertile were sometimes placed near the god's shrine (see Chapter 12). Carvings of women suckling children are said to have been placed in shrines and temples, although none has been recorded *in situ*.

Miscellaneous items may accumulate in a shrine room over the years, their origin and first significance forgotten after a generation or so. Relics of dead priests and priestesses – for example, their pipes – may be placed near the god they served. Pottery vessels, funerary terracottas and clay pipes, found in the bush, and neolithic axe or adze heads are also put there because they are in some way special and a shrine room is therefore the most appropriate place for them. Today family elders who have a shrine or stool room in their trusteeship place old objects there to prevent younger or disaffected members stealing and selling them.

Such items do not form the focus of, or serve as mnemonics for, any traditions; they become part and parcel of the furnishings, as it were, but are worthy of little remark in themselves. Large accumulations give the impression that the god is old-established and powerful, but it is not felt necessary to recall the history of individual items. Articles of courtly origin are different: swords, umbrellas or gold or silver lunates proclaim the god has aided a ruler and received formal recognition.

Images thus played a fairly small part in nineteenth-century religion. The power and character of gods was conveyed by the possessed dancing of their priests, their prophesying and apparent miracles. The reputation and wealth of a god was demonstrated by the size and decoration of its shrine and the number of its attendants and worshippers.

Unlike several of their neighbours the Asante have no tradition of masks and masquerade. Masks existed among different groups to the north-west and among the Adangbe people to the south-east. A masked cult, *Sakrabundi*, was seen by Austin Freeman at Odumase in Bron country in the 1880s and had probably travelled down trade routes from north of Bondukou in the Ivory Coast.[17] Masks may also have been used in Aowin areas to the south-west of Asante and, perhaps, in some Fante towns in Christmas and Easter parades. In the 1920s they were in use in Akwamu.[18] A mask existed near Nkoransa a few years ago, probably from the Bondukou Gbain witch-finding cult.

Although the Asante did not use masks, they cannot have been ignorant of them. There seem to be several reasons for their non-adoption. Firstly, many of the northern masks are owned and danced by closed associations who keep their activities secret. It is possible that Asante rulers actively discouraged the importation of masks as these would undermine their political control. It is striking that the only nineteenth-century masks were recorded in the 1880s when the Asantehene's powers were diminished. Secondly, the *akomfo*, being the mediums of the gods, did not need masks to help represent superhuman powers. They may also have opposed the introduction of new cults. Thirdly, the Asante lack any system of male initiation with which masks are used in some parts of the continent.

None of these reasons is entirely convincing, especially in view of the dramatic changes which occurred in Asante religion after 1900. After that date a large number of new protective medicines (*aduro*) and fetishes (*asuman*) were imported from outside Asante and used to combat witchcraft and other non-physical attacks which were widely believed to be destroying the local community. Many came from the general area where masks were found.[19] The spread of these cults was facilitated by the decay in the political system resulting from the impoverishment and defeat of the monarchy under Kofi Kakari, struggles between rival candidates in the 1880s, and the British removal in 1896 of the King and many major chiefs. New cults, whose priests required virtually no training and who gained their powers by purchase rather than the inspiration of a god, spread rapidly throughout the kingdom. Although individual cults were suppressed by the colonial government, others continued to be imported and to gain adherents. The traditional priesthood did little to resist the establishment of these cults which drew off adherents and deprived it of income. The failure of these new cults to take up masks to express their power remains puzzling. Masks would have been an exotic, mysterious element in keeping with the mysterious bundles of magical materials believed to give adherents protection against witches and other malefactors.

These cults were referred to as *asuman*, a term covering a vast range of objects of less power and more specific functions than *abosom*. *Asuman* can be obtained for almost any purpose: to protect a hunter, to keep thieves from a house or a farm, to bring money, or make an enemy sick. A person seeking a *suman* for a particular purpose will approach someone (usually a man) who is reputed to have such a *suman*. If the owner agrees, he will make one, showing the new owner how it is done, and in return receive a stipulated counter-gift (*aseda*). Most *suman* have names, and those who own them may have to keep a number of prohibitions: for example, avoiding the consumption of food with snails in it, or whistling near the *suman*.[20]

There is an element of secrecy about *asuman*, for their true purpose is usually known only to their owners. People are therefore suspicious of them, for they are never sure whether they are protective or aggressive. For example, many houses have *asuman* hanging over their doors from the street. The purpose of these may be to prevent thieves entering, to harm those who wish to harm the inhabitants, or perhaps to cause sickness to those who enter to commit adultery with occupants of the household – no outsider can ever be sure.

Muslims sold *asuman* for protection in war. These *safi* or *sebe* usually took the form of a short Islamic text, prayer or magical formula on a scrap of paper. The paper was later covered with a piece of folded leather so as to make a small square or rectangle, about 2.5 cm long and perhaps 1 cm thick. They were

Above (left) A talisman worn around the upper arm by major chiefs, the leather pouch covered with gold foil. Offinso state regalia. Ht 8.5 cm.

Above (right) The central *suman* (fetish) of the Abirewa cult of 1906, which promised to protect people against the mystical attacks of witches. The knives thrust through the bundle symbolise its power to kill wrong-doers. Ht 28.6 cm.

either worn around the neck on a leather thong or sewn to a garment. In the case of great chiefs the talisman might be covered in gold or silver sheet, worked in a variety of repoussé patterns, or the leather covering might itself be stamped with various designs and then have a thin layer of gold foil applied over it. Some also were covered in coloured leather, leopard skin or red imported cloth. They were sewn on to cotton smocks, made by non-Asante northerners, called *batakari*. The Asantehene and great chiefs showed their wealth and power by the number of talismans which festooned these *batakari*, and the Asantehene's Great *Batakari* (*Batakari Kẹse*) is believed to have strong protective power against gunshot and cutlass wounds.

After the British seized control of Asante a large number of new cults were imported to give protection against the attacks of witches and others who were believed to be subverting the moral basis of society. The first was Abirewa. Anyone who wished to harm mystically or to attack someone protected by the Abirewa medicine would be 'caught' by being made sick and, unless he confessed publicly, would be killed. Those who took the medicine and then tried to commit evil would be caught in the same way.

Abirewa probably originated on the southern borders of the Ivory and Gold Coasts, and the rapidity of its dissemination throughout Asante and the southern Gold Coast thoroughly alarmed the colonial administration which feared it might produce a united resistance to white rule. After evidence had been obtained that confessions to witchcraft were apparently encouraged by ill-treatment and that the corpses of those 'killed' by Abirewa were mutilated, the cult was suppressed.[21]

Abirewa was followed by a number of other imported cults, Hwemso, active in the early 1920s, Tigare, Brakune, Dubi, Kankamea and many others which flourished from the 1920s to the 1950s. All offered mystical protection and especially protection against witches. They all originated outside the boundaries of Asante, normally in the savannah areas to the north, and changed in character once brought into the forest zone. Most were suppressed by the colonial authorities.

The shrines of many of these new cults and many later imported *asuman* had small wood-carvings placed in them to represent the spiritual helpers (*boafo*) of the power. Apparently, they were produced in secret by local carvers and

A figure taken from a shrine of an anti-witchcraft power of the 1920s. A silver shilling is set in the top of the head to express the cult's power to attract money, and the right hand ends in a scoop, probably to receive money. Ht 29.6 cm.

70

clandestinely placed in the shrines. Many of them them have coatings or lumps
of medicine (*aduro*, *dufa*) on them. They were intended to impress those who
came to the shrines, and in some cases each 'helper' was given a name and to
some extent treated as an individual entity with special powers. It is possible
that carvings of this sort were spread from one or two centres by those who
were instrumental in disseminating the cults, but the exact place of carving of
most examples has yet to be established. One of these carvings, now in the
British Museum's collections, has an articulated arm ending in a small scoop or
cup, which was probably meant to receive offerings or payments made to the
power. The money-getting side of the cult is also indicated by the silver shilling
set in a plaster of medicine (*dufa*) on top of the head of the carving. Other
related carvings have knives stuck into them or tied to them indicating the
power of the *suman* to catch and punish malefactors, and are also heavily
coated with medicines. The images are rarely carved with any great skill, and
the form of many was almost entirely concealed by the *materia mystica* with
which they were covered and also, in many cases, by the lengths of cloth with
which they were 'dressed'. Most of these figures are carved in an ordinary
standing posture, and there is little or no attempt to give them a particularly
aggressive or threatening pose.

71

5 Gold and gold-working

By the nineteenth century the Asante government had developed into a series of specialised offices based on Kumase linking with local office-holders or performing specific diplomatic, trading or tax functions. The powers of the rulers of the founding states had been diminished and more direct control established in those areas subsequently incorporated into Asante. A complex bureaucracy was evolving. Rival groups struggled for power and influence and in the last quarter of the century rivalries sometimes became so acute that violence and assassination were prevalent.[1]

The rulers of the developing state used their riches to impress the public, to signal amongst themselves differences in rank, and to commemorate major events in their history. Those successful in government or trade sought the Asantehene's permission to convert newly achieved wealth into regalia to be transmitted to successors. While regalia would bedazzle and impress the populace and visitors, it conveyed more subtle messages to those learned in court traditions. Sometimes this was done verbally, for many items were intended to call to mind proverbs or aphorisms.

The Asante use of gold far exceeded anything Europeans encountered elsewhere in West Africa; but almost from the moment they landed on the Gold Coast they were aware that local leaders adorned their bodies with gold. The meeting between the Portuguese and the local ruler, Caramansa, in the place which became Elmina ('The Mine') gives a good idea of the use of such gold: the King, attended by servants and musicians, 'came naked, and his arms and legs and neck were covered with chains and trinkets of gold in many shapes, and countless bells and large beads of gold were hanging from the hair of his beard and his head'.[2]

This account suggests that gold-casting was well established on the coast by the late fifteenth century; it also encapsulates a moral and categorical problem which was to recur in subsequent centuries. Caramansa is 'naked', but at the same time his body is adorned with gold, produced and shaped in ways which indicated considerable technical skills. Europeans tended to see nakedness as an indication of an animal rather than a human nature. Because newly discovered peoples seemed to show no shame at their lack of clothing, some Europeans tended to see them as beings without a proper culture. To others nakedness and lack of shame indicated a lack of awareness of sin and guilt, without which a proper form of human, Christian society could not be built. For these and other reasons it was often assumed that local people had only the crudest forms of social system and religious beliefs and were incapable of either abstract thought or subtlety or delicacy of feeling. Yet the high technical skills of local people often conflicted with this view, posing unanswerable paradoxes.

The European greed for gold drew more and more traders and adventurers

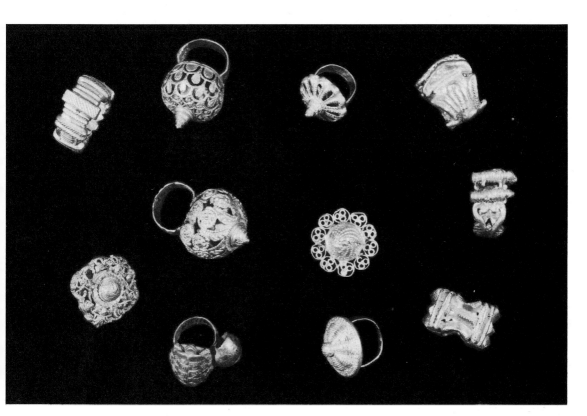

A selection of 19th-
century royal gold
finger or toe rings.

to the region; some left accounts of its local use, the way it was worked and the
quantities obtained. Thus Portuguese records show, for example, that a ship
from Elmina in 1502 returned with 250 marks of gold (each of 227 g) 'all in
manillas and jewels which the negroes are accustomed to wear', and it was
claimed that twelve to fifteen ships a year each brought the same quantity.[3]
Many accounts mention that the gold received was a mixture of dust and
made-up gold. Accounts of a voyage by John Lock in 1554–5 also indicate
items apparently made for white visitors.[4] 'Some of their women weare in their
bare armes certain foresleeves made of the plates of beaten golde. On their
fingers also they weare rings, made of golden wires, like a knot or wreathe, . . .
Among other things of golde, that our men bought of them for exchange of
their wares, were certaine dog-chaines and collars.'[5] A voyage in 1693 obtained similar made-up gold: 'The gold they took here was all in Fetishes,
which are small pieces wrought in many pretty figures, which the Blacks tie to
all Parts of their Bodies for Ornament, and are generally very good gold.'[6]

As far as we can tell virtually all worked gold was melted down by
Europeans. A few items – rings, gold hatbands, buttons, staff tops or snuff
boxes copied from European prototypes – were no doubt treasured, but most
local work was valued only for its bullion content.

Inevitably, not all gold was pure. Bosman noted that the gold from Denkyira
was pure but also contained 'fetiches' cast in moulds made of a sort of 'black
and very heavy earth'.[7] To get pure gold white traders were forced to take
these, although they were alloyed with copper and silver. The black earth

contained in some 'fetiches' deceived the unwary as to their true weight. Bosman distinguishes between 'fetiches' – those of pure gold, kept by the local people for wear, and those of alloy, which were cut up into bits and used as a sort of fiduciary currency: 'They are called Kakeraas [modern Asante, *Kakra-kakra*, 'small-small'], the word expressing something of little value; and the Gold itself is indeed very little worth . . . yet it passes current all over the Coast.'[8] The heavy black earth he mentions suggests that these items were cast by the lost-wax process (see p.80), being probably the clay and charcoal mixture used in the process. Lost-wax casting was certainly established in Asante by the early 1700s, for at that time the Dutch sent up cakes of wax as gifts to the court.

Cheating was rife. Local people faked or adulterated gold, probably in a vain attempt to tilt the balance of exchange in their own favour. Again they showed technical skill: 'Some pieces are cast by them so artificially that quite round for the thickness of a knife they are very fine Gold, and the vacancy filled up with copper, or perhaps iron. This is a newly invented cheat of theirs.'[9] Bosman also noted that silver, copper and ground-up coral were mixed with gold-dust and that gold had to be checked with a touchstone or put in a bowl and blown upon to remove the lighter material.[10]

Barbot recommended traders to have twenty-four gold needles, each of a particular purity for purpose of comparison, and warned that when local people blew away impurities from gold and then seemed to add more gold they actually removed metal under one of their finger nails.[11] Europeans also cheated, 'many of our Europeans making no scruple to weigh the gold by a heavier weight than they ought'.[12]

Barbot has left the earliest illustrations of Akan gold castings,[13] which are very similar to nineteenth-century Asante castings and may have been based on items taken back to Europe. Depictions of other objects – stools, weapons, etc. – are far less accurate and possibly based on descriptions only, as the items were not valuable or interesting enough to be shipped to Europe.

Gold was the key to local life and European contact. By the late seventeenth century, possibly earlier, most of the central and southern Gold Coast was committed to gold-dust currency. This greatly facilitated exchanges and encouraged the steady development of market-orientated production. It also led to a flowering in the art of gold-weights. But the problem of adulteration remained. On the coast emerged a new group of intermediaries, the gold-takers, who were responsible for testing all gold entering a white trading establishment and seeing their masters were never cheated. Some of these men may have been of mixed African and European parentage. Many are listed as serving European traders. In 1662 the New Africa Company specified that one of its staff at Cape Coast was to be a gold-taker, two appear (with three goldsmiths) in a list of the Company's personnel at Cape Coast Castle in 1749, and many later records mention these key men.[14] One proudly proclaimed his occupation and master on an ivory bracelet now in the British Museum's collections: 'John Acca Gold Taker Captain Baak' and on the other side 'I am the prince of Apolonia [*sic*] Tradesman'.[15]

By the nineteenth century coastal gold-takers were men of importance, appearing in public with servants and umbrellas, their hair and dress showing their profession: '. . . their heads entirely shaved, with the exception of a small patch a little on one side, from which hung a very handsome gold ornament, they had no European beads on, but round their wrists were bracelets of aggrey beads, mixed with strings charmed by the fetish man, or priest; also heavy gold manillas in the form of snakes, round each ankle was a string of gold ornaments, made in the shape of little bells, stools, musical instruments, weapons etc'. They also wore thick finger rings and elaborate sandals, 'the strap of which had a large tuft of many coloured silk'.[16] Some of this splendour derived from commission on all transactions. In the nineteenth century their task was not only to ensure the purity of the gold taken but also to discourage payments in the miscellaneous coinage used in coastal towns: gold-dust was far more profitable when exported to Europe.[17]

Varying estimates have been suggested for the quantities of gold produced in this region from its earliest exploitation until the end of the nineteenth century. These range from between 1,474,200 kg for the period AD 1500–1900 down to 396,900 kg for the period AD 1400–1900.[18] Whatever the quantities produced, the effects of gold in Asante were spectacular, for a proportion of all produced went to adorn the ruling group.

Virtually all royal insignia made use of cast gold. Bowdich's description shows the use of such gold: 'The sun was reflected, with a glare scarcely more

A gold neck torque.
Max. diam. 24 cm.

supportable than the heat, from the massy gold ornaments, which glistened in every direction . . . and massy gold necklaces, intricately wrought; suspended Moorish charms, dearly purchased, and enclosed in small square cases of gold, silver, and curious embroidery. Some wore necklaces reaching to the navel entirely of aggry beads; a band of gold and beads encircled the knee, from which several strings of the same depended; small circles of gold like guineas, rings, and casts of animals, were strung round their ancles [*sic*]; . . . manillas, and rude lumps of rock gold, hung from their left wrists, which were so heavily laden as to be supported on the head of one of their handsomest boys. Gold and silver pipes, and canes dazzled the eye in every direction. Wolves and rams heads as large as life, cast in gold, were suspended from their gold handled swords, which were held around them in great numbers; . . . immediately behind their chairs (which were of a black wood, almost covered by inlays of ivory and gold embossment) stood their handsomest youths, with corslets of leopard's skin covered with gold cockle shells, and stuck full of small knives, sheathed in gold and silver, and the handles of blue agate; cartouch [*sic*] boxes of elephant's hide hung below, ornamented in the same manner; a large gold handled sword was fixed behind the left shoulder, and silk scarves and horses tails (generally white) streamed from the arms and waist cloth: their long Danish mukets [*sic*] had broad rims of gold at small distances, and the stocks were ornamented with shells. Finely grown girls stood behind the chairs of some, with silver basins. . . . The executioner, a man of an immense size, wore a massy gold hatchet on his breast; . . . The king's four linguists were encircled by a splendor [*sic*] inferior to none, and their peculiar insignia, gold canes, were elevated in all directions, tied in bundles like fasces. The keeper of the treasury, added to his own magnificence by the ostentatious display of his service; the blow pan, boxes, scales and weights, were of solid gold'.

The Asantehene 'wore a fillet of aggry beads round his temples, a necklace of gold cock-spur shells strung by their largest ends, and over his right shoulder a red silk cord, suspending three saphies cased in gold; his bracelets were the richest mixtures of beads and gold, and his fingers covered with rings; his cloth was of a dark green silk; a pointed diadem was elegantly painted in white on his forehead; also a pattern resembling an epaulette on each shoulder, and an ornament like a full blown rose, one leaf rising above another until it covered his whole breast; his knee-bands were of aggry beads, and his ancle [*sic*] strings of gold ornaments of the most delicate workmanship, small drums, sankos, stools, swords, guns, and birds, clustered together; his sandals, of a soft white leather, were embossed across the instep band with small gold and silver cases of saphies; he was seated in a low chair, richly ornamented with gold; he wore a pair of gold castanets on his finger and thumb, which he clapped to enforce silence. The belts of the guards behind his chair, were cased in gold, and covered with small jaw bones of the same metal; the elephants tails, waving like a small cloud before him, were spangled with gold, and large plumes of feathers were flourished amid them. His eunuch presided over these attendants, wearing only one massy piece of gold about his neck: the royal stool, entirely cased in gold, was displayed under a splendid umbrella, with drums, sankos,

horns, and various musical instruments, cased in gold, about the thickness of cartridge paper: large circles of gold hung by scarlet cloth from the swords of state, the sheaths as well as the handles of which were also cased; hatchets of the same were intermixed with them: the breasts of the Ocrahs, and various attendants, were adorned with large stars, stools, crescents, and gossamer wings of solid gold'.[19] In short there was gold almost everywhere.

The gold used in such profusion came to Asante rulers in several ways: from mines worked by unfree labour, by taxes, fines, levies and death duties, from trading, from the occasional washing of the soil in the great Kumase market and from thanks-offerings (*aseda*).

To some extent the royal administration was self-financing: a proportion of the gold received was retained by the office-holders who handled it at each level. Those who travelled through the villages of the kingdom collecting taxes, equipped with leather satchels, weights and scales (*togyefo*), were allowed to keep 15 per cent, and other collectors were allowed a greater proportion of what they took. Gold-dust weighed out for thanks-offerings was traditionally made up of a major and a minor unit of currency, the latter called *mataho* or *kyekyerekon*, 'something stuck or tied on the neck' of the larger packet of gold-dust. The lesser sum went to the court official who had helped settle the case: 'a headless packet of gold dust does not go to the palace'.[20]

All nuggets were supposed to be surrendered by the finders to the local chief for transmission to the Asantehene in Kumase. It appears that the Asantehene returned a proportion of the nugget's value in gold-dust to the finder. A group of craftsmen was employed to convert nuggets (and possibly, in times of emergency, cast gold) into gold-dust for royal use. These '*buramfo* (from *ebura*, 'forge' or 'furnace') operated under the supervision of the Adwomfohene, also in charge of the royal goldsmiths. Nuggets were mixed with red earth and heated in crucibles, and when the gold was molten, the contents of the crucible

77

were shaken to intermingle the metal and clay. The contents were then pitched into cold water and suddenly cooled. As the metal and clay cooled at different rates, the gold was split into many particles, later recovered from the water vessel.[21]

The Kumase treasury was strictly organised. The main reserves were kept in the **Great Chest** (*Adaka Kese*), about 210 × 90 × 60 cm. It has been estimated that this contained 11,340 kg of gold when full, worth about £1,500,000 at nineteenth-century rates.[22] The gold was stored in cloth bundles of given values, and the chest was under the direct care of the Gyaasewahene who, according to an early source, held the only key to the room where it was kept. 'The **King of Ashanti** was bathed every morning to the accompaniment of the rattling of the treasury keys. The *afoto sanfo* were also the royal barbers and manicurists. The Gyase chief was always the head treasurer . . . carrying as his badge of office a golden key, while the assistant treasurer was the Gyasewa chief, who carried a silver key.'[23]

An Asantehene-elect had to gain control of the Great Chest to secure his position. The captives Ramseyer and Kuhne noted that Kofi Kakari's predecessor was said to have collected more gold than any Asantehene during his long, peaceful reign: 'It was weighed out in a large scale held by four strong slaves, but it was not until three months later that the elders allowed Kari-Kari to take possession.'[24]

Smaller containers held lesser quantities of gold for use in everyday court business. Sums of gold were also apparently kept with the royal skeletons at the Bantama mausoleum. Gold was handled on a day-to-day basis by a group of officials under the Fotosanfohene who was responsible for weighing sums in or out as required. Withdrawals were recorded simply: a cowrie shell was put aside for every *peredwan* (approximately 70 g) of gold-dust removed. The state's wealth was great: there is some reason to believe that the war chest taken on the 1820s' campaign before the battle of Kantamanso contained about £500,000 in gold-dust.[25]

If gold flowed into the court in great quantities, much was kept in circulation. Gold was used to buy weapons, powder and shot, and also to obtain European metalware and cloth for resale and luxury items such as liquor. The imported liquor available favourably impressed many grateful visitors. The British mission of 1817, for example, dined at the King's retreat outside Kumase. They were offered roast pig, ducks, fowls, stews and pease-pudding, oranges and pineapples with port and madeira, spirits and Dutch cordials: 'We never saw a dinner more handsomely served, and never ate a better.'[26] Almost thirty years later Freeman recorded that the Asantehene 'sent us some refreshment, consisting of Madeira wine, brandy, cherry brandy and liquors, with a supply of delicious water, all neatly served up in decanters on a tray, with tumblers and wine glasses'.[27] Winniet, the visiting British governor, was given a large dinner which included plum puddings served with ale, wine and spirits. In the 1870s Ramseyer and Kuhne came across a man carrying champagne for the King from the coast.

Politics and negotiation in Asante were accompanied and often expressed through formal gifts. A proportion of the gold coming to the court was recirculated in this way, often handed out by the King when he sat in public state twice in every forty-two days (see p.53). The philosophy behind such gifts was expressed by Asantehene Osei Bonsu: 'I must give them [northern visitors] gold and provisions and send them home happy and rich, that it may be known in other countries that I am a great King, and know what is right.'[28]

Gold-dust was essential to the stability of the kingdom; adulteration was punishable by death. The coastal people, in Asante eyes, were particularly prone to adulterate gold-dust as well as the gunpowder and liquors which they traded. One Asantehene complained about Fante debasement: 'He will send the English his trade; he will send them good gold like what he wears himself [showing his armlets] not bad gold like he knows the Fantees make', and 'The Ashantees take good gold to Cape Coast, but the Fantees mix it; he sent some of his captains like slaves to see [that is, incognito] and they saw it'.[29]

Nevertheless, such heinous crimes occurred nearer home. One of the most spectacular cases occurred when the King was persuaded by a senior chief to honour him by eventually attending his funeral. The man's treasure was examined after the funeral, and it was found that his gold contained large amounts of brass filings. His corpse was dug up and decapitated. The King of Dwaben who was defeated by the Asantehene's forces in the 1820s destroyed much of his property to prevent its seizure. The victors captured a quantity of gold-dust, but this 'had been mixed with copper and thus rendered comparatively useless'.[30] A similar disappointment met the British victors of 1874: '. . . among the loot we had brought away from the palace were several bags of fine brass dust, which we had taken for real gold dust.'[31]

Gold ornaments were cast by highly skilled specialist craftsmen (*sikadwinfo*) using the lost-wax technique (see p.80) which was probably introduced down the northern trade routes. Traditions suggest goldsmiths were regarded as valuable personnel in the early kingdom. Some Kumase goldsmiths claim descent from those captured from the defeated rival states of Denkyira, Takyiman and Akwapim. In the nineteenth century Kumase goldsmiths were under royal control, and some of their present-day descendants claim that outsiders were forbidden free access to their part of the town.

Generally speaking, goldsmiths could cast major items of adornment for senior chiefs only with the Asantehene's permission. Those who had acquired large fortunes and wished to increase the dignity of their office by turning gold-dust into inheritable regalia required royal permission; in one recorded case a levy of 20 per cent was taken. Descendants of royal goldsmiths claim that formerly royal officials weighed out the gold-dust to be used at the start of the day and the remaining dust and finished work at the end of the day to prevent cheating. It is possible, however, that they were allowed to keep a percentage as their due, as occurred when Bowdich had some small castings made.[32] Some goldsmiths were expected to accompany Asante armies to war to make effigies of slain enemies which would later adorn major stools or swords.

It is now impossible to discover the number of goldsmiths active in the pre-colonial kingdom. Much of the jewellery taken from the court in the last quarter of the nineteenth century does, however, appear to have been cast by a small number of craftsmen. Nevertheless, a colonial survey of 1909, probably based on incomplete returns, lists eighty-five goldsmiths in or around Kumase, with ten others from coastal towns, and twenty-five at Bekwae. Licensing returns from 1912 indicate that the capitals of most major states (for example, Mampon, Ejisu, Dwaben and Kumawu) had about six registered goldsmiths each.[33]

The lost-wax technique used by Asante goldsmiths is basically a simple one. In essence the item to be cast in metal is first modelled in wax and a clay mould built around it. A hole is made through the mould and the mould and wax heated until the wax melts so it can be poured out through the hole. This leaves a cavity in the shape of the original wax model into which molten metal is poured. The metal cools and hardens, the mould is broken open, and the casting removed and cleaned up. This is the basic technique; the Asante version has important refinements.

Asante casters use wax (*akaa*) from the hives of wild bees. The combs are broken up and put into boiling water so that the wax floats to the top from where it is skimmed off. Impurities are removed by filtering the molten wax through cloth or rolling soft wax into thin sheets. The dark brown wax is easy to work: small pieces remain quite soft at tropical temperatures and can be made more malleable over a charcoal fire. The wax, once cool, is fairly tough. Complex forms made with warm, soft wax, soon set rigid.

The Asante metal-caster (*egufoo*) usually works in the courtyard of his house or under an open shed behind it.[34] He usually sits on a low stool, a small table or log placed in front of him. The wax is softened over a brazier, which may be fanned from time to time by a small boy of the household, and is then rolled and shaped on a wooden block with a wooden spatula (*adwin nua*) rather like a blunt paper-knife.

A modern metal caster modelling in beeswax. A block of wax can be seen on the right, and wooden modelling tools are lying on the table.

The wax model is usually built up by combining pieces rolled into strips, cut from a prepared thin sheet, or shaped with the fingers, a spatula, or a thin blade, needle or rod. Wax and tools may be heated from time to time, and the tools dipped into cold water to lubricate them and to harden the wax as they touch it. Prepared pieces of wax are joined by touching the point of contact with a hot metal rod or blade to produce a molten patch and then quickly placing the two pieces together. The surfaces of the wax model constructed in this way can be further decorated by careful incising. The technique allows great flexibility and control in modelling, for all shaping is done with easily worked wax.

When the wax model is complete, the goldsmith attaches one or more thin wax rods in places which will be unobtrusive in the final casting. These will eventually protrude through the enclosing mould and, when melted away, leave channels down which the molten gold can flow. The rods attached, the goldsmith begins to build up this mould (*foa dua*). The high quality of many Asante castings, the sharpness of their detail and their lack of faults are largely attributable to the materials and techniques used in forming a mould around the wax. This is built up layer by layer. The first layers are made of a very fine clay paste mixed with finely ground charcoal, which may form more than two-thirds of the mixture. The wax model is dipped in this or the mixture painted on with the tip of a fowl's feather. The second method is preferred as the wax tends to repel the watery paste and the feather helps ensure all areas are properly coated. After the first coat dries, others are carefully added until a layer of about 3–6 mm is built up. An outer casing of clay is next formed around this, layer by layer, or by carefully pressing it around the initial coatings so as not to crack them. Fibres obtained from boiling up palm nuts to obtain their oil are sometimes added to strengthen this clay. The complete mould is allowed to dry for several days to eliminate the non-combined water in the clay which would turn to explosive steam on heating the mould.

When the mould is dry, it is heated in a cylindrical clay-walled furnace (*ebura*) filled with charcoal and then taken out and inverted. Any molten wax which has not soaked into the mould walls is tipped out, usually into cold water from where it can be collected for reuse. A small clay cup (*semoa*) containing pieces of gold is next grafted to the mould around the hole left by the wax rod. Clay is plastered heavily around the two to make a solid and perfect joint. Once the joint is thoroughly dried, the casting can be done. Mould and cup are placed in the furnace, the cup downwards, and left until the gold is considered to have become completely molten: the charcoal fire is kept at full heat by pumping air through it with bellows. The mould and attached cup are seized with a pair of tongs and rapidly inverted: this action makes the molten gold rush down the channel and into the cavity. The mould is held in this position, or carefully placed on the ground, while the gold is allowed to cool and harden. It is then smashed open (which requires considerable force as the mould has become baked in the fire) and the casting is picked out. This is next cleaned by picking off the black moulding material and scrubbing it in water mixed with the juice of limes. As craftsmen always calculate to use more gold than will fill the cavity left by the wax model, some of this is attached to the casting as a rod or sprue, formed in the channel down which the gold runs. This is carefully trimmed off. The trimmed casting is finally polished with a paste of very fine clay and water and finished with a soft cloth.

Any lost-wax casting can go wrong because there is insufficient metal, because this solidifies before it reaches all parts of the mould, or because bubbles of air or gas are trapped in the mould and so keep out the metal. The first cause is easily avoided and the other two are minimised by the Asante technique. As the metal to be cast and the mould are heated together, both metal and mould are at a very high temperature and the metal has little chance to cool as it rushes into the mould. As comparatively small quantities of metal are used, it is easy to melt fully and to pour. Furthermore, the inner layers of the mould contain a high proportion of charcoal: it seems that this absorbs air trapped within the mould and any gases produced by the hot metal reacting with the clay.

The high standard of Asante casting is clear: at its best Asante goldsmiths were able to produce castings of great delicacy and intricacy as well as larger, simpler pieces which impress more by their size than their complexity. Many pieces were clearly worked upon after casting. Some circular pectorals, worn by royal *kra* servants, were cast as plain discs with edge decorations made from wax threads, and the surface later decorated by repoussé work. Many pieces were also treated to appear more red. This, according to Bowdich, was

A cast-gold sword ornament in the form of a lion. Ejisu state regalia.

A pair of royal sandals with cast-gold decorations. Offinso state regalia.

achieved by boiling them up in a mixture of fine red clay and water which helped deposit a rouge-like coating in their lower areas.[35]

Many different types of castings were made in this way, as Bowdich's description of his reception at Kumase indicates. Large gold torques were made to be worn at the neck by the Asantehene, apparently as a sign of war-like intentions (lesser chiefs wore iron ones). Open-work beads, cylindrical and square-section, were cast and worn at the ankles or around the wrists, or below the knee, with small representational castings, such as jaw-bones, molar and incisor teeth (representing defeated enemies), drums, shells, beetles and elephant tails. Often such bracelets incorporated fibres and glass beads which were thought to have special powers. The Asantehene and Amanhene also wore large armlets (*benfra*), usually cast in two halves and secured with a pin. Talismans (*asuman, safi*), probably of Islamic origin, enclosed in square or circular leather pouches around which gold foil was fixed, were worn at wrist and elbow. The enclosing leather was decorated with punch-marks and the gold foil pressed into these. Occasionally these talismans incorporated an animal tooth or claw. Nowadays cylindrical ones are often interpreted as lengths of resilient *babadua* reed (see p.109) or as 'clubs' which strike those wishing to harm the wearer.

The Asantehene and Amanhene also wore gold rings (*mpetea*), often several at a time, on their fingers and toes. These show geometrical seed forms, mudfish, lions, globular open-work structures, sometimes referred to as birds' nests, cannons, tortoises and many other subjects from local life, usually calling to mind proverbs. A few rings seem to be based upon European forms and show, for example, miniature human heads and torsos. Castings in gold, or carved wooden forms covered in gold and silver foil, were sewn to the Asantehene's sandals and, in the present century, to cloth bands worn around the head. As the King's feet could never touch the ground, it was usual for a second pair of sandals to be carried in case the strap of one of those worn broke. The extra pair also, of course, served to show his wealth. The best sandals were elaborate affairs with strips of red, white and green leather threaded through holes in the sole to give the appearance of complex multi-colour stitching. While ordinary people went barefoot, the sandal straps of minor chiefs were decorated with patterns, often rosettes, cut in leather, and those of more senior chiefs with representational gold castings depicting, for example, ground-nut flowers, stars, the *aya* leaf and cowries. The latter two are in a sense visual puns: the word *aya*, with an alteration of tones, can mean 'insult', and the sandals therefore warn against careless talk before chiefs. The cowrie (*sidee*) approximates to the term *sire* ('smile') and is said to express not only the King's wealth but his pleasure in it.

One of the most widespread items of gold-work was the pectoral disc worn by the young servants of the ruler, referred to as his 'souls' (*akra*). These circular castings were suspended from whitened pineapple-fibre cord. The role of *kra* had many aspects but it often served as a training for higher office. The discs showed the wearer's close connection with the King. Those which survive show a variety of styles and decorations. Most are only 7 or 9 cm across but a few larger ones are known. Some, possibly early ones, have decorative motifs of bows and arrows, which were carried by some of the King's young servants who were said to be free to seize what they could from markets to support themselves. Other *kra* discs show rosette and foliate motifs which seem to have a European source.

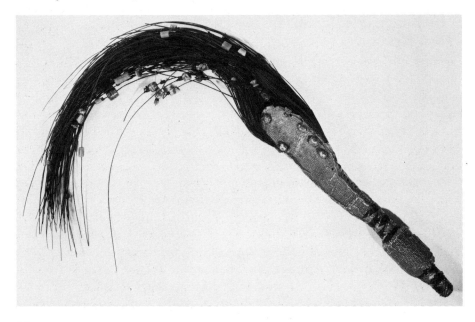

An elephant-tail fly-whisk, the handle covered with sheet gold.

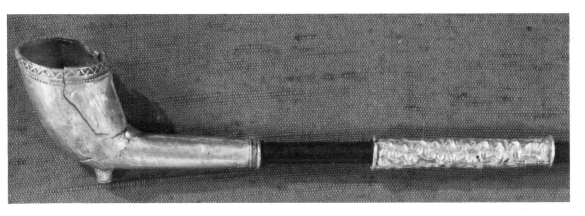

A chief's cast-gold pipe in the form of a 17th-century European clay pipe. The bowl is 8.1 cm long.

There is evidence to show that throughout Asante history old forms were increasingly elaborated to meet the needs of a society of growing complexity. As early as the seventeenth century on the coast elephant tails were used as fans or fly-whisks and brought prestige. Usually carried before the ruler by men (*ahoprafo*) who pretended to brush away danger or dirt, they became in the nineteenth century more elaborate and were given out to those who had made their fortune by trade.

Gold-casters also made tobacco pipes for the ruling group. Tobacco was introduced into Africa by Europeans who had obtained it from the New World. Most tobacco (*taa*) used in Asante seems to have been grown in the Americas. Local taste still favours uncut black tobacco, heavily impregnated with molasses, which can only be kept alight by placing a burning coal on top. Until the present century the Asante made clay pipes for their own use and gold pipes were carried in public by rulers and senior officials.

It is unclear how and when tobacco smoking entered the forest zone. Excavations in the savannah north of Asante seem to suggest that tobacco smoking could have been transmitted from that direction rather than from Europeans on the coast. However, the earliest locally made pipes found so far on the coast, dated to around the middle of the seventeenth century, are clearly derived from the European clay pipes. The long clay stem of imported pipes was fragile and difficult to make locally; as a result local pipes were soon made with short-stemmed bowls into which a hollow wooden tube or reed fitted as stem. Pipe bowls were made of stone or brass, but most were of fired clay. Bowls became larger and stems longer as pipes were used as items of display. Bosman speaks of pipes with stems almost 2 m long smoked with the base of the bowl resting on the ground. Pipe bowls were reinforced at the base with a 'foot' to take the weight of the pipe where it touched the ground. The internal angle between the short integral stem and the bowl became more acute until, by the nineteenth century, it seems to have remained constant at about 30–40°, although a few pipes have a much more acute angle.

The great majority of Asante pipes (*ebua*) were made in clay in both representational and non-representational forms, but a small number of cast-gold display pipes were made for chiefs. Many representational pipes are modelled to draw parallels between parts of the pipe and various aspects of objects, people and creatures. An early gold pipe, collected before 1837, has the bowl modelled in the form of a clay pot, and many clay pipes use the body of a person or an animal as the body of the pipe. One pipe removed from Kumase in 1874 appears to be the closest known to the prototype European clay pipes: it has a small forward-tilted bowl with a protrusion beneath it. It is unclear whether this is a genuinely old gold pipe, preserved at the court, or a late copy of a very early style.

Although the majority of these gold pipes were carefully modelled, some have casting faults which prevented their being smoked, and few, if any, of the well-cast ones show signs of having been smoked. Many, therefore, seem to have been used purely for display, either carried by royal servants, or held to their mouths by chiefs as they were carried in their palanquins. Stems were often as long as 1.2–1.5 m and fitted with cast-gold mouthpieces; most were bound at intervals with thin gold wire which was sometimes made to stand away from the stem in coils. It is said that the stems were cut to length so that the user could smoke comfortably while seated. A few cast-brass pipes are known: presumably these were owned by lesser chiefs who were not permitted to have gold ones. The adoption of alien forms, such as pipes, for the use of the rulers is, as we shall see, a common feature of Asante court art.

A 19th-century clay pipe with a bowl in the form of a *sankofa* bird.

6 The court and regalia

The use of gold to adorn rulers and their servants was intended to impress: 'The royal gold ornaments are melted down every Yam Custom, and fashioned into new patterns as novel as possible. This is a piece of state policy very imposing on the populace and the tributary chiefs who pay but an annual visit [to Kumase]', claimed Bowdich.[1] Many gold castings represented creatures, such as antelopes, scorpions and snails, to which proverbs or sayings could be attached. The proverb could, in some circumstances, be used to express general ideas or truisms. Indeed, Asante tended to interpret regalia as having meaning beyond their form. When a local man saw the British sappers in the 1874 invasion, he claimed: 'The axes they carried were to show that Ashanti would be cut down, and the spades indicated that Ashanti would be rooted up.'[2]

A clear theme in Asante history is the way once-functional objects were elaborated and made to serve as regalia which could identify the rank and purpose of the bearer and also express ideas about political and moral relationships. The eighteenth- and nineteenth-century development of regalia derived from the growth of central government and the problem of running a large empire without a literate class. Although literates were enticed into the Asantehene's service and written records made, most state business relied upon the integrity of those concerned and their ability to follow verbal instructions, supported by systems of checks, spying and reporting to ensure they did not exceed their brief. Instantly identifiable items of regalia, which could be obtained only from the King's court, helped smooth and speed the way of those appointed to carry out the decisions of the King and his council.

The Asante made early attempts to provide themselves with European-speaking literates. In 1743, for example, fourteen Asante children arrived at Elmina: it was Asantehene Opoku Ware's intention that they should go to the Netherlands 'to read and write and be taught music', but instead they were enrolled in a local school run by a Dutch-educated ex-slave. An Asante emissary, however, was taken to Holland and returned with impressive gifts for the King.[3] By the 1820s or 30s, possibly earlier, the King and court had small numbers of literates available, often visiting outsiders. Here the difficulty was that the Asante could rarely check what they wrote or read. Asante fears in this connection were well founded: the copy of Bowdich's Anglo-Asante Treaty left at Kumase differed in a number of important points from that which he took to the coast.[4]

Throughout the century Asantehenes attempted to attract literates to their service and maintained a regular correspondence with the coast. In 1818 Osei Bonsu hoped to have people educated by the British; opposition among senior officials apparently prevented this (the Gyaasewahene argued that written accounts would limit peculation). In the 1830s two of the Asantehene's sons, Owusu Ansa and Owusu Nkwantabisa, were schooled at Cape Coast and later sent to England, and two more Asante were educated in the Netherlands. By the mid-nineteenth century the Asante were using trained literates, mainly from the coast, at least one provided by Governor Maclean in 1836. In 1859 Asantehene Kwaku Dua had a Dutchman in his service, and the Wesleyan catechist Watts, who was in Kumase from 1862 to 1871, served as a secretary for some purposes.[5] Literate Muslims were also used in the treasury.

Towards the end of the century the use of written records and communications had made some headway. Europeans like the Frenchman Bonnat were absorbed, albeit briefly, into the system, and Asantes like the Owusu Ansa brothers, mission educated, were fully literate. Written messages were sent: for example, in 1889 Prempe I received a written account of the fate of a force dispatched against recalcitrant Ahafo towns. The writer described himself as 'Chief Miner', possibly an Elminan. The year before the King received a letter from a Muslim divine, Abu Bakr B. Uthman Kamaghatay, setting out terms for his return to Kumase. Both letters were kept until removed from Kumase by British forces in 1896.[6]

However, despite the regular written communication between King and Europeans on the coast, literacy made little headway in government as a whole. Diplomatic negotiations at the highest and lowest levels were still carried out by preference through speech, where the rich allusiveness of Asante oratory could hint at a range of possibilities, explore them, and find the most suitable solution with a subtlety and flexibility entirely lacking in any written document.

The growing complexity of the Asante government, its members' need to communicate internally and externally, to show their differences in standing, and to reward allies or placate potential enemies are reflected in the way many items, such as swords (*afena*), were elaborated in the eighteenth and nineteenth centuries. What began as a functional weapon ended as an object whose significance was indicated by its size, shape and a variety of attachments, often in gold. The sword gained an increasing richness of meaning over the years until colonial rule removed many of its uses, ending its development but stimulating the growth of other forms of court art.

The first reports of swords in Akan society are inevitably from the coast. Local swords may derive from Islamic weapons passed down the trans-Saharan trade routes. Early visitors were quick to associate the swords they saw with Turkish or other Islamic weapons. Towerson wrote of 'great daggers . . . which be on both sides exceeding sharp, and banded after the manner of Turkie blades'.[7]

At the end of the sixteenth century de Marees noted two-edged swords with handles covered with fish (probably ray) skin or sheet gold. Some with sheaths were adorned with large red shells, others with the heads of 'Apes' or 'Tygres'.[8] Dapper and others add slightly different details and indicate that jaw-bones of enemies were fixed to sheaths.[9] There is substantial agreement on the form of the sword: a curved blade, broader towards the tip than the handle, encased in a skin sheath, the handle made of two globes separated by a cylindrical grip, sometimes with a cow's tail attached. Most writers stressed the skill of local craftsmen in working iron for making weapons (and for repairing imported firearms).[10]

Some swords showed the achievement or status of their owners: 'They [the swords] have a wooden Guard adorned at one side, and sometimes at both, with small globular Knobs, covered with a sort of Skin, whilst others content themselves with bits of Rope singed black with the Blood of Sheep or other Cattle, with the additional Ornament of a bunch of Horse Hair, among People of Condition thin Gold Plates are usual.'[11] These added items indicated power and wealth: the imported red shells were expensive, and heads of slain beasts presumably showed hunting prowess. Some swords were carried when a town chief walked abroad. A sword-bearer had an important role, sometimes being sent as ambassador to other courts.[12] Barbot mentions a sword adorned with a cast-gold monkey head, and Loyer's account of Assini shows gold-adorned swords. Behind the King stood two of the royal wives 'each carrying on her shoulder a large gold sabre with a gold handle, from whence hung a figure with a sheep's skull in gold, as big as the life or bigger. On the sheath was a long shell of the same material round which was strung a hundred tyger's teeth bored'.[13]

A few swords were brought to Europe in the seventeenth century. In Ulm there is a sword from the coastal kingdom of Fetu, probably dating before 1650. The guard, pommel and sheath are decorated with ray skin, the grip and end of the pommel with gold leaf, a horse or cow tail is attached, and the blade

Asante diplomats with swords showing their status.

is pierced and stamped. Two similar swords were accessioned in the Danish Royal Collection in 1690, their handles decorated with ray skin and gold leaf. A further early sword, adorned with a red shell, is shown in Eckhout's painting of an Akan warrior, probably done in South America.[14]

Many Asante swords had gold adornments: 'Wolves and rams heads as large as life, cast in gold, were suspended from their gold handled swords.'[15] One function of swords was identified by Dupuis: 'The royal messengers stood behind the sovereign, shouldering by the blades large crooked sabres, the emblems of their offices, and displaying the reversed hilts, cased in thin gold sheathing.'[16] Those chosen by kings and chiefs to deliver messages or conduct important negotiations carried, or were accompanied by men carrying, gold-handled swords. These people were frequently encountered on the roads and paths of Asante. Visitors were often guided and controlled by sword-bearers. Huydecoper, travelling to Kumase in 1816 for the Dutch, was met by a sword-bearer of the Asante general Appia and later, nearing Kumase, met by another four sword-bearers; two went to report his arrival to the King, returned, and all four accompanied him towards the capital. Four more sword-bearers arrived and told him to dress correctly to meet the King. Later he witnessed two sword-bearers sent to stop Appia exceeding the terms of his mission. When the King wanted Huydecoper to clean the European silver at the palace, he sent a sword-bearer to command him.[17] Similarly, Dupuis was escorted into the capital by two royal messengers, one of whom was a sword-bearer,[18] as was Winniet in 1848.[19] As Ramseyer and Kuhne passed through Dwabęn in 1871, 'A messenger of the prince, distinguished by a gold sword, from which hung a large golden shell, . . . conducted us to the palace'.[20]

Kumase traditions place this use of swords to the earliest days of Asante history, relating how the King of Denkyira sent officials to Kumase demanding gold-dust. Among these men (who included his goldsmith to test the gold paid over) was a sword-bearer carrying the *afenatene* ('the long sword').[21] This use of swords continued until the break-up of the Asante kingdom: in the 1870s the Dwabenhene, who had left the confederacy, sent a sword-bearer to the Gyamanhene to help organise armed resistance to Asante rule.[22]

Messenger swords (*asomfofena*) were numerous in the last century. According to one recent Asante authority, the present Asantehene has five *asomfofena* which are borne in parade to accompany the Golden Stool,[23] but these would have been too few to support the vast amount of pre-colonial state business, even if some was devolved to senior officials with their own sword-bearers.

A second class of sword, *domfena*, was carried by generals: '. . . a general is appointed to the command of an army, by receiving a gold-handled sword of the King's from his hand (who strikes him gently with it three times on the head), swearing to return it encrusted with the blood of his conquered enemies.'[24] The captains used these to swear before the King: '. . . the captains rose and siezed their gold-headed swords from their attendants . . . each then directed his sword to the King . . . and swore by the King's head that they would go with the army that night, and bring him . . . the heads of all the Fantees.'[25]

The most important swords were thought to have a special spiritual significance. According to a recent Asante writer, these form a distinct class, *keteanofena*, of two divisions, the *bosomfena* and the *akrafena*. This general class of sword is said to be closely associated with the King's spiritual health: '. . . they are laid at the edge of the King's bed when he goes to sleep. It is believed that the spiritual force residing in the swords will protect him while he sleeps.'[26] It is said that the *akrafena* are used in various rituals connected with the cleansing of the King's soul, while the others are used for the swearing of oaths and for sending messages within Kumase. Such swords for swearing are also referred to as *nsuafena* ('oath swords'). It is unclear exactly how far this disinction is a recent development. The Asantehene's most important sword is *Mponponsuo*, a large sword on which senior chiefs swear their allegiance. The hilt and sheath (*boha*) are covered with leopard skin; a gold casting (*abosodee*) in the form of a snake holding a diminutive antelope in its mouth, and several gold- and silver-cased talismans are fixed to the sheath. It has two circular gold bosses (*nem*) between the blade and handle. The bearers of oath swords wore hats made of eagle feathers with a pair of gold rams' horns in front. Some major swords, and particularly those called *Bosommuru* and *Bosompra*, are linked to particular groups within the administrative order of the state.

Another class of swords, *afenatene* ('long swords'), were principally for display: they usually have long and elaborately worked blades and, sometimes, multiple gold-covered handles with representational carvings similar to the

A long sword (*afenatene*) of the type displayed within the royal palace at Kumase; the handles are missing. Ht 1.20 cm.

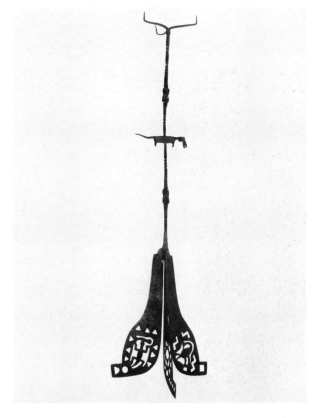

finials of umbrellas and linguists' staffs (see p.95). In many the blade is formed of a long, thin strip, twisted or even knotted, turning into a large flat sheet, pierced with geometric patterns or to indicate the outline of a crocodile or *sankofa* bird. A few of the largest have two or three blades springing from a single thin shaft. The three-bladed swords were stood, handle uppermost, near the King when he was sitting in state within the palace.[27] Gold-handled swords were among the items (chairs, palanquins and stools) consciously distributed as a way of rewarding or influencing the leaders of groups on the periphery of Asante rule, so bringing them into a common system of meaning, and this practice seems to have continued until the final quarter of the last century.

The main attachment to sword sheaths is a representational gold casting (*abosodeε*). Early reports from the coast mention the skulls of beasts tied to sheaths, perhaps displayed as trophies or for magical protective purposes. Some nineteenth-century Asante *abosodeε* seem to have had a proverbial dimension; others may have been mainly intended to show the ruler's wealth in a direct way. Recent Asante explanations tend to emphasise their proverbial aspects. Bowdich mentions a snake upon a sword, and it has been suggested that this represented the well-known proverb about the snake which after a long time finally caught the bird which had borrowed from it.[28] The meaning of the *abosodeε* of a snake holding an antelope on the sword *Mponponsuo* is unclear. A ram's head thinly cast in gold, similar to one described by Bowdich, was taken from Kumase by British forces in 1874. Two cast-gold heads now in London may also have been sword decorations, the larger of the two with a suspension loop by which it could have been attached to a sheath.

A cast-gold sword ornament in the form of a teapot. Offinso state regalia. Ht 13 cm.

A gold casting of a 'pot', clearly copied from a European vessel, today interpreted as an *abusua kuruwa* ('family pot'), can be seen attached to one of the Asantehene's swords in a photograph taken in 1884. It has been suggested this was seen by the missionary Thomas Birch Freeman about forty years earlier: '. . . an immense gold sword, to which was fastened a golden decanter, holding about a pint.'[29] *Abusua kuruwa* pots represent the unity and mutual dependence of the lineage group. European-derived pots of this sort today adorn swords in the regalia of the Amanhene of Bekwae, Ejisu and Mampon. Formerly this image may have been interpreted as an indication of the King's access to exotic goods and also, because it is a vessel, of his ability to provide for those he ruled.

The Offinso stool has a beautiful casting, made in the 1920s, of a European teapot (it is unclear if this was a replacement for an earlier version). The Offinsohene interprets this vessel as an *abusua kuruwa* and states that the sword is used to emphasise the idea of mutual dependence and co-operation. Others, while finding this an acceptable meaning, say that the subject was chosen because it was attractive (*efe*) or because it showed the stool's willingness to adopt progressive Western customs and goods.

All *abosodeε* are cast by the lost-wax process (see p.80); many have openings in the surface and were stuffed with imported red cloth to accentuate the colour of the gold. Sword decorations seem to have been treated carefully and only recast when severely damaged. Some, however, were apparently concealed or melted down in that troubled period just before and after the establishment of colonial rule, and many now in use seem to have been cast or recast since the 1920s.

Some sword images express the wealth of a chief and his stool. A sword from Ejisu has an *abosodeε* in the form of the blow-pan used for removing impurities from gold-dust. A Kumawu sword has three kola pods attached. This is seen as expressing wealth through trade; a proverb says 'when the kola went north, that was when the northern cloths came to Asante'. However, other interpretations are offered: the kola is seen as a sign of respect because the Kumawuhene takes kola to the funerals of other (?Muslim) chiefs, where its red and bitter qualities express grief. Informants also offer the saying 'the ant clings aimlessly to the kola tree, it won't fall down, yet it won't pick the fruit and chew it'. Crocodiles on swords, either on their own (Mampon) or biting a mudfish (Kumawu), give rise to several readings, some opposed: 'if a mudfish gains anything, it is ultimately to the benefit of the crocodile' or 'only a bad crocodile harms the mudfish with which it shares the river'. When two creatures are depicted, a saying may be offered which turns on one or more characteristics of each. It is reported at Mampon that the crocodile is seen as standing for the Omanhene, one of whose praise-names is 'the great crocodile that swallows a stone every year'.

Several swords bear images which relate to the military powers and prowess of the chief or his predecessors. Some bear military items: shields, sometimes with a sword resting on them, cannon, or a bird with cannon mounted on its wings, a powder barrel and gun, or the head of a slain enemy, usually called a

Worosa head after the King of Banda who was slain by the Asante some time after the middle of the eighteenth century.

At present the significance of any single *abosodeɛ*, like that of other items of regalia, is always open to discussion and argument. The Asante freely acknowledge that many parts of their culture are understood only by particular groups within their society. Many ordinary villagers today express ignorance of the significance of *abosodeɛ* beyond the fact that they represent the power and wealth of the ruler. It is possible knowledge was more widespread in the past. However, even among those who have spent much time at the courts there is never full agreement as to the significance of any particular sword ornament. As in other areas of their life, the Asante accept an essential ambiguity or indefiniteness about meanings: anything may be understood in different, even contradictory ways, according to the situation in which it is manifest and the interpreter's inclinations or presuppositions. The image forms a starting-point from which verbal formulations may proceed and, as they develop, be adjusted to the needs of the prevailing situations.

Today swords are still used as items of display, and newly enstooled chiefs swear their allegiance on the appropriate *bosom* sword. Since the last century there has been no change in the overall form of swords. The recasting of sword ornaments which occurred in the 1920s may have arisen because minor chiefs felt free to assume types of regalia previously restricted to their superiors. A British official commented upon the sudden changes when the Asantehene returned from exile: '. . . the upstart Etipinhene, Kwekua Dua, clad soberly, [appeared] without as much as a gold ring to adorn him and under an ordinary black European umbrella: compare him with Kobina Safo of Akropong in his palanquin with eight gold sword-bearers and three large umbrellas, and with the chiefs of Kwaso, Fumesua, Tafo and many others who have been regarded by Government as small fry and now come into their own again.'[30]

The role of swords has diminished since 1896, and their bearers have taken over no new functions. Messenger swords are no longer needed for state business. While the evolution of swords has largely ceased, another form of regalia has developed greatly – the staffs carried by the *akyeame* of major chiefs, the men who act as their public spokesmen or 'interpreters'. These staffs provide a further example of the way Asante adopted exotic items and used them to show status and communicate at a distance.

The *okyeame* today acts as a ruler's spokesman: in public assemblies, in discussing state business or at trials the *okyeame* repeats clearly the remarks of all involved. He wittily rephrases these in diplomatic language, stressing their importance while avoiding offence (*casa frenkyem*). He also acts as witness (*adansee*) to important business and is responsible for remembering major decisions correctly. *Akyeame* provide a main element of continuity in chiefdoms: they know state traditions and help instruct a new chief in these and the duties of his office. None the less, there is a clear separation between the ruler and his linguist expressed in the adage *Asembone nka 'kyeame fie* ('a crucial matter doesn't stop at a linguist's house'), meaning that major affairs are always referred to the King for judgement, and by the saying *kyeame dane ohenepa, yekye* ('it is something hated and avoided for a linguist to act like a chief'). Major chiefdoms usually have several *akyeame*. The role has changed and declined from pre-colonial days when *akyeame* were often influential figures helping to frame policy and undertaking crucial negotiations for the state.

Today the wooden spokesman's staff (*kyeame poma*) is elaborately carved, between about 1.4 m and 2 m in height and is often constructed in two or three pieces which fit together by means of simple rod and socket joints. The (detachable) finial (*poma akyi*) depicts creatures, objects, or humans, singly or in combination, often communicating an aphorism or proverb (*ɛbɛ*). Staffs are covered with gold leaf or, rarely, silver (*dwete*) foil attached by gold, silver or copper u-shaped staples or adhesives. Whenever the linguist speaks on important matters, he holds the staff for all to see. *Si poma* ('to set the staff') is thus sometimes used to indicate that public business is to be transacted. Staffs are usually kept with the other stool treasures in the royal palace or, when a linguist is very highly respected, by the linguist himself. The staffs are among the most elaborate and striking of all items of court art, second only to the great umbrellas (see p.107).

Asante traditions say little about the general history of staffs, for they tend to focus on the origins of particular offices, their peculiar regalia and the events regalia memorialise. Although an office may be identified by enduring material items, these are not considered to have origins or existence separately from the office and the makers of individual items are not remembered by name for more than a generation or so.

Two Asante theories about staffs have been published recently. In 1964 Kyerematen suggested staffs developed from clubs like those used nowadays as symbols of authority by northern Ghanaian chiefs. He also suggested staffs were in use before the end of the seventeenth century when King Obiri Yeboa is said to have introduced a new form decorated with monitor lizard (*mampam*) skin. He also recorded that at the beginning of the seventeenth century a staff was surmounted by a carving of an okra (*nkruma*) pod recalling the proverb 'the nkruma does not reveal its seed from the outside'. Kyerematen adds that the Asantehene's own linguists had staffs with tops only after Prempe I's return from exile, copying those used by linguists of lesser Asante chiefs.[31] Other published traditions are contradictory, implying staffs were created for two Kumase linguists during the reign of Kwaku Dua I, or were in use *c.*1700–20.[32]

These indigenous sources can be supplemented by European ones which indicate that these staffs have their origin in canes used by Europeans on the coast in the seventeenth century or earlier. Wooden staffs or canes were long used as markers of status and items of formal 'dress' in Europe. The moral or physical decay which could befall a European on the Gold Coast was indicated by his neglect of canes: 'most of the factors [traders] . . . have dwindled from the genteel air they brought; [and] wear no cane nor snuff-box', wrote one visitor.[33] Despite this doleful observation, canes remained in use and local goldsmiths had 'good skill in making spoons, buckles, buttons, *heading canes* or tipping the deer's feet' (the latter, presumably, to make snuff boxes).[34]

Gold-topped canes, therefore, were a part of European coastal life. Whites needed to communicate with local people, the potential source of wealth. To do this they evolved several systems: for example, to indicate that a ship wished to trade a cannon was fired or a flag hoisted. For more complex interchanges pidgin languages based mainly on Portuguese and English developed. A few people were taken to Europe to learn its languages and customs. A perennial problem for whites was how, without native literacy, to communicate with people out of direct contact. It was essential to have messages and replies delivered accurately, and to know the bearer of a message was acting with the sender's full authority. The first problem was largely solved by the growth of a class of Africans or mulattoes proficient in remembering messages and repeating them accurately. Early in the eighteenth century European canes began to be used to solve the second problem.

By the late seventeenth century at least a few staffs were in local possession. Müller mentions one and talks of an 'Obcjammi' (*okyeame*) who translated the King of Fetu's words into Portuguese for visiting whites,[35] and the missionary Kemp[36] recorded in 1892 that the Fante chief of Mankessim possessed 'a silver headed sceptre' presented in 1701 to a predecessor by the Dutch Governor-General. That this survived for nearly two centuries shows the high value placed on such gifts. By 1721 canes were used to show their bearers were official messengers: 'A man soon arrived with John Conny's [an important local trader] stick to demand the customary payment.'[37]

The limitations of communication imposed by a non-literate culture and the fact that Europeans were rarely able to travel very far from their coastal forts clearly required insignia of credence. By the end of the eighteenth century if a European, mulatto or native was dispatched upon an embassy to a native chief, he would carry a decorated staff to show he was on important business and acting on behalf of the power which issued the staff. Eventually the staff came to imply that a speedy interview was required with the local ruler and the message borne was no ordinary one.

Gold- or silver-topped canes were easy to carry, durable and not easily counterfeited – many probably had engraved inscriptions identifying donor and recipient. Occasionally other odd items of undoubted European origin were pressed into use. Sometimes flags, hats and even ebony rulers were used in this way by Europeans and Africans, and the latter, of course, used gold-decorated swords.

The Dutch Governor-General Daendels' journal for 1815 to 1817 records several aspects of the use of staffs. He planned 'to send a flag or stick to the Ashantee General' to inquire the reasons for Asante military activity near the coast. He also noted that 'One of the Ashantees, who carried the staff, now beginning to speak, said that they had come with positive orders from their King'. The rivalry of the European powers in the distribution of staffs and other regalia also comes out clearly: the 'English [that is, in English employment] Interpreter told them [the local people] that they should have an English flag and staff, to which they replied that they had no other Masters but the Hollanders'.[38] A 'large cane with silver knob and chain' and other rare, expensive gifts from Holland were conveyed to the Asantehene by the Dutch

Right The Golden
Stool, placed on its
side on the *hwędọm
tea* chair. The gold
effigies represent
slain enemies of the
Asantehene.

Below The hands of
the Omanhene of
Kumawu, showing
typical gold finger
rings and armlets.
He is holding a
gold-encased fly-
whisk.

Sword-bearers of the Kumawu paramount chieftaincy. The sheaths are decorated with golden castings.

Above A sword-bearer wearing an eagle-feather hat decorated with golden ram's horns.

Right Leather cap with silver and gold decoration, worn across the back of the head by the Asantehene, senior chiefs and officials.

Left The Omanhene of Kumawu seated beneath a state umbrella, with gold-handled swords in the foreground.

Opposite (top) A gold-decorated European table knife, probably from the Kumase court.

Opposite (below) Gold *kra* pectoral discs (*akrakǫnfomu*), worn by servants of the Asantehene and some paramount chiefs.

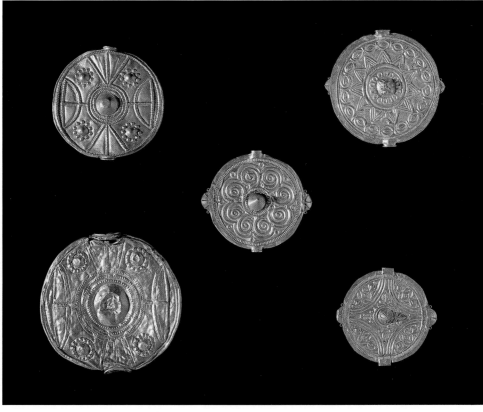

Above Women of a local matrilineage (*abusua*) at the funeral rites of a lineage co-member, wearing mourning colours of red and black.

Right Four protective wristlets. Some of the gold castings represent stylised molar and incisor teeth.

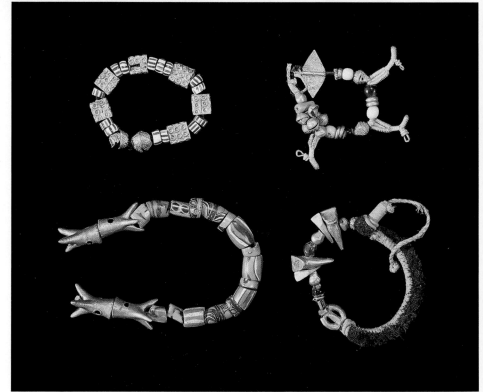

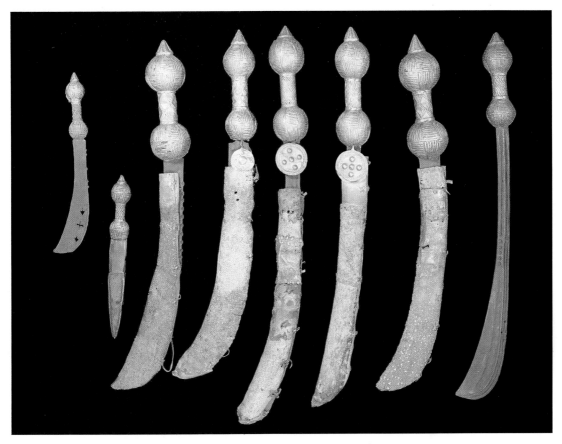

Swords (*afena*) with iron blades and wooden handles covered with gold foil. The sheaths are of ray skin.

A section of a war smock (*Batakari Kɛse*) from Ejisu covered with protective talismans encased in cloth and leather.

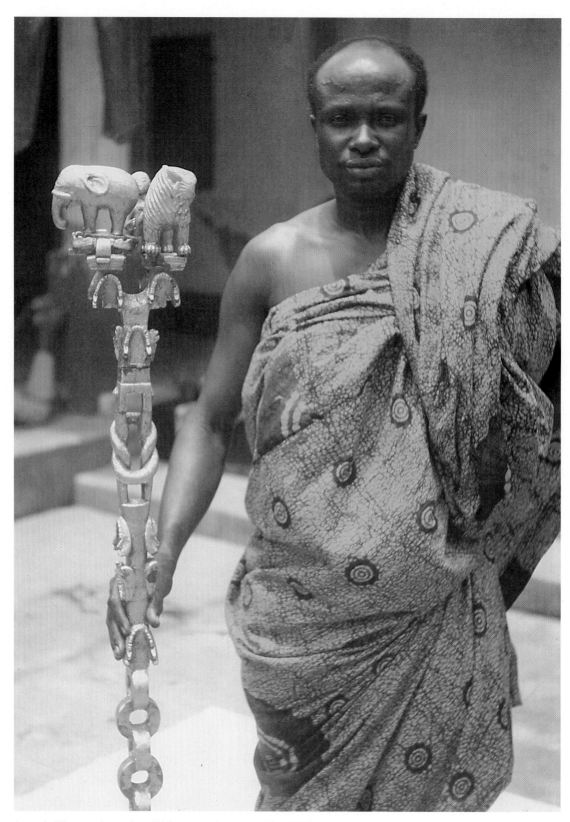

A man holding a spokesman's staff (*okyeame poma*) covered with gold foil.

Boakye Tenten, senior Asante diplomat and Asantehene's spokesman, at Kumase in 1884. In the foreground are two spokesman's staffs.

emissary Huydecoper who noted that the King soon appeared in public with this Dutch staff – a minor diplomatic triumph.[39]

Staffs were given to local rulers for political reasons, and they were subject to political manœuvrings and changes. If flags and canes were seized by insurrectionist or conquering states, the original donors (or their political successors) had to decide if the forced transfer of the object also marked the transfer of the earlier relationship to the new holders. Conversely, an attack upon a cane and its bearer was seen as an attack upon the issuing country. When a cane and its bearer were seized in the Wassaw area, the Dutch took it as a defiance of their authority and were little mollified when one of those suspected of involvement claimed 'he would never dare to panyar [seize for ransom or security for a debt] the least whiteman's Cane and young man, much less a Governor General's'. Governor Daendels threatened to go personally to regain his 'gold stick'.[40]

Eventually the term 'staff' became almost a synonym for negotiation: 'The staff is not back yet, I sent it yesterday but have not yet got any reply', a junior official wrote to Daendels. Without such staffs messages lacked authority and force. When Huydecoper encountered an Asante general, he promptly gave him a Dutch flag from the store he carried for just such a purpose. When asked why he was not given more, he explained that 'the Asante messenger had come to the General [Daendels] without cane or sword'[41] and therefore, Huydecoper claimed, the Dutch were unsure of both the messenger's credibility and his master's status. Staffs could be put to more sinister uses. Daendels suggested: 'If we . . . wish to arrest a Caboceer of considerable property and influence we must send the Staff to him and request him in a friendly manner to come into the fort'. Ironically, about the same time the Dutch complained of illegal seizures of people 'with the help of the cane of the King of Elmina'.[42]

The use of canes within Asante is described by Bowdich, who himself used both canes and flags. In making formal visits to the King the English 'never did without the flag, canes and soldiers'.[43] Whenever an interview was urgently sought with the busy Asantehene, servants with canes were dispatched to stress the gravity of the request: for example, two were sent to ask for the prompt surrender of a detained letter. It was proposed to send a servant south to collect supplies, and he was to have a cane to prove he was not trying to steal the expedition's resources. Conversely, when the Cape Coast 'messengers' in English employ refused to support Bowdich they were deprived of their canes and with them their official standing.

The canes used and distributed at this date by Europeans were wooden sticks about 1.2–1.5 m high, tapering towards the bottom, capped with a gold or silver knob and with a band encircling the body. The Asante canes were also of simple form. Bowdich recorded that they were the 'peculiar insignia' of the Asantehene's four linguists, and he saw 'gold canes . . . elevated in all directions, tied in bundles like fasces' carried by the linguists' attendants. Bowdich's illustrations show these bundles: the canes seem to be straight untopped staffs covered with gold. It is unlikely that any were topped with representational carvings, although some may have been copies of European-style sticks with gold or silver knobs.[44] Bowdich's widow refers in a novel to the King of Asante sending 'a man with a gold-headed cane' to show that white travellers 'were under his protection'.[45]

Canes in the European style were in use among the Asante and in coastal areas well into the twentieth century. Cruickshank, speaking of the coast, mentions 'silver-headed canes', and Beecham talks of 'nobles' with their attendants 'bearing gold headed canes'.[46] Boyle, writing in 1874, reports a southern chief 'carrying a stick with silver handle'.[47] It is noteworthy that decorated linguists' staffs are not among the detailed list of the things seen by the British in 1874 in the Asantehene's Stone Palace. Decorated staffs are not mentioned by the three white captives Bonnat, Ramseyer and Kuhne: despite their extensive opportunities to observe courtly and diplomatic practice in the early 1870s, all they record are 'staves straight and crooked, with gold and silver knobs'.[48] Elaboration came much later.

Over the centuries what began as a purely European object became part of a changing system of meaning for Africans and whites. To most local people canes were status markers and proof of the ability of local leaders to gain access to the goods and the ranking system introduced by the whites. Between whites and local cane-holders the canes expressed more or less enduring political alliances, and at times they signalled that the sender wished to communicate an urgent or important message.

These changes in meaning were not associated with a change in the physical appearance of the canes. Where semantic change occurred, the source of change was located in the context of use, or in alterations in other communication systems used alongside the canes – for example, in the verbal messages of their bearers. For a long time the form of the canes remained constant while their meaning altered. By 1817 canes had become status markers for the Asantehene's linguists. Locally copied canes were shown in large numbers, in a form of visual hyperbole, and here meaning depended mainly on the quantity rather than the form of canes.

Staffs of European origin with decorated or emblematic tops came into use in coastal and southern areas during the late nineteenth century. During the 1873–4 Anglo-Asante war British naval forces sent messengers to local chiefs bearing 'palaver-sticks, i.e. long Malacca canes with a ferule at one end and a gold or silver ornament representing an alligator or tortoise at the other'. Burton gave an umbrella with a silver elephant on top to the King of Apollonia; he had seen that the king already had a cane in that form.[49]

Two 19th-century spokesman's staffs with silver tops.

A series of photographs, almost certainly taken in early 1884, show scenes at the court of Asantehene Kwaku Dua II.[50] All the staffs in these are of simple form – straight sticks, about 1.2 m long, decorated with strips or sheets of gold or silver in their upper halves. None has a representational top. This type of staff appears in photographs taken well into the 1930s.[51] Some canes illustrated from this period may have been of European manufacture for 'message sticks' were still being distributed in the early 1900s to chiefs loyal to the British interest. Rattray recorded traditions in the 1920s that the linguists of some (unnamed) major chiefs had 'gold and silver staves'. The staff of the Asantehene's linguist was supposed to be made of gold, the Mamponhene's of silver, but that of Dwaben had only a top of gold. Those of other major chiefs' linguists were covered with red felt. He commissioned carvings to show people of different ranks and roles in Asante: one was of an *okyeame* carrying a simple staff with a plain knob.[52]

The impetus towards having more elaborate staffs seems to have entered Asante from the south. Fante groups began to develop staffs with carved tops towards the end of the nineteenth century. Large numbers of elaborately carved and painted staffs, sometimes only 60–90 cm long, were collected before the 1920s, probably among southern Akan groups, although their exact use and original ownership are still unclear. By 1917 some southern Akan

The top of a modern spokesman's staff, carved from wood and covered with gold foil, representing a saying that the hen knows when dawn will break but leaves it to the cock to make all the noise. Offinso state regalia.

linguists carried plain, metal-knobbed staffs, while others carried staffs entirely covered with gold leaf and topped by representational carvings in the forms of the backward-facing *sankofa* bird, two men facing each other and a man seated at a table or desk. Such sticks were not used in Asante until after the mid-1930s. At the restoration of the Asante confederacy, for example, no photograph located so far shows a linguist staff topped with a representational carving. Asantehene Prempe II's linguists carry two staffs, probably of European origin, at the ceremonies.

The elaboration of the form of linguists' staffs occurred mainly after the linguists who used them had lost their old positions within the Asante political structure, when their long-distance negotiating skills were no longer required. In the 1940s increasingly complex and grandiose staffs began to be produced. These often have elaborately carved shafts incorporating clocks, chains, wisdom knots and other motifs, which are usually interpreted as expressing some aspect of chiefship, for example, joining or binding the state together. However, the sayings by which this association are made vary from informant to informant. There is considerable diversity in the representational tops. Many depict creatures or situations which, through their associated sayings, express ideas of inequality in power. A staff top of an elephant stepping on a trap is intended to convey that when an elephant does this it is not caught but smashes the trap, a comment upon the superior powers of ruler and also a warning to those who wish to ensnare him. Another staff top, of a hen and a cock, has an associated saying to the effect that the hen knows when dawn will break but leaves it to the cock to make all the noise. The ambiguity of this is obvious: one party may know something but not shout about it, but whether the party is the chief or his people will depend on different viewpoints.

Swords and staffs show the way alien objects were taken up, elaborated and used by the Asante to give form to political competition and alliance, and to distinguish those who claimed power from those they ruled. The firearms and weaponry so essential to Asante military expansion were treated in a similar fashion. The two most important items were the guns themselves, initially flintlocks but later cap-guns, and the belts (*ntoa*) containing small wooden containers for powder, knives (for removing the heads of slain enemies) and pouches containing shot and gun flints. These were worn diagonally across the upper part of the body or around the waist.

The weapons and ammunition belts of chiefs and retainers were often elaborately adorned to show their owners' wealth. Bowdich noted that the 'corslets' of the gun-bearers of the Asantehene were made 'of leopard's skin covered with gold cockle shells, and stuck full of small knives, sheathed in gold and silver, and the handles of blue agate; cartouch [*sic*] boxes of elephant's hide hung below, ornamented in the same manner. . . . Their long Danish mukets [*sic*] had broad rims of gold at small distances, and the stocks were ornamented with shells', and other soldiers' ammunition belts 'were embossed with red-shells and small brass bells'.[53] Decorated ammunition belts and guns of this type have survived as stool property, while undecorated guns and pouches, formerly in the majority, have since 1896 been allowed to decay and disappear. Most which survive are in collections outside Ghana, many of them obtained by British forces on the battlefield.

Gun barrels were wrapped with brass wire or tightly bound cloth to minimise the risk of bursting, a perpetual problem with ill-maintained poor-quality firearms, charged or overcharged with unreliable gunpowder. The addition of golden 'cockle' shells was less obviously functional. The way such shells came to adorn guns and ammunition belts again indicates how the exotic was assimilated into Akan culture.

Today many Asante knives, ammunition belts, gunmen's caps and guns are decorated either with much-worn red shells or with closely similar gold castings. Other castings used in the same way look more like insects, with the carapaces divided along the length of the back and separate head sections with two eyes. Today informants are unsure what, if anything, these castings represent. Some suggest they are a creature of some sort (*boa bi*), others that they may be a fruit of similar shape called *adam*, and still more explanations are offered.[54] However, it is highly likely that all these castings are ultimately derived from the red sea shells initially used on the coast to decorate war-gear.

There are early accounts of war-gear adorned with shells. Bosman noted how local males 'have a cap on their heads made of a crocodile's skin, adorned on each side with a red shell'.[55] De Marees records the use of such shells on swords: '. . . at the end of the sheathe . . . they put a great red shell, as broad as a man's hand, which is in great estimation with them.'[56] A painting by Eckhout of an Akan wearing a sword at his belt, and which dates from the first half of the seventeenth century, shows it adorned with a red shell. Loyer records the practice of adorning swords with gold copies of shells of Assini.[57] The matter began earlier. Duarte Pacheco Pereira noted that among the items traded at Elmina by the Portuguese in the fifteenth century were 'certain red shells which they prize as we prize precious stones'.[58] Roger Barlow, in a volume based on a work by the Spaniard Bachiller Enciso published in 1518

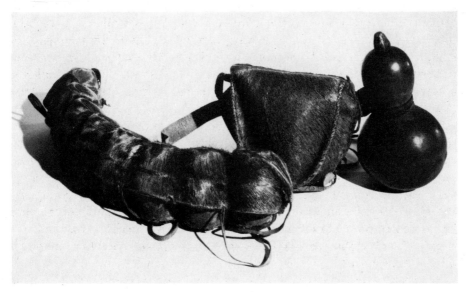

A 19th-century war belt made of animal skin, with gourd and wood containers for powder and shot.

and based on earlier sources, says of the area between Cape Three Points that 'they give the gold in truck of ringes of latyu [brass] and coper and for certain red shelles of fysshes'.[59] Other early accounts leave no doubt that these shells were an important item by which gold could be obtained. A document by Hernando del Pulgar states that shells from the Canary Isles could be exchanged profitably at Elmina: '. . . he who carried out very great shells of the sea demanded 20 or 30 pesos of that gold for each shell.' He provides a reason for the demand: '. . . because in those districts many thunderbolts fell from the sky, and those savages believed that any man whatever, who carried one of those shells, was protected from the thunderbolts.'[60]

This passing observation suggests why such exotic shells came to be associated with swords, guns and warriors' accoutrements. Throughout West Africa it is believed that thunder and lightning have a physical form: during severe storms thunderbolts fall and can later be found on or near the surface of the ground. The Asante believe each burst of thunder and lightning contains a thunderbolt and they may look for these near any object struck in a storm. The items they perceive as thunderbolts are the worn-down remains of Neolithic axes referred to as *'Nyame akuma* ('God's axes') which continually wash out of the soil. Trees or buildings hit by lightning or death by lightning blast are believed to be caused by *'Nyame akuma* hurled from on high.

It is unclear why red shells should originally have been considered as protection against *'Nyame akuma*. However, it is possible to speculate that their use on weapons of war arose from an intermediate conceptual stage: a stage in which local people made a link between the noise and flash of firearms, the wounds they inflicted, and the harm which was already known to be caused by thunder and lightning and which was conceived as being caused by *'Nyame akuma*. European guns may thus have been seen as projecting a form of *'Nyame akuma*. We may therefore speculate that the Asante decoration of war-gear with shells and gold derivatives of shells is a distant continuation of the fifteenth-century beliefs and practices reported from the coast. If exotic shells were seen as a protection against thunderbolts, they could also have been taken up as a protection against gunshot and so been adopted as an important protective addition to the equipment used in fighting. This is speculation; what remains, however, is evidence that the most important types of military equipment were adorned with items originating far from Asante and which could be obtained only by trade.

Firearms made obsolescent the shields used formerly, but these have retained a symbolic role. Large shields (*ekyem*) were made by attaching a hide cover to a wicker or wooden framework. Such shields are depicted in numerous gold-weights, both as frames and complete shields, and many of the latter have their outer surfaces decorated with bells and metal plates. A few, apparently early, shield weights show them decorated either with elephant tails and keys or representations of these: presumably these indicated the sword-bearer's high status. Weights also show shields being held by men on foot or by mounted warriors.

Shields clearly became used less often in battle as spears and bows and

arrows were increasingly replaced by imported firearms. They were, however, used in Asante until Prempe I was forcibly exiled, and were again brought out for the enstoolment of Prempe II.

Early sources indicate that shields were used to show the status of the owner as well as to protect him. The more important people had leopard, crocodile or elephant skin upon their shields, and Bosman records that a man who had achieved high status was permitted to carry two shields.[61] The earlier coastal custom of dancing with shields was continued in Asante: at one point in his installation the Asantehene dances bearing the *Bosommuru* state sword in his right hand and a shield in his left. Until recently, however, the symbolic significance of these shields was not understood.

A clue to this was recently discovered among the accounts of a planned slave rising in Antigua in 1736.[62] The slaves involved were clearly Akans, although not necessarily Asante, and in planning their revolt they made use of ranks and practices from their homeland. It is clear that these shields were used in a ritual, a 'shield-dance' in which a ruler, having danced with a sword and spear, swore to prosecute a planned war with the utmost vigour and not to desert the field. The shield thus remained as a special indication of warlike intention and is still used to stress the military, aggressive role of a newly installed ruler.

The strong verbal component and the subtleties of meaning of major regalia within Asante were often misunderstood by Europeans. Perhaps the clearest case of the conflicting assumptions of Asante and European negotiators arose

Above Shields, photographed during the 1930s.

Right Gun-men wearing war belts decorated with golden shells.

from the diplomatic use of the Golden Axe, *Sika Kuma*, an item of regalia dispatched from Kumase only on the most major diplomatic missions. Like messenger swords it was intended to show unequivocally that the mission bearing it came from the Asantehene and his council and was empowered to conduct especially important negotiations and investigations. In 1806 the Asantehene dispatched a party to investigate a dispute in the south, sending officials to one of those involved 'with two gold-headed swords and a gold axe, and requested him to remain quiet'. A rival group seized the royal negotiators, killed them, and took the swords and axe which, it was reported, were later passed to a Fante group to raise support.[63] A Dutch source gives an account from the Asante viewpoint: two chiefs, regarded by Asante as ruling areas within their realm, came into dispute. One rejected the Asantehene's intervention and fled to Fante with his supporters. An envoy from Kumase was sent to obtain their return, but the Fante refused to co-operate. 'The Asante Monarch then sent an envoy on whom [he] hung his golden sword and before whom was carried the Golden Axe of his forefathers as proof that this [envoy] represented his person. But the Fante scoundrels – who are the worst people on earth – murdered the Envoys and robbed them of the golden axe and Sword and everything else they had with them. After this [the Asantehene] having sent [envoys] for the third time, they [the Fantes] answered saying that their great fetish had taken the axe and Sword to Heaven.'[64] This serious defiance of the authority of Kumase was one of the factors which lead to the 1807 Asante invasion of Fante.

In 1881 a crisis occurred in relations between the British and Asante, and the Golden Axe was brought out again. A refugee from Kumase fled to Cape Coast and claimed British protection. A day later a senior delegation arrived, bearing the Golden Axe, and demanded he be returned to Kumase. The British saw the axe as a symbol of aggression and a threat, taking a literal view of its meaning. Griffith, the Lieutenant-Governor, later wrote: 'The refusal of a demand from Ashanti accompanied by the Golden Axe, means war on the part of the Ashantis, that they will cut their way to the accomplishment of their purpose. The Golden Axe was sent down in 1863 and 1873 and war followed.'[65] The British were told by a number of local people that the real meaning of the axe was more subtle: it showed the Asante determination to cut through all blockages on the path to a settlement. The British refused to see this, and, although a second embassy followed, the matter was unresolved and both sides feared that war was likely. One of the most experienced officials, Boakye Tenten, one of the Asantehene's *akyeame*, was then sent to the coast with a mission numbering about 400 people. He carried about 57 kg of gold, raised by a special tax, to offer to Governor Rowe towards the heavy indemnity imposed in 1874 and as an indication of the Asante desire for continued peace. He stressed that the British were not to see the Golden Axe as a sign of war.

'The Prince [Boakye] further explained that Asante had two symbols of war, a peculiar sword and a certain cap; whereas the "Gold Axe" being "fetish" and endowed with some magical and mysterious power, is never sent on a hostile errand'. This garbled version of indigenous exegesis continues: 'The weapon, said Prince Bwaki, is so old that no one knows its origin, and it is held so precious that in procession it precedes the Great Royal Stool, or throne of Asante. The leopard skin, bound with gold upon the handle, symbolises courage in the field; the gold is wealth, the iron strength.'[66] Boakye is also quoted as saying that in future the Golden Axe, so open to misunderstanding, should not be used: 'The Queen of England presented a silver-topped cane to Quaco Duah [the Asantehene] this cane the King has, and he proposes to have it copied in gold, and to send the cane with his messengers in future, so there shall be no mistake about the meaning, as there was about the axe.'[67] Governor Rowe indicated these peaceable overtures would carry more weight if the Axe were handed over to the British. The matter was referred to the Kumase council at the end of April, and in late May of 1882 a senior official arrived from Kumase explaining how, after lengthy debate, it had been decided to present the axe to Queen Victoria.

The largest, most striking items of regalia were the multi-coloured umbrellas (*kyinie*) used to shade senior chiefs whenever they appeared in public. By the time Bowdich visited Kumase these were central to the displays connected with kingship, and they had probably been used in Asante long before 1817. Chiefs using umbrellas for shade were observed on the coast in the seventeenth century. It is possible that the Akan learned of umbrellas from the north: an umbrella topped by a golden bird was used to shade the ruler of Mali in the fourteenth century.

The umbrellas seen by nineteenth-century visitors were generally circular, but a few square or rectangular ones were also reported. Circular umbrellas were usually, perhaps always, made to fold. The frame was made of a hard, evenly grained wood, *twafoyeden* (*Harrisonia occidentalis*), in three parts: the central shaft, perhaps 7.5 cm in diameter and about 3 m long, and two sets of ribs. The top set of ribs supported the cloth covering and folded downwards; the lower set braced the upper ones and was attached to a wooden

The Golden Axe of Asante presented to Queen Victoria. Reproduced by Gracious Permission of Her Majesty The Queen.

collar which slid up and down the shaft. The inner ends of the lower ribs were hinged to slots in the top of this sliding collar, and a hole was drilled through each outer end. The upper ribs were similarly hinged to a wooden ring fixed at the top of the central shaft. These upper ribs were about two or three times as long as the lower ones, and each was drilled between a third and half-way along its length from the centre. A single length of rope was threaded alternately between the holes in the outer ends of the lower ribs and those in the upper. When the lower collar was slid up the central shaft, the ribs were pushed outwards, the rope was tightened, and the upper ribs, to which the cloth covering was sewn, were forced outwards and rigidly braced. The collar was then fixed in position by a wooden peg, a nail pushed through a hole in the shaft or a sprung clip. Umbrella making was a skilled task: in the early nineteenth century there was a village of umbrella makers just outside Kumase, presumably supplying the palace and the senior functionaries of the capital, and most major states seem to have had their own umbrella makers into the present century.

The coverings for umbrellas were clearly intended to be spectacular, and imported cloths were mainly used, both for the dome and for the hanging valance. The predominant colour in many umbrellas is red, but many also

The King of Nkoransa, *c.* 1897, seated beneath his state umbrella.

108

have areas of coloured velvets (yellow being preferred) and pieces of vari-coloured patterned prints. A small umbrella given to Bowdich, and described as a 'child's' umbrella, is covered with several types of imported cloth. A few very important umbrellas are covered with thick multi-coloured *nsaa* cloth, made by the Fulani from sheep or goat wool. The umbrella used to shade the Golden Stool and known as *Katamanso* ('the covering of the nation') was made of this, and so is one used by the Bantamahene.

An umbrella was obviously used to keep the chief physically cool, but it was also intended to promote a condition of spiritual peace and coolness (*dwo*) and to create around him a particular symbolic space. Rattray quotes a well-known saying: *Onyame nhu ohene apampam* ('God should not see the crown of the King's head'),[68] and the umbrella serves to isolate the King from above in the way that his sandals prevent his ever coming into direct contact with the earth beneath. The Asantehene was covered with an umbrella whenever he left the palace and when he moved from one part to another: even when he and other senior chiefs held audiences at night, they sat beneath umbrellas.

One obvious function of the umbrella was to signal the presence of the chief. When the streets of the capital were crowded with the vast unruly throngs celebrating the Odwira festival or in the confusion of the battlefield, these huge umbrellas, towering high above men's heads, could be seen easily. When a chief walked, his umbrella-bearer (*kyinie kyimini*) made the umbrella 'dance' to the music of the drums and horns that accompanied his chief, sounding his praise-names and recounting his deeds. The bearer raised, lowered and spun the umbrella pole to make the valance flap and twirl to produce a cool breeze and to show the umbrella's colours to best advantage. The umbrella thus combined the element of display and spectacle with the idea of the necessary coolness of the chief, a coolness to which the great fans and elephant-tail whisks which were used around the King also contributed.

The umbrellas seen and described by Bowdich were topped by a variety of images: '. . . crowned on the top with crescents, pelicans, elephants, barrels, and arms and swords of gold; they were of various shapes, but mostly dome, and the valances (in some of which small looking glasses were inserted) fantastically scalloped and fringed; . . . a few were roofed with leopard skins, and crowned with various animals naturally stuffed.'[69]

These tops (*kyinie akyi*) are detachable: they usually have a square socket in their base which fits over a block protruding from the top of the umbrella, and a pin or nail is pushed through a hole in both to keep the finial in place. There exist a number of documented nineteenth-century umbrella tops, and several more are depicted in photographs taken in the last two decades of the century. This evidence makes it clear that the most common type of umbrella top was the one showing a *babadua*, a type of cane with rings running around it at short intervals. A number of explanations of this top are now proffered: according to some, the *babadua* was used in constructing barricades during war; according to others, it was particularly strong and resilient (it is often used in house construction). Other sources suggest that a path of *babadua* was put down, and when the cane broke under the weight of warriors the army was big enough.

Clearly the underlying idea is of resilience and toughness. Asantehene Kwaku Dua II, who reigned briefly in the mid 1880s, was photographed seated under an umbrella topped with a *babadua* cane, and umbrella tops of the same type were used by the Amanhene of Nsuta, Nkoransa, Kokofu, Bekwae and Wankyi in the 1890s.[70] The umbrellas under which Prempe II was shaded after his installation were also topped in this way, and the great majority of those used by senior chiefs at the parade following the installation were topped with carvings of *babadua*. The predominance of this type of umbrella top is indicated by Rattray's remark: 'The ornamental tops of state umbrellas are called *Babadua*.'[71]

Another common umbrella top depicts a war-horn (*akoben*). Tops of this type ('crescents') were observed by Bowdich and are today among the regalia of several major states as well as a number of Kumase chiefs. A number of proverbs are put forward to give the significance of this horn, but all turn on its importance in war and the fact that only the victorious have the right to sound it: 'When an army is defeated a horn is not blown in its honour.'[72] It is possible that this type of top is ultimately derived from the Islamic crescents which often decorated the umbrellas of Muslim rulers, an exotic image which has been interpreted by the Asante in terms of their own culture.

Three other common images are the *sankofa* bird, a chevron-patterned fern called *aya*, and the top of a strong-smelling plant, *prekese*. The fern *aya* is said to be a form of visual pun: the plant is considered beautiful because of its symmetrical form (just as the *babadua* is admired for its regularity), but its name, spoken with the tones slightly altered, also means abuse. The top is

Above (left) Umbrella top, in the form of five *sankofa* birds, made of wood covered with gold foil.

Above (right) Umbrella top in the form of the *aya* leaf. Offinso state regalia.

110

therefore said to be a warning against ill-considered speech in the ruler's presence.

A number of other nineteenth-century umbrella tops are known in a variety of forms: at least one top made from animal skin is preserved within Asante, in the regalia of the Bantama stool, and is a model of an elephant. Other tops, of unclear provenance, depict a lion, a hand holding a pistol, and a hand with a thumb raised in the air.

The earliest explanation of the significance of these tops is, inevitably, given by Bowdich: 'a small black wooden image, with a bunch of rusty hair in the head'[73] was intended to represent an Akyim chief slain by the chief to whom the umbrella belonged. The majority of images, however, now seem to have a far more indirect and generalised significance than this. On one level these images are considered pleasing because they are well carved and show things or creatures which are themselves considered beautiful or powerful, and on another they are given a wider significance by having various verbal formulae attached to them. These sayings, aphorisms and proverbs are interpreted as making truistic statements about the chiefs who are sheltered under the umbrellas and their political position.

In the past there also seems to have been some restriction placed on who could possess umbrella tops of particular types. Rattray claims 'they varied according to the rank of the chief. The top of the King of Ashanti's umbrella was of gold and might represent a war horn, *akoben*, a hen covering her chickens, *akokobatan*, or a palm tree, *abe*. The *Babadua* of *amanhene* were of silver, with the exception of Juaben, who being of the King's clan might have one of gold. Gods have their umbrellas for their shrines just as kings and princes, but they are made of white material and are generally surmounted by a gong (*odawura*)'.[74] The views Rattray expressed were probably a statement of the ideal rather than the practice at the time he wrote. Nowadays most umbrella tops of Amanhene are covered with gold leaf, and a number of nineteenth-century umbrellas possessed by *abosom* are of red and not white cloth.

7 Stools and chairs

In 1482 the Portuguese held a formal meeting with the ruler of what grew into the great trading town of Elmina. He, Caramansa, came with members of his court, signalled by 'a great noise of bugles, bells and horns', and 'attended behind by naked page boys with seats of wood, like stools, to sit upon'.[1] It is clear from this and later accounts that wooden stools have long been an essential element in local life. Today they remain important, and the stools once used by dead forebears are preserved and periodically have sacrifices offered before them.

All Asante stools (*nkonnua*, *dwa*) have the same basic form although with many variations in detail. Essentially, the stool comprises a rectangular base, from which a central column rises; this supports a more or less rectangular seat, usually larger than the base, which curves upwards at each end. Distinct, named types of stool are created by varying the size and shape of these elements, by adding more supporting columns or adding surface decoration. The Asante, as in other areas of their culture, have carried the elaboration of basic forms to great lengths. Wooden stools must have been invented at a very early stage in African prehistory; they are used widely throughout the continent, and most cultural groups have evolved distinctive forms. Asante stools are very like many of those used among southern Akan peoples, and closely similar ones were used on the coast of Dahomey in the nineteenth century, possibly derived from Akan prototypes.

It is still impossible to establish a chronology for Asante stools. Some depicted as gold-weights may date to the early eighteenth century or before; coastal stools were illustrated, but unreliably, in Barbot; a few types are linked in tradition to particular rulers; and it is possible that a few remains of fragmentary eighteenth-century stools are preserved in stool rooms: none the less, this evidence is incomplete and difficult to evaluate. The earliest datable Asante stool was purchased by Bowdich in Kumase in 1817 and its form is indistinguishable from one of the most common types of stool still made, the *mmaadwa* stool. The earliest Akan stools were possibly circular like those reported from the coast in the seventeenth century. Stools with lobed oval or rounded seats are depicted as gold-weights and actual examples were collected in the last century, but today virtually all known Asante forms (with the possible exception of the Golden Stool) are basically rectilinear. Many stools were probably invented to serve the needs of the increasingly complex society which evolved in Asante in the nineteenth century. Some forms have now become rare, and stool-carvers can produce them only after consulting photographs in Rattray's books. A few types of stool have apparently disappeared completely: two blackened stools in the British Museum are of a form no longer seen.

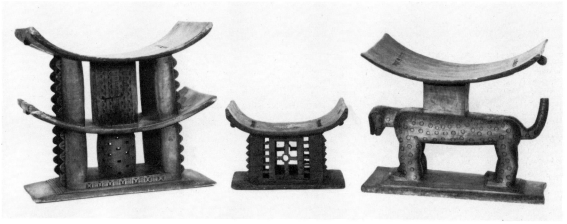

The great majority of stools are carved out of the pale wood *ọsẹsẹ* (Bowdich's *zezzo*), chosen for its even texture and paleness (it is *fittaa* – 'light', 'bright'), and because it gives a fine, smooth surface. The stool is carved from a single block with the usual carver's tools, and the grain normally runs horizontally, which tends to make supporting pillars crack as the sap dries out. A few stools were carved from another light wood, *'Nyame'dua*.

The most common class of stool is the *nkonnua fufuo* ('white stool'), formerly used by men and women for everyday purposes. These were used in the central court of a house or within rooms, or outside when attending important discussions, usually carried by a small boy from the household. Stools were also used when men and women were working, for example, when men were weaving or when women were seated around the hearth cooking or preparing food. Ordinary stools were unadorned but were periodically scrubbed with water and fine river sand, sometimes with lime juice, and this treatment gave them a clean, white colour. In use stools became rather yellow, displeasing to Asante eyes, and also acquired a coat of dirt (*efi*), undesirable for something so closely associated with a person. A stool is still linked with the personality and spiritual state of its owner and is cleaned before any major ritual involving an individual or household, such as *adae* rituals and, formerly, soul-cleaning (*kra dware*) ceremonies.

113

The longest list of stool types – over thirty – was compiled by Rattray in the 1920s.[2] He indicated that certain designs were restricted to particular ranks or roles within Asante society and that some were carved for the exclusive use of the Asantehene and never sold on the open market, a restriction enforced by the death penalty. Among such restricted stools were those in which the seat was supported upon an image of a leopard or an elephant (*osebo dwa* and *esono dwa*), creatures being used to express the King's greatness and fierce nature. The *mmaremu* ('cross') and *kontonkorowi mpenu* ('divided circular rainbow') stools were also supposed to be used by the King. Shrines of gods were placed on stools in which the seat was supported on a carving of a crocodile with a mudfish in its mouth (*odenkyem'gwa*), the predatory, amphibious nature of the

The Omanhene seated on a *hwedom* chair, his personal silver-decorated stool beside him.

crocodile suiting the deity living in the world and yet out of it. All traces of royal control over stool types has now vanished. Particular types of stool were also once associated with one or other sex: the *mmarima* ('the men's stool') is now also used by women. Many stools are named after elements in their design – for example, the *damedame* ('draughts') stool has a pierced chequer-board design to its central pillar, and the *pantu* stool has a pillar shaped like the square-sided spirit bottle after which it is named. The hierarchical nature of Asante society is expressed in a stool in the form of one shallow stool on top of another, the *obi-te-obi-so* stool: 'someone sits on top of someone else' or, more loosely, 'there is always someone above you and bearing down'.

Stool-carving seems to have been a more or less full-time occupation for some men, and stools were sold to the public. Some, possibly, were made for sale in markets or to casual customers; but probably most were made on commission and payments for them spread over time, for most Asante transactions of this sort contain an element of continuing mutual obligation and indebtedness. The prices of some stools were comparatively low: the fairly large stool Bowdich bought cost the equivalent of 6d,[3] and certain small, simple stools were referred to as 'tuppenny stools', that is, they cost a *damma* of gold-dust.

The personal stools of chiefs were larger and more elaborate than those of commoners. Those of the Asantehenes and queen mothers were decorated with repoussé-patterned sheets of gold or silver produced by the court goldsmiths, and many of these metal facings incorporate European motifs. The stools of other senior office-holders were also decorated with silver. Major stools had leather cushions placed on their seats. Since Rattray's books in the 1920s, it has been claimed that silver decoration was restricted to a very small number of chiefs, especially the Omanhene of Mampon, but the large number of stools decorated in this way indicates that the practice was formerly far wider. The simplest decoration is a small disc of metal at the centre of the seat, sometimes called *otadee* ('like a pool'). Patterns on these relate closely to those of the pectoral discs worn by royal servants, and they may have been made by the same people. It is possible that these discs evolved from the practice of nailing silver coins to the centres of stools. More elaborate decoration consists of gold or silver strips radiating from the central disc, pieces around the supporting columns and strips on the base running parallel to its sides. The metal is usually fixed to the wood with small staple-like pieces of wire forced into pre-drilled holes.

The stools of major chiefs are still carried in public by the chief's stool-bearers. Distinguished by their peculiar hair-style of a bald patch shaved across the head, they carry the stools resting on the napes of their necks with the seats forward. As Bowdich observed, 'Their stools (of the most laborious carved work, and generally with two large bells attached to them) were conspicuously placed on the heads of favourites'.[4] The large, highly decorated stools of chiefs mark the importance of their users, and many of the decorative elements are said to have a relevant meaning. The personal stool of the late Asantehene Prempe II, for example, had reef knots covered with gold foil carved on its outer supporting columns. These 'wisdom' knots are said to have been chosen by the monarch on installation to express his wish to bind the nation together again.[5]

Stools have a particularly close association with their owners, especially those of senior people and office-holders. Once installed, an office-holder is forbidden to touch the earth with bare feet or to sit on the ground. Such contact between the body and the earth (Asase Yaa) is considered polluting, bringing *mmusuo* and causing famine and sickness to the community for which the office-holder is responsible. This rule is kept scrupulously: if rivals wish forcibly to remove someone from office, they seize him, pull off his sandals and seat him on the ground. A stool is thought to receive some spiritual element from its user, and Asante often explain their habit of tipping stools on to their sides when not in use as a precaution against a stray bad spiritual power (*sunsum bone*), possibly from an executed person or an accident victim, entering the stool.

The Asante make a basic distinction between plain white stools and blackened ancestral stools (*nkonnua tuntum*). White stools are converted into blackened ancestral stools for only a very few people. Only office-holders who die properly and in office leaving behind successors and who have led successful, untarnished lives are potentially ancestors. Deaths caused by disfiguring or wasting diseases, such as leprosy, by snake-bite or attack by wild beasts, by drowning, lightning, falling trees or by suicide are shameful and polluting; those who die in these ways cannot have their stools blackened.

If an office-holder is judged worthy, it is usual to blacken his or, in the case of a queen mother, her most frequently used personal stool. The corpse is generally placed on this for its post-mortem bath and then arrayed in the finest of cloths and jewellery for display before burial. After the funeral, and on a propitious day, the stool is placed with existing ancestral stools, and hair and nail parings from the corpse are placed in the hole which runs vertically through the central column. The stool is blackened with soot mixed with raw egg, and blood and fat from a sheep are added. The blood congeals and darkens, the white fat darkens, and the stool eventually becomes encased in a shiny black deposit.[6] These stools are usually kept together in a windowless room of the palace, resting on a bench or low clay altar, and covered with cloth or a coarse woollen *nsaa* blanket of Fulani origin. Formerly, metal vessels (*kuduo*) containing gold nuggets or dust were placed before the stools of important chiefs. Today pottery vessels of various sorts normally stand before the stools. Many ancestral stools have brass bells attached to them or fetters fastened around their columns. The bells are to call the ancestors, and the fetters express the desire that their souls may be firmly attached to the stools. These are sometimes attached to the stool in its user's lifetime.

Stool rooms are holy and pure (*kronkron*). Only the most senior and worthy people can enter them, and enormous respect is shown in the ancestral presence. In some areas Europeans are not allowed to see ancestral stools, and formerly any mutilated person, including until recently those who had been circumcised, was forbidden access. Stools were taken from the stool room on

116

important occasions, and especially on major campaigns, so that ancestral assistance and support would be available. If there was serious danger of defeat, those involved would make one last, terrible attempt to arouse the fury of the ancestors and turn this against the enemy: they demeaned the stools by standing upon them.

Blackened stools form a focus of respect at the pinnacle of each unit within the political system. An incumbent makes libations, offerings and prayers at his predecessors' stools on behalf of all those he represents and for whom he is responsible to the office-holder above him. The ancestors are believed to take a continuing interest in their descendants, warning them in dreams and visions of impending dangers, and punishing them for secret transgressions. An office-holder appears before the stools as the inheritor of jural authority over the living but in a position inferior to the ancestors. On entering the stool room he shows respect by slipping his feet out of his sandals and standing on them, and rolling down his cloth to expose his left shoulder. An old cloth is usually worn to show his inferior position.

The greatest and most famous stool of Asante is the Golden Stool, Kofi (*Sika*

A 19th-century *asipim* chair. Ht 65 cm.

Dwa Kofi, 'the Friday-born Golden Stool'). According to modern oral traditions, this stool was brought from the sky by the great priest Anokye to rest upon the knees of Asantehene Osei Tutu. The stool was believed to incorporate the spirit (*sunsum*) of the Asante nation and to symbolise its unity. The earliest accounts of Asante history make no mention of Anokye, although Bowdich has left a brief description of the Golden Stool as it was in mid-1817: '. . . the royal stool, entirely cased in gold, was displayed under a splendid umbrella.'[7]

On the death of an Asantehene the stool, which is never sat upon, and other regalia were held by the *wirempefo*. Real power could be exercised only if the candidate chosen as Asantehene could command the allegiance of a sufficiently strong group within the kingdom and gain access to the treasury and important regalia. Possession of the Golden Stool gave a symbolic and clear confirmation of the transfer of resources and power to a new leader. The Asantehene-elect Kofi Kakari, for example, did not gain custody of the Golden Stool until about three years after his installation ceremonies.[8]

The role of the Golden Stool has, in the last hundred years, largely been to simplify or obscure the complicated manœuvrings by which rival groups attempted to control Asante. In 1896 a British governor demanded it: according to some accounts, he asked why it had not been produced for him to sit on. The Asante refused to hand the stool over, and it remained hidden until 1920 when certain Asante began to remove from it pieces of gold and the golden bells tied to it. When this came to light, the nation went into mourning. The colonial regime saw that the perpetrators were tried and exiled, although the Asante wanted their execution. The remains of the stool were placed in the royal mausoleum and later reincorporated into a new stool. The exact form of the original Golden Stool is far from clear, but gold castings hang from the present one to represent defeated enemies of the Asantehene including the British governor Sir Charles Macarthy, defeated and beheaded in the 1820s. Like other important stools, it has Islamic talismans fastened to its central column.

Stools come from an early level of Asante culture, but carpentered wooden chairs were also used during the last century, possibly earlier. All were derived from European prototypes and until recently remained entirely in the hands of the ruling group.

There are three basic kinds of chair. Today the most common is that called *asipim*. These are usually no more than about 1m in height and have a wooden frame with a hide seat and back stretched over it. The outer surfaces of the frame are usually decorated with large numbers of round-headed brass nails and are often adorned with large semi-spherical brass castings attached by nails driven through the centres. The backs have cast-brass finials. The upper parts of the fronts and backs of these chairs are also occasionally decorated with sheet brass with repoussé and incised designs. A few chairs have open-work wooden backs bearing geometrical designs somewhat similar to those found on the handles of gold-dust spoons. The hide seat is usually supported by a webbing of hide strips each about 2.5 cm wide.

Asipim chairs are nowadays kept in the palaces of senior chiefs for use when
men gather to discuss important matters. When not in use, they are tilted
forward against a wall, a practice apparently derived from the Asante habit of
leaning unused stools at an angle. *Asipim* chairs seem to have few or no ritual
connotations: they may be paraded with other more important items of
regalia, and a few are kept in stool rooms or those which house the shrines of
deities; but no sacrifices are made at them and they are not linked in any
special way with former owners. They seem to be based on seventeenth- or
early eighteenth-century European chairs.

The second type of chair *akonkromfi* (?'mantis') is more elaborate. These are
based on imported folding chairs in which the two pairs of legs cross at the sides
in the shape of an x, pivoted at the point of crossing. The framework of these
chairs is often decorated with brass-headed nails or larger semi-spherical
pieces of brass, and some have motifs such as knots carved into the frame. The
backs are usually made into complex open-work patterns, some of which
appear to be derived from European heraldic designs. A number of these
chairs are so closely similar that they may be the work of a single maker or
workshop. The most famous *akonkromfi* is possessed by the Asantehene and
called *kodie* ('eagle'). The arms are made in the form of birds, and there are
two inward-facing birds on the finials. This chair, or its decorations, was

119

probably made after 1874 when similar gold birds now in the Wallace Collection, London, were removed from Kumase.

The third type of chair is called *hwẹdom*, a term sometimes interpreted as 'facing or looking at the army'. These chairs were possessed by a number of the states near Kumase and are closest of all to their European origins. They have flat backs and seats with legs and stretchers copied from turned prototypes (some parts may have been made on a lathe and imported into Asante). Both *hwẹdom* and *akonkromfi* chairs were used by senior chiefs when seated in public and especially on the stepped circular platforms (*sumpi* or *sumpene*) outside their palaces. A number have talismans fitted beneath the seat. It was unusual for a chieftain to have more than one such chair.

The greater importance of *akonkromfi* and *hwẹdom* chairs is indicated by the fact that they are usually far larger than *asipim* chairs. In creating their own chairs the Asante elaborated and extended the decoration of the originals. The frames of the Asante versions were covered with imported brass nails and incorporated figurative elements such as birds and knots. The chairs, or parts of them, were given a verbal dimension for parts of the design were linked with proverbs and sayings. Thus an *akonkromfi* chair from Berekum has a design associated with the proverb *Konim ne Besehene yefa no Benyansafo*,[10] about the

A 19th-century *akonkromfi* chair. Protective talismans (*asuman*) are fixed beneath the seat. Ht 102 cm.

difficulty of distinguishing between two similar leaves, and other chairs have metal decorations or finials linked verbally to the moon, segments of orange, and the stars. Decorated chairs were well established by 1820. Dupuis described the 'royal chair': 'Its arms and legs were carved from the solid into grotesque forms and embossed with little ornamental casts of gold.' He also saw the 'royal seat' of the recently defeated King of Gyaman 'studded all over with gold and silver ornaments, and silver coins of different European states'.[9]

An actual prototype for some of these chairs recently came to light. This was a large chair of Spanish or Portuguese manufacture probably dating from the seventeenth century. It was removed from the Asantehene's palace in 1896 on the day Prempe was seized by the British. The back and the seat are of hide and are stamped with elaborate scroll-work and floral designs. The chair has been well looked after, but there is no evidence to show exactly how it reached Kumase.[11]

Some of the basic forms of stool bases and supports are also found in the wooden gaming-boards used in playing the various forms of *oware*. In this game the two players have to redistribute counters (usually seeds) so as to gain, or make their opponent have, a particular number in one or more holes in the board. The boards used by kings were sometimes decorated with strips of gold.

A 17th-century Portuguese or Spanish chair found at Kumase in 1896.

8 Gold-weights

The vast quantities of gold mined and panned within the Asante kingdom were used for trading with outsiders, for making regalia and personal adornment and as an internal currency. The search for gold and the desire to control its production was one of the main stimulants to state formation in this area. Many technical and cultural innovations entered the forest zone through the gold trade. By the beginning of the eighteenth century, if not earlier, gold-dust was the sole Asante currency, although an iron disc currency may have preceded it in some areas.

Gold-dust was used by mass and, except on the coast, was never cast into pieces which were given a particular value. This necessitated the local production of large numbers of brass weights for measuring out units of gold-dust among the Asante and related groups. Virtually all were cast by the lost-wax process (see p.80). Two broad categories were made: representational weights which showed objects, creatures and situations from local life in miniature; and geometric weights in the form of pyramids, discs, truncated double cones, rectangles, etc., often with linear and cursive decoration on one surface. Geometric weights outnumber representational ones by perhaps ten or fifteen to one. A few weights were made by adapting an existing object of roughly the right mass: beads, bits of European brass, or brass castings from groups near Asante, or seeds, especially those of the *Abrus pecatorius* bush (*damma*).

Until weights fell out of use towards the end of the last century every person engaged in trade owned or had access to a set. Gold-dust was used from the humblest of petty trading to major national enterprises. The basic equipment was simple. The dust was weighed in a simple set of beam scales (*nsania*). A weight (*abramoo*) was placed in one pan and the gold-dust in the other, usually with a sheet-brass spoon (*saawa*). Impurities in the gold could be removed by placing it in a sort of scoop (*famfa*) and blowing across it. Gold-dust was usually kept in tied twists of cloth placed in small brass boxes (*adaka ketewa*, *abampuruwa*), occasionally in quills plugged at the open end.

Gold-weights are in many ways the most fascinating of Asante arts. The large numbers made, probably over a period of at least 300–400 years, their different sizes, and the many subjects depicted produce an impression of almost infinite variety. Many weights show keen observation and are modelled with great sensitivity and understanding of sculptural form.

Weights were not an Asante invention: they, and units in the weight system, were introduced from outside. The great proliferation in weight forms, however, was a product of Akan society. It is probable that the earliest gold-weights in the forest zone were introduced from the north by Manding-speaking traders, perhaps in the fourteenth century, and based on Islamic units. The Islamic units *mithqal* and *uqiya*, the first for weighing gold, the second for silver and other materials, were widely used in northern Africa and the western Sudan, although the actual weights of each nominal unit varied somewhat from area to area. It has been plausibly argued that certain shapes of weight, particularly those in the form of two truncated cones joined at their bases, are derived from Islamic prototypes (although there is no proof when weights of this shape first appeared in Asante).[1]

It cannot yet be established exactly when weights were first used in Asante, but they were in use on the coast when the Portuguese arrived.[2] Bowdich recorded in Kumase a tradition that the Asante weight system was derived from the Inta people, a term indicating little more than that this group was somewhere to the north.[3] Other traditions record that weights were obtained from the defeated Takyiman kingdom in the early part of the eighteenth century, but this late date is improbable.[4] It has been suggested that the units used in nineteenth-century Asante were derived essentially from four exterior systems, namely, the Islamic *mithqal*, the Islamic ounce, the Portuguese ounce standard and the troy ounce standard. Attempts have been made to show that the named Akan units of weight, which range from fractions of a gramme to several hundreds of grammes, relate to units in these systems.[5] A statistical analysis of the weights in three large museum collections has strongly suggested that, whatever the ultimate origins of weight units, those examined have an underlying 1.46 gramme unit in multiples of 3, 4, 4.5, 6, 8, 9, 10, 11, 12, 24, 36, and 48, and possibly 1.5, 2 and 7, producing the complete range of weights. Weights were carefully adjusted by removing metal or adding solder or bits of wire to achieve an accuracy of one-half gramme in the case of lighter weights and between one and one-half grammes in the case of heavier ones.[6]

A selection of geometric gold-weights.

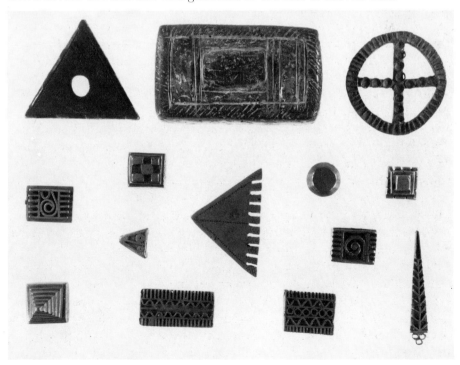

Each weight user would check his own weights with those, supposedly of the same unit, of the person with whom he was dealing to ensure that the latter were actually equal. Some sources claim the weights of senior chiefs were heavier unit for unit than those of ordinary people. Possibly those in power used their position to call weights by the name of lesser units to benefit themselves.

Anyone involved in trade would have available a set of scales, gold-dust containers, spoons and weights, and the number of these was related to the person's position and prosperity. Most weights would be geometrical, a few representational. Some people would also possess representational weights made by encasing a real object (a beetle, seed, or flower) in a mould and then heating mould and object until the latter turned to dust: the cavity left was filled with molten brass to reproduce the original item, a process sometimes called the 'lost-beetle' method.

The hundreds of thousands of representational weights made in the eighteenth and nineteenth centuries show an astonishing variety of subject-matter, unequalled in any other African plastic art. What led to this flowering of creativity, and what, if any, were its limits? One factor which encouraged variety was the lost-wax technique used (see p.80). This is ideal for producing small, delicate castings, and the ease with which wax can be shaped encourages the craftsman to produce many different forms. The ready availability of wax and imported brass encouraged the production of large numbers of weights depicting numerous subjects.

Gold-dust scales.

Another factor encouraging variety was the economic situation in which the Asante increasingly found themselves. Trade links to the north and with European groups on the coast, the settlement of previously unexploited land, and the military predominance which came with imported firearms seem to have produced an unstable and generally expanding economy. Although many groups were largely self-supporting, some goods were traded widely – mainly cloth, pottery, metal and leatherwork, from both local producers and coastal importers. From the latter came items used by at least some Asante – brassware, silver vessels, guns, powder, liquor, tobacco, and so on. Markets grew up throughout the country, and the existence of an almost infinitely divisible gold-dust currency facilitated internal and external trade. The economic vitality of Asante for most of its existence with expanding production for sale rather than use within the producing group required weights. In addition, the developing state system required levies, taxes and fines in gold-dust. Most trading and most political activity therefore required gold-weights.

When we consider the subject-matter of weights, we can, perhaps, glimpse other forces shaping what was depicted. While at first glance it appears that representational weights show virtually every aspect of Akan culture, a more detailed examination shows that there are subjects which are curiously absent.

The constraints on weights made by casting from a natural object (the 'lost-beetle' technique, p.124) are obviously greater than those made from a wax model. Only small items which can be reduced to powder when heated inside a clay covering can be used. Nevertheless, the range of these is considerable, including small knots of leaf-fibre, seeds, the efflorescences of palm flowers, tiny bunches of developing plantains, small fruits, the claws of fowls, ground-nut shells, crabs' claws, beetles, insect heads and *pupae*. Occasionally these were used in combination with wax models, or castings were made by joining several natural objects together – for example, half a dozen insect heads. Such objects do not seem to have been chosen in order to produce something of proverbial significance, although some have associated sayings – for example, at least two sayings accompany castings of crabs' claws: 'the crab is feared because of its claws' and 'take the claw and eat the meat without cracking it'. It appears, therefore, that this sort of casting was made because certain natural items were available and would make weights of a useful size. The use of comparatively tough items such as crab or fowl claws suggests that this method of casting could have been extended to many more objects, but it is unclear why this did not occur.

The range of subjects made by lost-wax casting is far greater. It is clear that some subjects (for example, shields, war-horns, drums) are represented in comparatively large numbers; others (for example, hares, butterflies, royal palanquins, tobacco pipes, Europeans) occur relatively rarely. An exact numerical analysis of subjects would be difficult and probably unilluminating: we cannot estimate how far existing weights represent a true sample of those formerly in circulation.

Weights show most of the items used around the house, in farming or by Asante craftsmen: axes and adzes, metal-bladed digging-sticks, various types of bill-hooks and long knives, hammers and tongs, bellows (copied from European prototypes), parts of looms, lamps, basketry scoops, the grinders and ladles used in preparing and serving food (sometimes resting on a cooking pot), *oware* gaming-boards, and many sorts of stool. However, a number of things which might be expected to fall in this category are not represented: the domestic hearth, metalworking forges, and the house itself. There is no technical reason for these omissions: it was no more difficult to cast a model house than to make a model of a wicker and wooden fowl house, examples of which exist.

A large proportion of Asante weights depict animals, birds, fish and amphibians. Many are so well modelled and cast that the species can be recognised. Among the most popular animals are various antelopes, some of which can be identified as the oryx (*otwe*), the bushbuck (*onwansane*) the larger *okoo*, the reedbuck (*gyamframa*) and the elusive bongo (*tromo*), a creature which, if slain, had a funeral ritual performed to free its killer from its dangerous spiritual power (*sasa*). The elephant and leopard are also favourite subjects, the latter sometimes depicted vainly attacking a tortoise: 'a hungry leopard tries to eat any animal'. Various sorts of fish and birds are also modelled: some castings of the former show the catfish from the internal rivers and the sawfish from the coastal waters. Among castings of birds are hornbills, chickens and cocks. Other creatures depicted are porcupines, monitor lizards, snakes, baboons and monkeys, tortoises, snails, snakes and chameleons.

Everyday events are also depicted, often in a lively manner. Men and women are shown going to their bush farms, tools resting in flat wooden bowls balanced on their heads, or returning with bundles of wood for the cooking fires. Women are modelled suckling children, engaged in pounding *fu-fu*, or, occasionally, admiring themselves in mirrors. Men are depicted carrying mining equipment, gold-panning bowls, or with their guns and slain game over their shoulders, or playing *oware*. A number of proverbial subjects based on common acts are shown: men trying to scrape medicinal bark from trees single-handed, greeting long-lost friends, or walking along puffing pipes with gunpowder kegs balanced on their heads.

Weights show a number of religious acts: fibre-skirted priests dancing with the shrines of their gods on their heads, men sacrificing chickens into bowls of 'Nyame nua ('God's trees'), or killing chickens over *asuman* made from old brooms (because they had come into contact with all sorts of filth). In the latter the men stand with their legs crossed, left over right, a reversal of the usual and proper order of things required in dealing with dangerous *asuman*.

Weights also show aspects of the political system. Chiefly items abound – state swords, some with separately cast sheaths adorned with decorative *abosodee*, *asipim* and other royal chairs, elephant-tail fly-whisks and large wicker fans, decorated guns, and stools adorned with metal plates. Other objects also express power – ivory trumpets or 'horns' with the jaws of defeated enemies tied to them, large *antumpam* and other drums and, rarely, the palanquins used to carry chiefs. Chiefs and their servants are also shown, the chiefs usually seated on *asipim* chairs, or, occasionally, being carried in their

A selection of representational gold-weights.

palanquins; and a few weights show royal servants wearing gold pectoral *kra* discs. More numerous are weights showing warriors or executioners grasping severed heads.

There are other images of power: fully armed gunmen and mounted warriors bearing guns, shields and swords. Cavalry was of no real use in the forest where horses were killed by insect-carried diseases, but a few horses were kept at Kumase for prestige and in the northern savannah country they were of greater military use. Weights depicting drums and horns, or men playing these, or double or single bells, as separate castings or being sounded by hunchbacked criers, must be considered as images of royal power. By the early nineteenth century, if not earlier, the largest types of drums and horns decorated with jaw-bones could be owned only by senior chiefs whose towns or states had contributed in some major way to success in battle. There were also strict controls over what types of music could be made with these and what types of 'phrase', mimicking the tones of spoken language, could be sounded upon them. Double bells were used to announce royal decisions or edicts and were closely associated with chiefship.

Contact with outsiders had a profound influence upon what was depicted as weights. European cannon, for example, were modelled in large numbers. These were occasionally captured by Asante forces and displayed as trophies. Locks, keys and European bellows are also found as weights, as are stoneware liquor flagons and, occasionally, glass bottles. A few European sailing-vessels are depicted in weight form (although it is unclear where exactly these were cast), and scraps of European brass, sometimes bits of clock mechanism, were pressed into service as weights. The many hand-guns which appear as weights were all, of course, imported, and the practice of making barrels to contain gunpowder and other trade goods was introduced by whites, as were tobacco (perhaps shown in bound lengths of twist) and smoking-pipes. The shell decorations on war belts were also imported. A few weights show Europeans, usually identifiable by their dress and, especially, by their unpleasantly long and pointed noses. One shows a European politely doffing his hat, another has an almost naked girl on his knee, a third is seated at a desk with pen and ink.

A number of European goods do not appear as weights. Many of the slightly bizarre gifts sent to please or impress Asantehenes are not found – saddles, flags, lathes, magic lanterns, European swords, leather goods, and so on – and perhaps this is hardly surprising. An odd omission is any representation of the carriages exported to the Gold Coast in considerable numbers in the nineteenth century. In the absence of horses these were pulled by teams of men to convey Europeans and a few senior Africans up to 25 or 30 km at a time. One was conveyed to Kumase, with great difficulty, by the missionary Thomas Birch Freeman in the early 1840s and presented to the Asantehene.[7] Such vehicles must have excited interest among the Akan, and it is interesting that they do not seem to have been reproduced in weight form.

What factors led to the depiction of some things and the neglect of others? Although the Asante can suggest one or more proverbs applicable to the object, creature or situation depicted as a weight, it is unlikely that most weights were cast to fit proverbs. The association between most weights and proverbs is generally looser, sometimes non-existent. Only a few weights were demonstrably cast to call to mind one specific proverb. One of the most common of these shows two crossed crocodiles united at the stomach. This represents a saying to the effect that although the creatures have a single stomach the heads still compete to swallow the food, a proverb emphasising the futility of individuals trying to grab what is gained for the common good of their group. Another common proverb weight shows a backward-facing *sankofa* bird, indicating the saying that a person should not be afraid to try to undo past errors. The many weights depicting antelopes with excessively long horns represent the saying 'had I known' – regrets after an event (in this case growing very long horns) are in vain.

Obviously weights which show two creatures in conjunction or some specific event or activity are easier to link unequivocally to a single proverb than those depicting a single subject that may appear in several sayings. For example, a weight of a crocodile with a mudfish in its mouth can refer only to one or two proverbs in which these two creatures are linked, while weights showing the creatures singly can be associated with several proverbs. Equally a weight showing a man scraping medicinal bark from a tree is unequivocally intended to call to mind a saying which emphasises that such tasks are best done by co-operation between two people, while a weight of a snake seizing a hornbill refers unambiguously to a story of how the bird, which borrowed money and refused to return it, was eventually caught by its creditor.

Such a direct, unvarying one-to-one relationship between a weight and a proverb is rare and implies these weights were made to match the proverbs rather than the proverbs invented to fit the weight. In the vast majority of cases, however, the association is looser. Single-subject weights – for example, a leopard or a drum – can be 'fitted' with large numbers of proverbs which mention these things, and in such cases it may well be that sayings are invented or modified to answer the 'problem' of giving such weights significance.

The depiction of human activities, to which one or more proverbs might be linked, tends to be stereotyped. Although humans are portrayed in action, carrying loads, suckling children, making sacrifices, the images have a repetitive quality and only a small number of activities are depicted. Such weights do not appear to be derived from their makers' free and direct observation of everyday life; the vision they manifest is channelled or circumscribed, and conversely many Asante situations are ignored completely. Perhaps the most striking of these is the lack of any weight which shows an offering being made before ancestral stools. Similarly, there are no weights showing funerary rites or corpses being carried in a form of divination formerly used to establish the cause of death. Warriors wearing talisman-covered war smocks are not depicted, and there are no weights which can be unequivocally shown to depict men or women dancing. Children are rarely, if ever, shown on their own. Few or no weights show carvers or blacksmiths at work. The absence of other subjects is less surprising, for they are not depicted in the public art of most cultures: weights showing childbirth, urination or defecation are not known, and only a handful of weights show sexual intercourse. Some of these subjects were probably excluded as too sacred (stool sacrifices) or too offensive or polluting (defecation, childbirth), but the other omissions remain puzzling.

A number of creatures and things are rarely, if ever, found as weights: the absence of hearths and houses has been mentioned, and cowrie shells (*sideẹ*) and neolithic stone axes (*'Nyame akuma*) are not found as weights; but the most striking list of exceptions relates to living creatures. The following are never, or very rarely, found in weight form: dogs, cats, pigs, cows, goats, sheep, the small rodent known as the grass-cutter, the tree-bear (a kind of potto), mice and rats, crows, vultures and hyenas, horses without riders, ducks and turkeys. There is no technical reason why such castings could not be made, and all these were creatures known throughout Asante in the nineteenth century. They also appear in many proverbs, so they were not excluded because they had no proverbial significance.

These exclusions do show, however, a certain consonance with the rest of

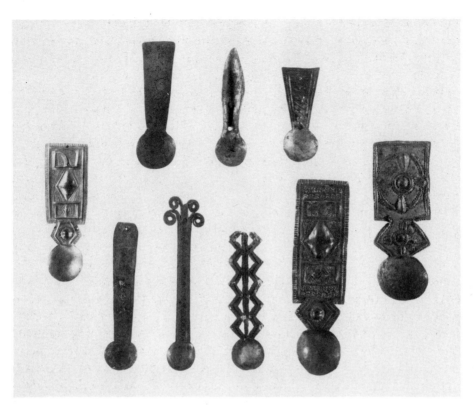

Sheet-brass gold-dust spoons.

Asante culture. The Asante classify living creatures in a number of ways, according to their physical form, their behaviour and where they live. The main, broad classes are animals which live above ground (*surommoa*), those with feathers (*ntakrammoa*) and those in water (*nsuommoa*). The most basic division, however, is between those creatures which live with or near man, the animals of the village ('*fiemmoa*, literally, 'house beasts') and those in the bush (*wurammoa*). The creatures which are not depicted as weights are, almost without exception, animals which are considered as especially close to man. The cat and dog are allowed into the house and are sometimes fed the same food as humans. The cat (*okra*) is thought to have a special link with humans and the human soul (*okra*): if a cat runs away, it is a sign its owner will soon die. Dogs and cats are given names, and new foods and medicines (*aduro*) are tried out on dogs to see if they are safe for humans. Sheep, goats, pigs and cows are village animals in that they cannot survive without human assistance, and the sheep, a 'soft' and 'cool' animal, is the ideal sacrifice. Vultures, crows and hyenas are creatures which live on the fringes of human society, eating its filth and carrion.

Excluded or unrepresented creatures are therefore those associated with the village and its fringes, the zone formerly separated from the bush by a symbolic barrier (*pampim*). They are treated as if they are, in diminishing degrees, part of human society, and some have what can only be described as a moral relationship with man. Cats, for example, could not be killed until after a mock trial: red palm-oil was smeared around their mouths and they were

130

then accused and convicted of stealing it. Sheep were the primary sacrificial animal, slain after the presence and assistance of the ancestors was invoked. In the past Asante slaughtered goats and cows not simply for their meat but in order to remove some danger or pollution.

It therefore seems that some conscious or unconscious process directed the attention of weight makers away from those creatures which were primarily associated with the world of man rather than that of the bush. The pattern previously noted in the physical structure of the village and its formal separation from the wild area of the forest seems to be repeated, in a negative way, in the subject-matter of gold-weights. The causation of this is obscure, but from all the thousands of representational weights made the pattern of exclusions, rather than of inclusions, of items avoided, rather than portrayed, indicates that Asante casters were not simply depicting whatever took their fancy.

The scales (*nsania*) used with gold-weights are of simple design: two slightly concave circular brass pans are suspended by three or four lengths of thread from the opposite ends of a horizontal beam. The great majority of scale beams are made out of a strip of sheet brass, sometimes decorated with incised or punched decoration; a few cast ones are known. The pans generally hung a long way beneath the beam: even in small sets of scales the distance between pans and beam would be 23–30 cm and was correspondingly greater in larger sets. The scale pans are often plain, but perhaps a quarter to a third of them are decorated with patterns of circles or intersecting arcs inscribed with the help of compasses.

It required skill to use these scales accurately. They could not, of course, be used in windy places, and old Asante relate that traders would attempt to blow surreptitiously on to a scale pan to exaggerate the weight it contained. Gold was usually placed in the scale pan with a brass spoon (*saawa*) to prevent it sticking to the fingers (some traders are said to have picked up small grains under their finger nails in order to steal them). The great majority of spoons were made from imported sheet brass, the bowl formed by beating and the stems or handles frequently decorated with cut-out, incised and punched designs. These spoons vary in length from 5–7.5 cm to 25 cm or more, and the degree of decoration on them also varies. A considerable number of spoons, which are probably datable to the second half of the nineteenth century, have their handles decorated with curls of metal produced by shaving off slivers from the edge which curled up under the pressure of the moving blade.

The larger spoons were most probably owned by chiefs, senior officials and the wealthy members of the emerging trading classes. The designs on the stems of some of these elaborate spoons sometimes contain motifs seen elsewhere in Asante metalworking. A few spoons of sheet silver exist, but they were probably used not for weighing out gold-dust but to place food offerings before the gods or in the outdooring ceremonies of the children of important chiefs. Two types of cast spoons are known, some very similar to sheet-metal ones, and a few with thin, curving bowls and elaborate handles. The former sort are now seen mainly in shrine and stool rooms and were probably never used for gold-dust. The latter are usually recovered from rivers and appear to date from a very early period in Asante history. Sieves (*ahuhuamoa*) for gold-dust were made from beaten and perforated sheet brass and were probably used to separate nuggets from gold-dust. The largest known was removed from Kumase in 1874.

An essential piece of equipment for trading with gold was the blow pan (*famfa*) made from sheet brass and shaped by beating. Gold-dust suspected of containing impurities was placed in the circular end of this and then shaken out to cover most of the surface. The gold-dust was blown upon very gently and the lighter impurities driven towards the open end from which they could be flicked or brushed away. Many blow pans were decorated with incised compass-drawn patterns.

Two sorts of boxes were used for gold-dust storage: those fabricated from sheet brass, joined by riveting and by folded joints, and those cast by the lost-wax method (see p.80). About equal numbers of each survive: the former were probably made by the group who also made sheet-brass pomade pots (*mforowa*) (see Chapter 9); the latter by the casters of gold and gold-weights. Sheet boxes are mostly circular or oval in shape, the lids usually decorated with punched and incised decorations, some with repoussé work. The lids and bases are made from two pieces of metal, the side piece with a flange bent out at an angle of $90°$, and the edge of the top or bottom piece folded around this, the two pieces

A large brass sieve, used at the Kumase court to separate gold-dust from nuggets.

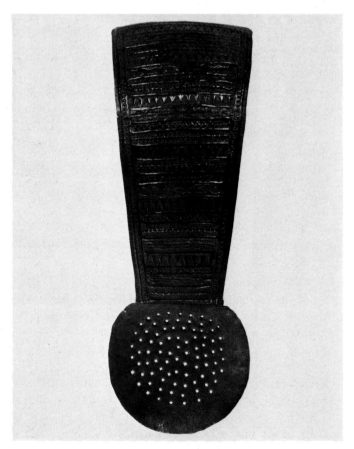

Gold-dust boxes and, lower centre, a scoop (*famfa*). The two lower boxes are made of sheet brass, the others are cast.

hammered or pinched together. Most of these boxes are small, no more than 5–7 cm long and 1–2 cm deep.

Cast-brass boxes are generally more elaborate in form. Some of the smallest of these, possibly the earliest type, have lids decorated with patterns virtually identical with those found on geometrical gold-weights, but other, generally larger boxes have lids adorned with representations of birds, cannons, human heads, scorpions and other creatures. Most have plain sides, but a few have raised designs on them or are decorated with the creatures modelled on the lids. The lids of these boxes have shallow walls on their undersides which fit into the sides of the base: in many the fit is far from perfect, and some boxes have holes caused by poor casting; some holes have been filled with solder or by running in molten brass. Holes did not make a box useless for storing gold-dust, for this was first put into little twists of cloth, which were tied at the neck.

The weights, spoons, boxes, scales and gold-dust were usually kept in a pack called a *fotoọ*, carefully bundled together in a piece of cloth which was in turn wrapped in a roughly rectangular piece of goat or antelope skin. The *fotoọ* was placed upon the ground and opened up when trading reached the stages at which the gold had to be weighed. This was usually done over it, so that any gold-dust which spilled would fall in the *fotoọ* and not on to the ground. These packs sometimes also contained a touchstone (*twaboọ*) for testing the purity of nuggets or cast gold, feathers for brushing tiny specks of gold from the cloth in which it was tied or from scale pans, and odds and ends, such as scraps of brass, beads, occasionally seeds and bits of stone, which could be used as weights if necessary. A few of these kits also contained bits of neolithic axeheads and what appear to be *asuman*, perhaps to bring good fortune in trading.

9 Brass vessels

Europeans trading to the Gold Coast were quick to discover a large and profitable local demand for brass. Soon vast quantities were being shipped out, both in the form of sheet, ingots and manillas (c-shaped rings with flaring ends) and new and second-hand bowls, pots and basins. Demand was not confined to the coast; much found its way to Asante and other inland forest kingdoms. Imported brass vessels (*yawa*) have remained important in Asante until the present day. They were used to make the shrines of gods, in the great Odwira festival, in nubility and funeral rites, and in the *odum* ordeal in which a decoction of the poisonous *odum* bark was drunk (vomiting being a sign of innocence). If ever a large container was required for some important rite, an imported brass bowl was generally used. A few richer houses also used brass basins and bowls for food and water, and in 1817 the Asantehene proudly planned to decorate his splendid new Stone Palace with flattened 'brass-pan'.

Brass bowls and vessels crop up again and again in Asante history and are often concerned with key events. Many groups have traditions that their founding ancestors, or the first inhabitants of Earth, descended from on high in a brass bowl, and such bowls are mentioned in several other myths. Until the end of the last century there was a very large European-made bowl in front of the royal mausoleum at Bantama. According to traditions collected in this century, this was sent from the earlier kingdom of Denkyira to be filled with gold. The Asante refused the demand and defeated the more southerly state. Also at Bantama were kept two English ewers made in the time of Richard II, apparently associated with the Asante defeat of groups towards the south-west (how these vessels reached the area is totally obscure). The Golden Stool itself was placed between two brass bowls before being concealed from the British by burial.[1]

It is highy likely that the first brass vessels to reach the forest zone came from the Islamic world by way of trans-Saharan trade routes. A number of bowls with Islamic inscriptions still exist in Ghana, although some recorded earlier in this century cannot now be located. It is impossible to establish when these bowls arrived in the area, but most, if not all, are now regarded as sacred or holy (*kronkron*), and they are often said to have descended from the sky, a statement associating them with non-human powers and with the distant past. Some of these Islamic vessels may have been used as shrines for gods and still exist, hidden away in rooms usually closed to outsiders, or placed inside larger vessels of European manufacture.[2]

The Akan and other groups also made brass vessels for themselves. It is not known when this practice began but it was established by the end of the seventeenth century. Shaw's excavations at Dawu produced pieces of mould used in casting vessels, and Bosman talks of 'Copper Ointment Boxes' which

A selection of *kuduo*, the ones on the extreme left and right showing patches covering casting faults.

were almost certainly the precursors of sheet-brass vessels made to hold the vegetable shea-butter used as a skin pomade.[3]

Vessels cast in brass by the lost-wax process (see p.80) are called *kuduo* by the Asante. The term embraces such diverse forms as open vessels with constricted waists, shallow vertical-sided pots with plain lids, and bulbous tripod-legged pots with lids like inverted chalices. The height and diameter of such vessels, and the several other forms, may vary from 7 or 8 cm to 60 cm or more, and they exhibit a considerable range of surface decoration. In Asante eyes, however, their defining characteristics are that they are locally cast in brass and suitable for a limited number of uses in special circumstances normally connected with the spiritual state of a person, his forebears and descendants.

According to Rattray, *kuduo* were classed as *agyapadie*, a term he translates as 'heirloom'. *Kuduo* were clearly regarded as items of great importance, and many thousands survive. Earlier in this century it appears the Asante were reluctant to part with these vessels to outsiders and, although many have since been removed from Ghana, some are still to be found in stool rooms or in the private possession of old people. Many of the *kuduo* which exist today are heavily corroded, indicating that they have, at some time, been buried.

Kuduo were used in a variety of special contexts. Rattray has left accounts of these uses based on the memories of the old men and women to whom he deliberately confined most of his inquiries. There is, therefore, an inevitable element of reconstruction and, perhaps, idealisation in what he was told. According to Rattray's informants, *kuduo* were used in rites connected with a man's *ntoro* group and also with his *kra*. Both terms are what we might call metaphysical concepts concerning the transmission and state of non-physical elements in human life. The *ntoro* was a named group with its own dietary and behavioural rules to which a man belonged through his father. *Ntoro* appears to have been conceived as some sort of spiritual element passed from father to son. The *kra*, a term often translated as 'soul', was believed to come from God (*'Nyame*) and to leave a person on death. Today Asante ideas about both, and the practices connected with them, are often vague and contradictory. Indeed, Rattray's own accounts seem slightly hesitant. According to the latter, how-

A selection of *kuduo*.

ever, a wife was expected to keep the prohibitions of her husband's *ntoro* group. When she was unmistakably pregnant, a ritual was performed in which food was placed in a *kuduo* besides which the couple had intercourse. The food was later given to their children and part also placed on the roof as an offering to 'Nyame and on the ground (presumably for the earth goddess, Asase Yaa).

Rattray also states that each week the Asantehene performed a ritual in which mashed yams (*eto*) and boiled eggs were placed in a *kuduo* in a special area of the palace before being consumed. The account does not make it completely clear whether this was a *ntoro* rite or a rite to cleanse the King's *kra* (*kradware*, 'soul-washing'), or whether the two were the same.[4] *Kuduo* were also placed before the blackened ancestral stools and food and drink offerings made at them. It is said that gold, in nugget and gold-dust form, and valuable beads were kept in these *kuduo* in stool rooms. They were also used at some types of funeral, and there is strong evidence that they were filled with gold-dust, and buried with important people: it is said that a trusted descendant was told of this so that the *kuduo* and its contents could later be dug up in times of need. (No doubt such concealment also helped preserve wealth from the death dues claimed by the Asantehene.) Occasionally in Ghana one sees recently excavated *kuduo* with specks of gold-dust stuck to their inner surfaces. *Kuduo* therefore seem to have been intimately connected with male affairs, and to have served as a sort of external expression of male powers or male spiritual condition in the same way as the fertility *akua'mma* expressed the female preoccupation with child-bearing and the physical continuation of the matrilineage (see Chapter 12).

Kuduo were obviously produced by skilled metal-casters, presumably men who would also have made gold castings and gold-weights. It is interesting, therefore, that it has not so far proved possible to find gold-weights by the same hand as the figures and creatures which decorate some *kuduo* lids. Nor has it yet proved possible to establish a chronology for *kuduo* or to establish if certain styles originated in particular areas within or outside Asante. Few metal analyses have been done and dating on stylistic grounds is rather unreliable, for if *kuduo* were carefully preserved as 'heirlooms', perhaps possibly in some cases transmitted patrilineally, and if they were dug up from time to time, it is possible that old forms were copied and recopied throughout Asante history. It is nevertheless a reasonable working assumption that some vessels which seem closest to Islamic prototypes are early, provided these prototypes arrived at an early stage of Asante history, which cannot yet be proved. Early *kuduo* would therefore include shallow convex-sided open bowls, those lidded *kuduo* which have sides which flare out sharply towards the base, those with bulbous bodies which frequently have lids like inverted chalices, and those whose sides are convex towards the base but then become vertical. It has been plausibly suggested that the last form is derived from Middle Eastern 'canteens' made of two or more interlocking containers and the preceding type is copied from lidded vessels made by fitting one vessel, upside down, on to another of ordinary bowl shape. Nevertheless, it remains extremely difficult to decide the age of individual vessels of each type: for example, small vessels may have been made in early periods when little brass was available; equally they may have been made later for poorer people. Wear and patination are poor guides to age, for vessels may have been accorded many different sorts of treatment. The actual distribution of *kuduo* inside Ghana may not indicate accurately their place and date of origin, for some were seized in war and others may have been traded over considerable distances.

The large number of surviving *kuduo* serves to indicate the growing wealth of Asante in the eighteenth and nineteenth centuries, its willingness to absorb exotic forms and, probably, the increased stratification of Asante society. The technical skill shown in *kuduo* making varies considerably: some with elaborate lids depicting animals or groups of humans show sensitivity in modelling and considerable expertise in brass casting; others are rather crudely modelled and poorly cast. It is unusual to find a *kuduo* completely without some fault originating in the casting process. The most common faults are holes caused either by an insufficiency of metal or the failure of the metal to reach all parts of the mould because of trapped bubbles of gas or poorly designed run-in channels. In many cases it is clear that holes have been filled by a later localised casting, and sometimes the original surface decoration has been extended by incising or punching the surface of the cast-in area. Holes in the bases, sides and lids of many *kuduo* have also often been mended by patches of sheet brass: holes were pierced through the patch and base, and short strips of thin brass threaded through these and bent over. Occasionally a separately cast area of rim is attached to the body by this method. A few (?old) vessels are composed almost entirely of sheets joined in this way, a method also used to repair (or perhaps to increase in size) some of the royal silver vessels imported from Europe.

The decoration on *kuduo* bodies shows great variation, and it is not uncommon to find different forms and styles on lids and bodies, which suggests the two parts were made at different times or new lids were made to replace damaged or lost ones. Most decoration was created during the wax-modelling stage, either cut and punched into the soft beeswax or built up by adding threads, strips or complete images of wax to the basic form. Many vessels are decorated with panels of cursive and straight lines, often enclosing or separated by compass-drawn rosettes. These decorations are almost certainly degenerate, highly stylised copies of the inscriptions on the sides of the Islamic prototypes of these vessels. Some *kuduo* decorations are similar in form to the low-relief mud plasterwork used on palaces, temples and richer houses. A few are also similar to the patterns found on geometric gold-weights, perhaps suggesting that some weights were originally made by cutting up scraps of imported Islamic brassware.

Although *kuduo* exhibit great variations in form and size, it is possible to identify a number of basic elements which, differently combined, make up most vessels. The basic forms are depicted in the photographs in this chapter; from these it will also be seen that while some vessels stand on three stumpy feet others have either open-work bases, with or without a bottom ring, or fully enclosed bases. Lids fit either inside the vessel by means of a cast vertical rim or over the outside. In many cases this fit is far from perfect, and the lid rims have obviously been cut, bent and hammered to make them fit at all, which may indicate the two parts were cast at different times or derive from different vessels. Some lids are hinged to the body: by loops on the lid fitting either side of a ring on the body, by a ring on the lid fitting betweeen two rings on the

The lid of a large *kuduo* showing a seated chief surrounded by court officials. The vessel was in use in Kumase towards the end of the 19th century, but the ruler's bare feet and facial scarification are non-Asante characteristics.

Three cast-brass oil-lamps. The largest is 22 cm high.

body, or by a ring on the lid and one on the body (presumably once tied together by a piece of cloth or fibre). Many *kuduo*, usually of the largest type, also have clasps hinged to the lid and engaging a ring which protrudes from the body. This presumably enabled them to be secured by a small lock or by a carefully knotted length of cloth or fibre. Most clasps are cut from sheet brass; only a few, on the largest vessels, are cast. In a few cases the lids or bodies have protruding fingers of metal which engage in sockets on the other part; these help keep the lid firmly in place.

A considerable proportion of surviving *kuduo* are lidless, but where lids survive these are usually the most ornate part of the vessel. While some lids are plain, or have a small amount of low-relief decoration in wax strips or threads, many depict objects or creatures and, in addition, have cast handles swivelling in sockets. Many have single handles, but it is not unusual to find paired handles in shapes ranging from straight to convex or concave; some are decorated with small images, usually of birds.

The most elaborate lids are those which depict animals or humans. The range of animals is not great: elephants, antelopes, porcupines and leopards predominate. A number of *kuduo* depict antelopes being attacked by leopards, occasionally with a hunter standing by holding a firearm. This composite image may represent a basic triad in Asante thought: the wisdom and aggression of humans is, in the realm of the wild, divided between the sinister rapaciousness of the leopard (always springing to the left in attack) and the wisdom of the duiker. The most complex lids show what are almost certainly royal scenes, generally a seated figure, the King, surrounded by warriors and musicians. Most large and elaborate vessels were probably made for use by the rulers of major states, and possibly by the Kings of Asante. Some are almost certainly of nineteenth-century date, but curious anomalies in the details of the figures depicted suggest they may have been made by a craftsman from outside Asante, even though they were used at Kumase.[5] Other lids, possibly earlier, depict single human figures about a variety of activities: men playing horns, a young woman sitting on a stool, combing her hair and looking in a mirror, a man playing on the stringed musical instrument, the *sanko*. The work of individual *kuduo* makers can often be identified among surviving vessels.

The motifs which decorate the lids and bodies of the less elaborate vessels include locks, leg irons or fetters, bows and arrows, and keys. These may be intended to have meanings which derive from the role these vessels played in rituals concerning the owner's health – that is, they have served to express a wish to lock or tie the owner's *kra* to him through these rituals. It may also be significant that bow and arrow designs are found on what appear to be early forms of the gold *kra* discs worn by royal servants, that arrows were ritually fired while the King drank in public on ceremonial occasions, possibly a time of spiritual danger, and that some of his servants carried small bows and arrows. A number of narrow-waisted, open *kuduo* decorated with castings of crocodiles seem to be by the same hand or, at least, from the same workshop. They are probably of nineteenth-century manufacture for few show any great wear, they exist in large numbers, and some still have traces of moulding

A sheet-brass *forowa*.
Ht 11.8 cm.

material stuck to them. The significance of the crocodile in this context is not known.

There exist a very small number of vessels in *kuduo* form made of sheet brass or, very rarely, constructed by combining sheet brass with cast elements. The vast majority of Asante sheet-brass vessels, however, have a different form and are classed as *mforowa*. These usually consist of a cylindrical body topped with a conical lid fitting outside it, occasionally with a clasp. In most cases the body is divided into two compartments: the larger is accessible on removing the lid, but the smaller, lower one is often completely enclosed, the base being a disc of brass or thin sheet iron. A few *mforowa* are rectangular or roughly triangular. The lid and body of a *forowa* is usually heavily decorated in repoussé and punched work, often with the edges of designs made sharper by incising. The basic function of the *forowa* was to serve as a container for a vegetable fat made from the seeds of the savannah-growing tree *Butyrospermum parkii*. This was used as a pomade for the skin, and accounts suggest that the Asantehene adorned his body with a mixture of gold-dust and this 'shea-butter'. The *mforowa* were sometimes stood over or near a charcoal fire to soften the white mass of this pomade, and many retain traces of it in their interiors, as do a number of *kuduo* collected around the turn of the century. *Mforowa* were also used for storing gold-dust and other valuables.

The method of making *mforowa* was the same as that used in making small gold-dust boxes from sheet metal. The main cylinder of the body was formed from a rectangular strip of brass riveted end to end, and the other parts were fixed together by bending one piece of metal over the next and hammering the joint together. Some of these vessels have open-work bases made by cutting the metal with a punch or chisel, and they generally show great skill in their manufacture. The surface patterns vary considerably with circular designs on lid and body usually being made with the help of compasses. In a few cases the repoussé design motifs on *mforowa* are also found on court gold-work, suggesting that the same craftsmen may have made both sorts of object.

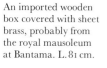

An imported wooden box covered with sheet brass, probably from the royal mausoleum at Bantama. L.81 cm.

It is probable that some of the best workers in sheet brass were employed by the Kumase court to make the brass-covered boxes in which were kept the skeletons of the Asantehenes at Bantama. At least one such box survives in Britain; its surface is decorated with elaborate repoussé and punched patterns, similar to those found on the backs of *asipim* chairs, and the metal is fixed to the underlying wooden box with a number of copper staples. The box itself appears to be of European manufacture and may have been used to pack goods for shipment to the Gold Coast.

The Asantehene also acquired prestigious vessels from outside, and these were rarely modified before being used at the palace or in parades. The Kings of Asante had a great liking for large silver vessels of European manufacture, which was fostered by many gifts sent from the coast. King Osei Bonsu took a keen interest and he asked Bowdich to identify the countries of origin of his pieces. His request to the mulatto Huydecoper was less polite: he told him to come and clean the silver. A few years later the Asantehene was asking for Dutch vessels in an obsolete style to be sent out for his use. Such silver probably provided some of the motifs used by court goldsmiths on sword decorations and *kra* discs – for example, hanging swags and floral patterns – as well as serving as prototypes for some *abosodeε*. Some of these vessels were used for serving palm wine.

An 18th-century European silver vessel used at the Kumase court.

10 Clothing and cloth

The earliest observers of Asante noted in passing that the clothing of those they encountered varied considerably according to their rank and the activities upon which they were engaged. Cloth has been worn in the Akan areas for a long time, perhaps for more than 400 years, and by the nineteenth century in Asante several different types had evolved. Each of these, and the way in which each was worn, served to communicate a distinctive message, and the subtleties of its significance were widely understood. The most expensive, complex and splendid cloths were, of course, worn by the Asantehene and the most senior chiefs, but even they at special times would assume deliberately humble forms of dress. The most elaborate cloths were woven specifically for the Asantehene, members of his family and for chiefs he wished to reward and honour. Many incorporated silk obtained by unravelling imported cloths, although the basic yarn was cotton, grown in the drier region north of Asante and spun there or in Asante itself. The patterns of these cloths were the prerogative of the monarch: in dress, as in so many areas of Asante culture, the hierarchical ideology of Asante politics was given physical expression.

In a society as complex as that of nineteenth-century Asante the distinctive role of any one group was indicated by a number of things besides dress: by the ornaments worn (for example, slaves and commoners ideally could not wear gold jewellery) and by the regalia carried; by the way the hair was styled (the Asantehene's stool-bearers had broad bald patches shaved across the tops of their heads, and the queen mother's servant women had tufts of hair shaped like curved swastikas); by physical mutilation (no Asante was scarified except for curative or prophylactic purposes, but northerners bore heavy facial scarifications); and by their dialect, vocabulary and ability to use and understand the rich, allusive language of the court (the missionary Ramseyer recorded how the people laughed at him when he first preached at Kumase, for they found his expressions coarse and provincial).[1]

Clothing was one of the most obvious and important marks of distinction in Asante society, and it remains so, although the rigid nineteenth-century differences between the apparel of political leaders and successful traders and those of the common people have become blurred. Nevertheless, basic distinctions in clothing remain: between the dress of the two sexes, and between people of different ages, status and occupations, depending also on the occasion for which the clothing is worn.

The most fundamental item of dress for women is a set of waist beads (*toma*). These are tied around a girl shortly after birth, usually at or just before the *ntetia* ritual at which the child is named, its paternity acknowledged, and at which it begins formally to enter the human social order. Hitherto its presence in the world has been treated as a temporary, unreliable event: the infant's hair and faeces are referred to as those of a ghost (*saman*), and it is believed that the ghost mother who had sent her child into the world may reclaim it and the infant die. These beads were a girl's sole item of dress for the first part of her life. When she reached five or six, a small strip of cloth, usually bright red, was worn threaded through these beads, front and back, to cover her sexual organs. When she entered puberty, her mother might make her wear a white cloth to discover when she first menstruated. A woman continues to wear a cloth (*etam*) of this sort for the rest of her life. Formerly, as a girl grew older she would add more waist beads, often given by her husband or lover. Old women, consequently, sometimes wear several strings of waist beads which form a thick and heavy girdle. Waist beads are never removed, even when bathing or sleeping, for without them a woman is shamefully naked. These beads also have a strong sexual connotation: if a man touches a woman's beads, he shows his wish to have intercourse. Formerly, if she chose to reject his advances, this act could lead to a charge of adultery against him.

At about the age of seven or eight girls traditionally began to wear a cloth skirt which reached from the waist, or slightly above it, to below their knees.

A gold-weight showing *fu-fu* being made. The woman (right) is wearing waist beads, the man a *danta*.

The cloth was wrapped once or twice around the lower body, and the top few centimetres rolled downwards and outwards at the point of overlap on the left side to secure the garment. Asante women went about with their breasts exposed and only began to cover them in the 1920s and 30s under Western influence. However, they usually wore a second, smaller cloth around the upper parts of their bodies to carry children on their backs, and this was tucked in and secured at the front. Senior women sometimes also wore a second piece of cloth over the upper parts of their bodies, covering their left shoulders. Shaped and sewn dresses were introduced for women only in the present century; they are still considered an innovation and not worn for important ceremonies of a traditional nature. Women would discard their cloths only for important rituals, the best documented of which was *mmumue*. This was performed in the main street of the village while the men were at war by a group of women wearing only their pubic covers and waist beads. This may also have been the dress worn by women taking the judicial *odum* ordeal, in which they either chewed *odum* bark (*Erythleum guineese*) or drank a decoction made with it. Vomiting the poison indicated innocence. At her nubility rite a girl would wear a fine cloth and many beads around her neck. Her body would be painted with white clay, often in patterns.

Men's clothing showed greater elaboration and a wider range of forms than that of women. The basic male garment was a length of cloth (*danta*) tied over the genitals and around the waist, a form of dress depicted in many gold-weights. By the time they were eight or ten, boys began to wear lengths of cloth wrapped around the body and secured by a knot behind the neck so as to leave both arms free. The usual adult male garment was and still is a long rectangular piece of cloth, wrapped carefully around the body, passed over the left shoulder and brought around the body once more before being tucked in. These cloths, given the general term *ntoma* (which includes women's cloths), can be 3 m or more in length and have continually to be hitched up and adjusted; today they are worn over tailored shorts, never over long trousers.

Normally the left shoulder and upper arm are kept covered by the cloth, restricting their movement. The left hand is considered inauspicious and dirty in some contexts (it is used in wiping excrement from the body and in certain reversed, 'bad' rituals), and covering of the left shoulder and upper arm befits the status of that part of the body. Occasionally the torso is bared by pulling the cloth off the shoulder and rolling it into a thick girdle above the waist. This shows respect before more senior people and is accompanied by slipping the feet out of the sandals. It is also done when men approach ancestral stools. The cloth is also pulled from off the left shoulder when vigorous exertion is planned: for example, by drummers before playing, or for some dances.

These large cloths, made either from locally woven cloths of narrow strips sewn edge to edge or machine-made, are the normal form of male dress. Occasionally men wore cotton smocks of the sort worn among groups like the Gonja and Dagomba to the north. Such smocks, covered with protective talismans, were worn by senior men during war and were probably imported from the north. The greatest of these smocks, which are called *batakari* by the

Asante, are completely covered with talismans encased in leather and cloth. The custom of wearing talismanic war garments was well established by the nineteenth century, and some were worn with other northern appurtenances. 'Their vest was of red cloth, covered with fetishes and saphies in gold and silver; and embroidered cases of almost every colour, which flapped against their bodies as they moved, intermixed with small brass bells, the horns and tails of animals, shells, and knives; long leopards tails hung down their backs, over a small bow covered with fetishes. They wore loose cotton trowsers [*sic*], with immense boots of a dull red leather, coming half way up the thigh, and fastened by small chains to their cartouch or waist belt; these were also ornamented with bells, horses tails, strings of amulets, and innumerable shreds of leather; a small quiver of poisoned arrows hung from their right wrist, and they held a long iron chain between their teeth, with a scrap of Moorish writing affixed to the end of it. A small spear was in their left hands, covered with red cloth and silk tassels; . . .'[2]

The Asante use of these garments can only be understood in the context of their ideas about mystical power. Power for special purposes (for personal or village protection, to catch witches or to bring wealth, etc.) is always sought from areas and people on the very edges of the Asante world about which they have little direct knowledge. Bowdich noted how Muslims at Kumase were

Right A *batakari* smock with protective leather-covered talismans, late 19th century.

Left A man wearing a stamped *adinkra* cloth.

thought to give protection by means of scraps of Koranic writing which Asante purchased for considerable sums; a Muslim, he concluded, could live for a week on a piece of paper.[3] The medicines of Western visitors were firmly believed to have an extraordinary efficacy and were sought so eagerly that visitors became infuriated by Asante importunities.[4] The savannah peoples, physically, socially and linguistically different from the Asante, were believed to have access to powers unknown in the forest zone and the Asante use of protective *batakari* is an example of this belief. Change, where it occurs within Asante, can only be countered by the introduction of new powers from beyond the formal structure of Asante society.

The most elaborate of these smocks, the *Batakari Kẹse* (Great *Batakari*), were possessed only by the Asantehene and major chiefs. The number of talismans on them showed the great sums expended upon them, and some were encased in sheet gold or silver with repoussé decoration by court goldsmiths. These smocks were usually worn with a talisman-covered cap, and sometimes with additional protective *asuman* hung around the neck. These costumes were worn during wars, and at least one in the British Museum's collection was obtained on the battlefield. Bowdich noted that the Asante believed the *safi* purchased from Muslims could 'make them invulnerable and invincible in war, paralyse the hands of the enemy, shiver their weapons, [and] divert the course of balls'.[5] Possibly such heavy costumes offered some protection against arrows or slugs cut from bars of lead and fired from poorly maintained muzzle loaders. There is an irony in the fact that one *batakari* was taken from the body of the Asantehene's Nsumankwahene, the chief in charge of all purveyors of mystical powers: he was killed behind the battle line by a stray bullet.[6] *Batakari Kẹse* were, and are, also worn in peacetime by chiefs during their installation, when their role as aggressive military leaders is emphasised. They are also worn during the funeral rituals for other chiefs to stress the scarcely controlled anger and violence which follows a leader's death.

Smocks of this sort, but without additional talismans, are worn by priests of great witch-finding *asuman*, like Tigare, Brakune and Dubi, imported into Asante from the north in the present century. By wearing them a priest shows the origin of the power he serves. Priests and priestesses also wore a distinctive skirt (*dosọ*) made from raffia during rituals for their gods. Similar skirts were worn by the priests of new anti-witchcraft powers early in this century, but now they have largely been replaced by cotton smocks. A number of smocks exist covered with writing in Arabic, or a degenerate copy of Arabic, and with what may be protective caballistic designs on them. It is likely that these were also obtained to provide protection during war.

A third form of dress has now disappeared from use: barkcloth. Barkcloth (*kyenkyen*) was manufactured from the bark of a forest tree of the same name (*Antiaris* sp.). A strip was cut from the tree by making incisions and inserting a chisel to prise off the bark. The inner layers were separated from the harder outer surface which was discarded. The inner bark was soaked in water to soften and then placed over a felled tree trunk. It was beaten with wooden mallets which had cylindrical heads with grooves running around them. The beating spread and softened the bark out, and felted together its fibres. The soft, white-grey cloth produced in this way had a texture rather like that of very thick, coarse paper. According to traditions, this was the earliest fabric worn.

Barkcloth was cheap, 'the garb of the poorest slave in the realm', and as recently as the 1920s it was used by hunters who wear old, cheap clothes as they are quickly soiled and torn by the thorny creepers and branches in the forest, the damp earth and the constant dripping from leaves. Barkcloth was also worn by the Asantehene during part of the Odwira festival. Here it was worn to contrast with the elaborate cloth robes worn in the rest of the ceremony, to give this part an archaic character and to show the King's position in relation to the crucial yam crop.[7]

These garments and fabrics and the ways they were worn signalled broad sexual, social and age differences and gave some indication of the wearer's purpose and activities. Colour gave further differentiation. Light cloths were worn to express innocence, rejoicing and justification. Predominantly white cloths, often with areas of pale blue, were worn by chiefs after making sacrifices to ancestral stools, by ordinary people for the outdooring of newly-born children or after a successful conclusion to a law case. For such events it was usual to mark the forehead, temples and upper arms with blobs or lines of white clay (*hyire*).

The garments worn for funerals and other mortuary rites were predominantly dark, usually a combination of black or deep blue (*tuntum*) and red or russet shades (*ko̱ko̱o̱*). Nowadays women usually wear dark blue cloths around the lower parts of their bodies and red ones over the upper, covering their left

A wooden stick and chisel used to remove a piece of bark (top left) from the *kyenkyen* tree, a barkcloth beater and (bottom) a piece of barkcloth.

shoulders, with either small black headscarves, or red headbands. Men wear either plain, deep red cloths or, more usually, brown, red, blue or green ones decorated with designs in black dye. These *adinkra* cloths seem originally to have been imported from the north, and the patterns upon them may ultimately derive from Islamic writing. One such cloth, in natural white, was collected in 1817 by Bowdich who was told the material came from Dagomba.[8]

Adinkra cloth is traditionally linked with the defeat of Adinkra, King of Gyaman, in 1818, although the piece collected by Bowdich clearly indicates it was in use before then. A Kumase court tradition written down about forty years ago claimed the cloth was introduced by the Takyimanhene Ameyaw when he was captured and brought to Kumase by Asantehene Opoku Ware.[9] Rattray gave the first good description of its manufacture. The cloth was first dyed, for example, with the bark of the *kuntunkuni* tree to produce the russet cloth with the same name, and then pegged out on a level place. The dye was made by boiling up pieces of *bache* bark with iron slag (*etia*) as a fixative. The tar-like liquid produced, *adinkra aduro* (adinkra medicine), was applied with stamps cut from a piece of calabash or with a wooden comb, dipped in the liquid and drawn carefully across the surface of the cloth.[10]

Designs used in stamping are also modelled in the low-relief decorations of houses, as ornaments on chiefly headbands and sandals, and perhaps in the trimming of hair. As generally occurs in Asante, there was a verbal component to these designs, and it is now usual to be given more than one verbal

150

Adinkra stamps.

explication for each stamp. Rattray indicates that a chevron design represented the fern *aya*, and at least two designs of paired curves were interpreted as versions of the *sankofa* bird. The pattern *'gye 'Nyame* ('except God') was said to derive from the thumb and fingers of the hand. Other stamps were interpreted in terms of the objects from which they took their names: war-horns, a *dono* drum, handcuffs (*epa*), a star, a heart, and so forth.

There seems little conscious significance in the overall designs of cloths, and motifs seem to be selected to build up pleasing overall patterns in blocks or panels rather than to convey a particular meaning. Darker cloths are worn to express grief and mourning after a death and are also worn by those wishing to destool a chief. Lighter shades are now worn as a sort of 'Sunday best' cloth, but it is possible – although unlikely – that they were formerly worn to express grief: Prempe I was photographed wearing a light *adinkra* cloth at Elmina Castle in 1896 on his way to exile. Nowadays some *adinkra* cloths are also decorated with long thin panels of coloured thread stitched through them. Some of these are made from long strips of factory-made cloth: they are stretched between two trees so their edges touch and the thread sewn through both pieces. A different-coloured thread is used at intervals of half a centimetre or so, usually in a regular sequence of, for example, yellow, *akoko sadee* ('because it is chief'), followed by red (*kokoo*), blue, green (*ahan'mono*), black (*tuntum*). It is said this makes the cloth look more beautiful: *na ema ntoma no ye fefe.*

The Kings of Asante made use of imported cloth and clothing to demonstrate their access to European goods and friendly links with European powers on the coast. Occasionally they seem to have worn the gifts more from politeness than for pleasure. Clothing was among gifts to rulers from the earliest period, and by the nineteenth century the practice was well established. Among Dutch gifts in 1816 were laced hats and a shirt and coat, but when the Asantehene found them too hot he quickly took them off.[11] He did, however, wear some of the other clothes and apparently met with acclaim. He is said to have preferred breeches which showed off his calves, and promised always to wear them in honour of their Dutch sender. British visitors thought differently: 'The King walked abroad in great state one day, an irresistible caricature; he had on an old-fashioned court suit of General Daendels' of brown velveteen, richly embroidered with silver thistles, with an English Epaulet sewn on each corner the coat coming close round the knees, from which the flaps of the waistcoat

151

Left A section of woven
narrow-strip cloth
dating from the second
half of the 19th
century.

were not very distant, a cocked hat bound with gold lace, in shape just like that of a coachman's, white shoes, the long silver-headed cane we presented to him, mounted with a crown, as a walking staff, and a small dirk round his waist.'[12]

To build up the English trade Bowdich encouraged the King's interest: 'I did not discourage the King's great anxiety for clothes of the English costume, considering that his example would be more auspicious than anything else to the introduction of these manufactures.'[13] Such gifts were occasionally put to unexpected uses: 'The King displayed . . . the flags . . . all sewn together, and wrapped around him as a cloth.'[14] 'An admiral's full uniform, richly embroidered' presented by Dupuis was also acceptable.[15] The use of European clothing was extended to other members of the King's family: 'The King presented one of our servants with gold, for making trousers for his child, and mending him a pair of drawers, which he thought it extravagant to put on under trousers or small clothes, and therefore wore them alone.'[16] Asante soldiers also wore European clothes; some may have been deserters from the coast, rewarded for turning up in Kumase with their equipment. One of the white-educated Owusu Ansa brothers was also seen in Kumase in the 1880s wearing full English morning dress.[17]

The most impressive of all Asante clothing, however, is undoubtedly that made from locally woven narrow strips in which dazzling complex patterns are produced. These colourful cloths are widely referred to as *kente*, a term apparently of Fante origin but now in general use throughout Ghana.[18]

It is uncertain how weaving was introduced into the forest area, but it almost certainly came from the north, possibly in the sixteenth century or earlier. Local looms produce cloth about 7.5 cm wide, and so large pieces are made by joining several strips edge to edge. This allows the weaver to manipulate the overall pattern of the finished cloth by mixing strips of different patterns or by aligning similarly patterned strips in different ways.

The earliest Asante cloth was of cotton, and cotton cloths with simple warp patterns were used by ordinary people into the present century. However, at least by the reign of Opoku Ware I, in the 1720s or 30s, imported cloths were unravelled to obtain coloured yarn, and especially silk. This was then woven to produce a mixed cotton and silk cloth. Cotton was obtained from the drier north and spun locally: it is said that Salaga, which fell under Asante control in the mid-eighteenth century, was then required to produce cotton for Asante.

Like many West African peoples, the Asante weave on a horizontal double-heddle loom, but the patterns they produce are the most complex and intricate of all those created on this comparatively simple apparatus. A small number of cloths called *asasia*, traditionally restricted to the Asantehene and his close kin, were woven using a third set of heddles. The weaving of such heavy, elaborately patterned cloths has now virtually ceased.

Weaving is almost always done out of doors in Asante, sometimes under a shady tree or a simple palm-leaf shelter, or nowadays on the verandah of a concrete-built house. The loom is fixed into a simple carpentered wooden frame and can be erected or taken down in a few minutes. One knows when a weaver is at work: the rhythmic click and squeak of the heddles, reed and shuttle are distinctive, and often one encounters lengths of thread stretched out between stakes as the warp is prepared or sees yarn being wound on to bobbins for the shuttles.

The weaver sits at one end of the loom, usually on a stool, with his bare feet stretched out in front of him. With his toes he grips the ropes which are attached to, and operate, the two pairs of heddles. (Chiefs are precluded from weaving as their bare feet should never touch the earth.) The warp threads are attached to a beam immediately in front of the weaver, and as the cloth is woven it is wound around this. From the beam the warp threads pass through the reed or beater, a rectangular frame with many vertical slats made from pieces of split palm-frond ribs. This is suspended from above and pulled hard towards the weaver after the weft has been passed through the warp to ensure the cloth is tightly and evenly woven. The warp passes successively through the two pairs of heddles (the first called *asatia*, the second *asanan*); each pair is linked by a cord running through a pulley suspended from the frame of the loom. Each heddle has different numbers and groupings of warp threads attached to it. As each is operated, a gap or 'shed' is created in the warp threads through which the weft shuttles can be passed. Each set of heddles can be operated independently of the other. A length of string runs down from the heddle ending in a disc of wood or calabash which the weaver grips between his big and second toes and pulls to operate the heddle. The warp threads, having passed through the heddles, run over a horizontal beam and from there stretch out another 5 m or more, weighted by a large stone to keep them in tension during the weaving.

It seems reasonable to accept that the simplest-patterned cotton cloths were

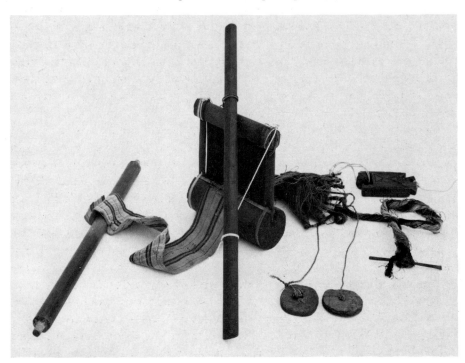

The main parts of a loom showing the reed, heddle and pulley. This may be the loom collected by Bowdich in 1817.

154

the earliest to be made. It has been suggested that these may have been copied from those called *kyekye*, woven in the Bondukou area and imported from there, perhaps from the sixteenth century onwards. In *kyekye* cloth the pattern runs the length of the cloth strip and is created by using warp threads of different colours, usually white (that is, undyed) and blue (indigo dyed). These cloths can be woven using a single pair of heddles and were possibly the most common locally woven fabrics for most of Asante history. It is probable that such cloths were imported from the north-west in considerable numbers until the end of the last century.

The next most complex cloths are called *bankuo*: in these, solid blocks of colour mask the warp threads, which in the case of dyed warps are hidden under solid blocks of white yarn. More complex patterns are produced by weaving small areas of geometric designs in between these solid areas of colour. The second set of heddles is brought into use to produce complex patterns: in the finest of all cloths the warp threads are completely concealed by the weft float designs.

The use of silk yarn to create areas of bright colour in a predominantly cotton textile can be dated at least to the first decades of the eighteenth century. The first fragmentary account of such weaving indicates that such cloths were used by the leaders of the Asante nation, and the demand for silk yarn, or cloths for unravelling, from both northern and coastal markets increased as the kingdom developed. The earliest silk weft floats were, apparently, used only to create small areas of colour. Larger blocks of silk weft-faced colour were known as *babadua*, presumably because of the similarity to the structure of the *babadua* cane. The small areas of weft floats, which can show remarkable variety, are sometimes called *adwin*, a term with connotations of skill or craft. Cloths containing these elements are distinguished from other, less rich textiles by being referred to as *nsaduaso*. Cutting across the distinction between cotton and silk cloths is a more general set of terms: *ahwepan* cloths which have only warp stripes; *topreko*, single cloths which have weft-faced areas and extra warp floats; and *faprenu*, in which the weft floats are even denser, giving the appearance of tapestry weave.

The nomenclature of Asante cloths is extremely complex, and today the names of most patterns are known only by weavers and by a few of the old people who grew up in court circles seventy or more years ago. There is evidence that many older patterns will not be woven again, for while the market for silk cloths has increased buyers are less knowledgeable and willing to buy fabrics woven outside Asante, especially from Ewe weavers. The full significance and basis of many pattern names cannot now be established.

Most cloths are named according to their warp pattern, and over 300 such names are known; *asasia* cloths, where the warp is completely concealed, are named according to the weft patterns. Weft-float patterns are generally given names of their own, although these are not used in naming the cloth as a whole.

Some cloth names are derived from the names of people, normally rulers: for example, Kwakye Asare, Amere, Ansaku, animal or bird names, *Kofi esono* ('Kofi the elephant'), *Higya* ('the lion'), plants or trees, *odum* tree, *emmọ* ('rice'), *nsankani koko* ('the nsankani flower'); things, *nsafonsia* ('six keys'), *kyemfere* ('potsherd'). Rattray recorded these [19] and many others in the 1920s. Some patterns were known by more than one name, and some were said to be worn only in particular circumstances which gave them their names: for example, the cloth called *Amanahyiamu* ('the nation has met together') was worn by the Asantehene at the Odwira festival. Other cloth names were linked with particular historical personages: the cloth Yaa Amanpene was said to be called after a daughter of Asantehene Osei Kwadwo, and Dado after the wife of a weaver. This practice was noted early, for Bowdich wrote: 'The beautiful Adumissa is still eulogised and her favourite patterned cloth bears her name.'[20]

In many cases there seems to be no direct link between the formal properties of the design and its name, the name (or names) deriving from an associated event or individual. Associations between the colour and pattern of a cloth and its name seem to have been made on several bases. The famous cloth *adwineasa* ('skill is exhausted' or perhaps 'the end of art') is named because of the complexities and intricacies of the weaving involved. 'Liars's cloth' (*nkontompo ntoma*) is said to take its name because an element in the warp design appears first at one side of the strips and then at another, never keeping to a straight and obvious line. *Sika futura* ('gold-dust') has a very large area of yellow in it, and the design *bodom* ('bead') has lines of colour similar to those in this type of bead. Similarly, the cloth *kontomerie ahahan* ('the tender leaf of the coco-yam') has a yellow warp and green weft, producing a cloth of similar colour and lightness to that leaf.

Rattray's evidence of the 1920s strongly suggests that the Asantehenes kept close control over the use and distribution of certain patterns and particularly the rich *asasia* cloths. Old members of the court claim that the Kings were supposed to be offered newly invented designs so that they could, if they wished, reserve these for themselves. Much weaving seems to have been done for the court, being commissioned by chiefs and leading officials, and the best cloths were never put on the market. Once the weaver had completed the work, he would be rewarded with a suitable sum in one or more instalments. Much of this weaving seems to have been carried out at Bonwire, a village a few miles to the south of the modern boundaries of Kumase and today the centre of Asante weaving. However, it is clear that weaving was done elsewhere in Asante, and Asante weavers also worked in distant northern towns such as Salaga, perhaps to be near plentiful cotton supplies and, possibly, to be free of the controls of the central region of the kingdom.

11 Pottery

Even today locally hand-made pottery has not been supplanted completely in Asante by more durable metal pots and pans produced in Europe. Until this century a variety of local pottery traditions existed in Asante. In all of these pots were shaped without the use of a wheel and built up by the usual hand methods: coiling, pinching the clay upwards from a mass, or by working up sheets or slabs. Pots were shaped with the simplest tools: pebbles, seeds, corn-cob cores and pieces of wood were used to smooth the surface or to make patterns on it, and sometimes small plaited pieces of fibre were rolled over the surface to decorate it. Regular impressed patterns were also made with the tips of wooden combs. After the pots had been allowed to dry out slowly in a shaded area, they were heaped together and covered with cane and branches. These were then burned, and the pots were fired at a fairly low temperature which sometimes left the innermost parts unfused. Pottery was produced in considerable quantities, some villages specialising in the craft and selling their goods through local markets. It was largely a female occupation, but according to Rattray, only men could model clay into the form of images for pipes or for funerary purposes. It is possible, however, that post-menopausal women were also permitted to make such forms.[1]

The Asante produced a large number of different pots. These ranged from small, shallow dishes used as cups and shallow soup vessels (*tasenaba*), with open lattice-type decorations around their edges (*ananane*), which were used for holding and melting shea-butter pomade, to large round-based water vessels (*ahena*) and cooking pots (*osene*). Food, and especially *fu-fu*, was usually served in a flat bowl with a wide wavy-edged rim from which all present would help themselves, each sex eating separately. The forms and types of typical Asante pots can be seen in the pictures in this chapter. Most of these pots were blackened after firing by placing the still-hot vessel on a heap of dry vegetation. This burst into flame, was quenched, and the pot was blackened by the smoke. Strong prohibitions surrounded the work of potters (*kunkunyonfo*): menstruating women could not make pots; unfired pots could not be removed from the village where they were being made, nor be counted; and pots could not be made while the army was away at war.

A number of pots show elaboration well beyond the point of functional usefulness. Some, which were used to contain water, stand on integral three- or four-branched stands and have elaborately decorated central columns, which occasionally are fitted with stoppers of rudimentary human form. The most elaborate of these vessels are usually called *abusua kuruwa* ('the cup of the matrilineage'), and the sides and central column are often decorated in low relief with images, including those of snakes, ladders, locks, crocodiles, fish and keys. These elaborate pots are still found in stool rooms and before the shrines

of gods: in some cases it appears they have been put there in the last twenty or thirty years to keep them safe. *Abusua kuruwa* were formerly used in one of the concluding parts of a funeral when the deceased's lineage ate together and placed food for the deceased on a small platform outside the village. According to Rattray, hair and nail parings of everyone in the *abusua* were then put in the family cup. This ritual marked the final severance of the deceased from the world of the living; after it, steps could be taken to reincorporate the dead person as an ancestor.

Human images in terracotta were made for use in the funeral rituals of important men and women, usually senior chiefs and queen mothers. The practice was far from universal in Asante, and as yet it is impossible to trace how it spread from one area to another or to understand why it was taken up or abandoned in different areas. Modelling in terracotta for post-mortem purposes is found among other Ghanaian Akan groups and appears to extend into the southern Ivory Coast. Early visitors to the Gold Coast, such as de

Above (top) A collection of flat food vessels and taller water vessels. The second vessel from the left has a coarse inner surface and was used, with a wooden grinder, to mash up cooked vegetables.

Above Three *abusua kuruwa* ('family vessels'), the surfaces decorated with images of snakes, heads, crabs and other objects, often with proverbial meanings.

Marees and Bosman,[2] reported that coastal groups made small earthen or clay images for use in funeral rites, and in the nineteenth century the experienced and sympathetic Cruickshank praised the quality of those made by one Fante group: 'They were nearly as large as life, and the proportions between men and women, boys and girls, were well maintained. Even the soft and feminine expressions of the female countenance were clearly brought out.'[3] It is probable that many archaeological sites containing funerary terracottas remain undiscovered in the forest and that eventual excavation of these, and more detailed local studies, will reveal variants in local practices and symbolism.

All the terracotta heads recovered in areas once, or still, within the Asante kingdom show the characteristic flattening of the head and exaggeration of the forehead found in other Asante depictions of the human form. The size of the recovered heads varies between about 8 and 30 cm. Many of the smaller heads, of very simplified form, appear to have been broken from the sides of large pots from which they originally protruded. Others have short plug-like necks with rounded ends, suggesting they were placed in the necks of other vessels or fitted into bodies made of some other material. The smaller heads or figures were probably intended to represent the slaves and dependents who might have been slain to accompany a deceased senior man or woman in death. The larger heads, sometimes placed directly on the ground or in the mouths of large pots, and in the southern Akan areas sometimes attached to terracotta bodies, represent chiefs and queen mothers. In these great attention is given to the depiction of hair-styles and, in some cases, to copying forms of scarification on face and neck which are now unknown in the area. In some the facial areas are coloured with red slip. Many of the larger heads are hollow, with a hole in the back leading to the central cavity. A few have only a small thumb-sized hole in the back of the head. It is unclear whether these cavities were intended to prevent the build-up of steam within the head during firing or whether something, such as clippings of the deceased's hair and nails, was inserted in them.

Accounts from areas outside Asante indicate that these terracotta figurines were used in the funeral itself (*ayi*), and not in the actual burial. Burial usually took place within a few days of death, after the corpse had been displayed in its finest garments and surrounded with evidence of wealth. The funeral was held at a later date, ideally forty days after death, and was a public occasion to which came those who had obligations to the deceased as well as friends and co-villagers. Women of the deceased's lineage mourned as a group and sang dirges, and his children sat in a particular posture of grief, legs straight out ahead of them. Grand-children, if any, expressed the confirmation of the proper order of things – that the old should die before the young – by dancing and singing that 'they would not fast' for grief and by pretending to pound *fu-fu*. The more senior the person, the more elaborate their funeral and, usually, the greater the time needed to organise it and to assemble the drummers, drink and necessary funds. In the case of paramount chiefs and kings it was usual to hold other ceremonies on the first and subsequent anniversaries of their deaths, and even on the fortieth anniversaries. Terracotta figurines seem, in some

areas, to have been used to represent the dead person at the actual funeral, when they were placed in public view, richly adorned or even, in the case of senior chiefs, paraded through the town in the royal palanquin. A number of heads are marked with red and white clay: it is possible that this was done when anniversary rituals were performed.[4]

Clearly these images are intended to represent in some sense the deceased person and those who served him or her. They were not, apparently, modelled from life, although in southern Akan areas it is recorded that the potter sometimes looked into a bowl of water or palm-oil in order to visualise the dead person's features. There is no tradition of exact portraiture in sub-Saharan Africa, no tradition of trying to copy a person's facial features in such a way as to express his essential character. In the Asante case attention is paid to hair, scarification and, perhaps, the general form of the face, but essentially it is status and an idealised form of beauty which are being depicted. The terracotta heads from any single site, such as Ahinsan in Adanse, show considerable variation in style, while at the same time it is possible to identify almost identical heads modelled by the same potter. In making these heads, therefore, there was no concern to depict exactly the physical features of the person portrayed; it was enough to create an image whose accoutrements, posture or context of use indicated the social role of the person it represented.

Left A funerary terracotta head from the Adanse area, probably 19th century. Ht 23.2 cm.

12 Wood-carvings

The Asante produced a considerable range of carvings shaped, more or less, in the form of the human body. These were used for different purposes, and to some extent use affected form. The most numerous and distinctive carvings are small black-painted dolls with flat circular or oval heads. These are usually referred to as *akua'mma* ('fertility dolls'), a term which goes back at least to the 1920s and is now widely used by literate Asante.[1] Tens of thousands of these were carved, and they form a distinct class by virtue of their shape, use and number.

The term *akua'ba* (pl. *akua'mma*) includes a large number of other images (*ohoni*, *mfoni*), generally in wood or terracotta, intended to represent the human form or significant parts of it: figures in shrines, those placed before sellers of medicines in markets to attract purchasers, loom heddle pulleys, and figurines used as snuffers for medicines. The latter have hollow legs which lead into a cavity in the region of the stomach and chest where ground medicine is placed. The open ends of the legs are placed in the nostrils, and the medicine is inhaled. This term *akua'ba* applies mainly to free-standing images but it may be used with some differentiating detail to designate figure carvings in, for example, stools or staffs. The term also includes mud figures modelled in play by children, crudely shaped male figures placed over blacksmiths' hearths, figures on clay pipes and funerary figures. The gold images of slain enemies hanging from the Golden Stool and figures on *kuduo* lids are also *akua'mma*, although figurative gold-weights are rarely called by this name.

A second less widely used Asante term has the same meaning: *abodua'ba*. Some informants claim this is not 'pure' or 'proper' Asante (*Asante kronkon* or *Asante paa*). It is unclear whether the term was once confined to certain areas or formerly used by incomers, free or constrained.

The great majority of *akua'mma* are the so-called fertility dolls, nearly all of which are carved in *oṣeṣe* (*funtumia* sp.). They tend to be about 15–22 cm in height; it is rare to find one less than 12 cm or more than 32 cm high. Almost all are coloured black, and in all the head is a thin circular or oval disc set, tilted slightly backwards, on a short neck. The neck, about 3–5 cm long, is carved so it appears to be a number of rings, one on top of the next; sometimes thick and thin rings alternate. The neck is usually of constant diameter, and the body is either completely cylindrical or slightly narrower towards the top. Two tapering horizontal protrusions represent arms, sometimes pierced to take loops of tiny beads. The spinal column is occasionally represented by a shallow channel. The breasts and navel are represented by small raised areas. Sexual organs are rarely depicted. In most carvings the body ends in a short, larger diameter cylinder or a stubby truncated cone a few centimetres deep with a flat base so that the doll will stand on a flat surface. Sometimes loops of beads are tied around the 'waist'.

The disc of the head dominates the carving making up about 50–60 per cent of what is seen from the front. The eyebrows are usually represented by a pair of linked arcs and the nose by a thin protrusion, slightly thicker towards the bottom. In about half of these carvings the eyes and mouth are also represented. These features are nearly always confined to the lower half of the head disc, giving the impression of a high, domed forehead. The ears are not usually depicted, although many carvings have looped metal ear-rings or strings of tiny coloured glass beads attached to the edge of the head.

In about three-quarters of these carvings the back of the head is decorated with a number of incised straight or curved lines, usually arranged symmetrically about the vertical axis. In a very few cases this carving is representational of, for example, a schematised fort or a ship. Most of these patterns show great variation both in form and complexity. About a third have chalk or white clay (*hyire*) rubbed into them. Perhaps fewer than one in a thousand carvings depict

Two *akua'mma* (fertility dolls). Ht 34.7 cm, 32.6 cm.

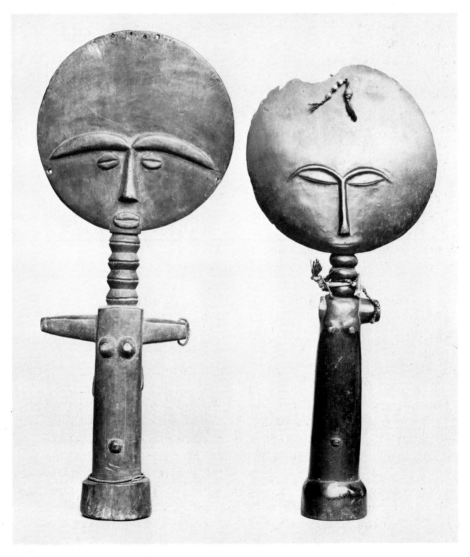

163

a figure with legs, usually with a simple representation of the vagina carved between them. Male sexual organs are very rarely indicated.

These carvings were found in very large numbers throughout all areas of Asante and among all strata of society. Although it is impossible to calculate the number carved in the past, field inquiries suggest that comparatively recently perhaps one woman in three or four possessed an *akua'ba* at some stage in her life. Large numbers pass through the hands of dealers. In 1968 an English dealer bought as a single lot over 7,000 such dolls from an African trader based in Kumase. In 1972 during a four-week period 200 such carvings were counted in the possession of a single, middle-rank Kumase dealer, and in 1967 about 2,500 dolls, collected over six months, were seen with another Kumase dealer.[2] In considering these figures we must also bear in mind that the pre-colonial population of Asante was smaller and that existing dolls represent only that proportion of the total which has survived wear, tear, concealment or loss.

It is difficult to establish how far back these dolls go in Asante life. The vast majority of those which survive were probably made in the four or five decades before the 1930s when production for local use seems to have more or less ended. The earliest doll known to the present author is dated to the 1860s or 70s on the basis of traditions that it was given to a female relative by Asantehene Kofi Kakari.[3] These carvings have two striking features: there is a high degree of similarity between them even though they were made by a large number of carvers and, secondly, they were produced in great quantities. To understand these features it is necessary to reconstruct their native use and significance.

These images were exclusively the property of women, and their function and form were inextricably connected with the essential role of women in Asante society. The following account of their use has been reconstructed from the memories of several old women, in their seventies when interviewed.[4]

The main reason a woman obtained a doll was a fear that she was infertile. It is almost impossible to over-emphasise the importance of successful child-bearing in Asante life. A woman was expected to bear many children. Failure to become pregnant, miscarriages and the deaths of young children were and are all matters of deep concern and fear which give rise to suspicions of witchcraft. A woman who has many children who survive is highly honoured; if she bears ten children, her achievement is recognised by a special ritual, the *badu'dwan* ('sheep of the tenth'). Such successful women also have to play a crucial part in girls' nubility rites.

The local matrilineage (*abusua*) is believed to be united by the blood passed by women to their offspring. Girl children who continue this line are more highly valued than boys. Asante women thus live under a double expectation: that they will bear children and that they will bear female children who can continue the matrilineage. One a girl's nubility rite has been performed after her first menstruation, she is expected to become pregnant within a few years: only women who are obviously sick or notoriously promiscuous are excepted. When a mature woman does not become pregnant, it is a source of great concern and distress to the woman, to her husband or lover (*adamfoɔ*), and to her local descent group. Formerly aid was sought in such cases from herbalists (*adunsinfo*), owners of medicines (*aduro*) or from priests of major gods (*abosom*). It was from the latter that instructions to obtain an *akua'ba* were usually obtained.

Supplications to a god were usually made on a *dabɔne* (bad day), one of the special days within the forty-two-day Asante cycle. Accompanied by her mother, or her mother's sister or a particularly close elder sister, the woman would visit the shrine, having fasted and also refrained from sexual intercourse during the preceding night. She would offer a small sum of money or gold-dust and an odd number of eggs (more than five) to the person acting as the spokesman (*okyeame*) for the priest. At this stage it was, according to informants, not usual to declare the purpose of her visit: gods obtained reputations from telling supplicants why they had come. The woman and her helpers would enter the room where the priest was seated, possessed by the god. Priest and supplicant might enter into a form of indirect dialogue, with the spokesman interpreting the words spoken by the possessed priest. As priests were often almost incoherent, their bodies twitching and shaking, and their phrases gabbled (*basa basa*), clarification was necessary. The god might in this way offer observations about the woman's conduct, her various relationships, and how these might be improved. Such consultations were often short and could end quickly if the priest (or his god) was not satisfied that everything had been brought into the open by the supplicant.

Several explanations could be offered for failure to bear children or for a woman ceasing to menstruate without a foetus developing: the woman was promiscuous; certain major crimes or sins (*akyiwadie kɛse* or *akyiwadie kɔkoɔ*) remained undiscovered among the local lineage, so offending the ancestors; or witches (*abayifo*) were active within this group. If none of these explanations was given, the priest might order the woman to return with an *akua'ba* on a specified day. The doll would be obtained for a small sum from a local carver, perhaps one suggested by the shrine *okyeame*. The doll would be handed over on the appointed day, placed for some time near the god, and then returned to the woman. Probably she would also be given a medicine (*aduro*) to drink or to bathe in and instructed in certain prohibitions (*akyiwadie*) to be kept until she had given birth. She would carry the *akua'ba* held on by her cloth on her back in the position in which a real child is carried. The doll was carried face forward with only the top of the back of the head protruding from the cloth. According to some informants, the doll was carried until the woman became unmistakably pregnant; according to others, until she was successfully delivered of her child. The rite at which the child was named and formally entered human society was performed on the seventh or fortieth day after birth. Later the mother and child would return to the priest, wearing white cloth and with temples and upper arms decorated with white clay to make a thanks-offering (*aseda*), generally to the nominal worth of a sheep. The child might have to keep behavioural or dietary prohibitions given by the priest until adulthood or throughout life. The doll was retained by the woman.

It is said that dolls were also bought (or even carved) by fathers or by husbands for daughters or wives. Young (pre-menarche) girls were given these carvings to play with: it was believed that by looking upon a well-formed doll a woman was influenced or assisted to bear a good-looking child. A link of some sort was conceived between the form and quality of the doll and the nature of the child eventually born.

Akua'mma are therefore a product of a woman's concern to have children, and formerly they were exclusively the possessions of women. The care with which they were treated accounts for the survival of many of them. Today, as in the past, such carvings are carefully wrapped in odd scraps of cloth and hidden in the rafters of their owner's room. Alternatively, they may be locked away in her wooden trunk or box where she keeps all her most prized and personal property.

Although *akua'mma* of this sort are believed to help women to have beautiful children, the Asante are unable to say much about how they achieve this. When questioned, senior Asante women and priests profess that they do not understand how the conception and birth of children is aided; at best they say that it is brought about by the god concerned. This lack of verbal explication is striking: literally tens of thousands of these objects with a singular fixity of form were made by many carvers and distributed and used throughout all ranks of society, and yet their users can say little more than they are used to help 'get children'. Although knowledge is not distributed evenly throughout Asante society, the widely declared ignorance of how *akua'mma* work is not an aspect of this stratification or specialisation of knowledge; it is a much more central and profound ignorance. The Asante are totally unable to put into words how or why these carvings help children to be born, yet they insist they have the power to achieve this and consequently are of the greatest importance.

There is one frequently repeated 'explanation' of the origin of these carvings.[5] There was once a woman called *Akua* (the usual name of a girl born on a Wednesday) who had no children. She applied to a god (*bosom*) for aid and was told by the priest to have such a doll carved. After that she bore children. From this such carvings are known as the child (*ba*) of Akua. Such folk etymologies are a feature of Asante theorising about the world, the past and, in particular, the names of things, people and animals but need not incorporate historical facts. This Asante word-play is facilitated by the tonal nature of the language. Similar words are differentiated by the high or low tones given to their syllables. By altering tones words of different meanings can be given the same meaning. Accounts of historic events are embellished or supported by word-play, puns and more or less forced interpretations of the names or titles of those involved.

Christaller's nineteenth-century Twi dictionary suggests another origin for *akua'ba*, giving *akua* as 'a human figure of clay' and including a text about wood or clay figures (*akua*) being used in funeral rites.[6] It is therefore possible that *akua'ba* is a diminutive of this older word. The tones given by Christaller for Akua, the woman's name, and *akua*, the figure, are different.

The available evidence suggests that most of these dolls were carved by nonprofessional male carvers, working for a relatively small local market and not dependent on making dolls or other forms of image for their livelihood. Carving *akua'mma* was a minor task additional to making stools, wooden bowls, grinders and mortars, except in the few villages where carving seems to have been on a much grander scale in the last century. When so many dolls were produced by numerous carvers to an almost fixed pattern, it is necessary to seek the social, technological or intellectual forces which controlled this form so closely.

The Asante carver (*adwinfo*, literally, 'one with skill or craft', or *asenfo*, 'one who cuts') tends to do most of his carving in the light, fairly soft wood called *osẹsẹ* (*funtumia* sp.). This is pale yellow when fresh, fading as it dries. *Osẹsẹ* has long been used: Bowdich bought a stool of 'zezzo' wood, and Christaller's Twi dictionary has the following entry for *osẹsẹ*: 'a certain tree; *dua fitae bi a wọde sen*

Two *akua'mma*.
Ht 27.2 cm, 30.1 cm.

akonnua, wode pam pon' which may be translated thus: 'a light (possibly even with the connotation of clean, shining, unblemished) wood used to carve stools and construct doors'.[7]

Osese has advantages for carvers using simple hand tools. It is evenly textured, fairly soft, straight grained and free from knots and bumps. The Asante carver prizes it for its light colour and its ability to take a smooth finish. The contrast between the raw materials available to the forest-dwelling Akan and to the craftsmen of the arid north, or the arid southern areas like the Ga-Adangbe plains, working with gnarled, slow-growing timber, is striking. With the large, evenly grained blocks of easily available *osese* the Asante craftsman is potentially free to cut with comparative ease almost any size or shape of object he wishes. The broad character of Asante carving owes a considerable amount to the easy availability of such excellent raw material. There is, however, one major problem with *osese*: when dry it tends to be rather weak and to split easily along the grain.

According to Rattray's informants, the *osese* tree, like the *kodia* and *tweneboa* (from which drums are made), was believed to have the potential to trouble those who cut it down: it had *sasa* and was *nye kora* ('no good at all'). Before felling an *osese* tree, the wood-cutter would say a prayer and make an offering to avert the sickness or misfortune which could otherwise come from the tree's *sasa*. Offering an egg, he would address the tree: *Osese, gye kesuadi, dadie (dade) ntwa me* ('Osese, take and enjoy this egg, and do not let my (iron) tool cut me'). Rattray added that later the 'wandering spirit' (*?sasa, sunsum*) was attracted back into the completed object.[8] Inquiries suggest this practice has now ceased, perhaps because carvers rarely fell timber themselves but buy it from contractors. Carvers today tend to use *osese* in a 'green', unseasoned state. This may lead to splitting as the timber dries out over the years. A sort of accidental seasoning of *osese* logs occurs, as these may lie about for years before they are sold to be made into carvings.

Actual carving is almost always done outside the dwelling-house, even when the house concerned has a large central courtyard. Some Asante say this is because adzing is noisy and produces wood chips and dust. Possibly the location of carving away from the courtyard, where much of the household's semi-public life takes place, is also determined by a general feeling that work activity (*adwuma*) should take place 'behind' (*akyi*) or away from the house, and because of the advantages offered by a more public work place.

Today if carvers live in a large town, or Kumase, they usually work in a small shed attached to one side of the house or, if space does not allow this, in front of the house on the main street. If they live in a bush village, they may erect near the house a simple shelter (*pato, asesewa*) with a flat palm-frond roof supported on roughly trimmed corner posts. It is useful to work where passers-by are able to see what is made.

The tools used by carvers are still comparatively simple, although practice, a good eye and a strong arm are needed to use them effectively. Many are still made by local blacksmiths and are either ordered directly or bought from market dealers in ironware. Nowadays many tools are made from scrap salvaged from wrecked cars or lorries. This metal is of high quality, even after it has been heated and reheated several times in a low-temperature charcoal forge and then quenched in cold water. In the past tools were made from both imported (European) 'bar iron' and iron obtained from non-Akan peoples to the north and west of Asante. The craft villages which Dupuis, Bowdich and other early travellers noted were working and shaping iron into tools; local smelting had ceased.[9]

Carvers' tools (*naade*, literally, 'irons', 'metal things') are few in number and comparatively easily made.[10] Principal is the socketed adze (*soso*, a term also used for the agricultural hoe). This has a haft made from an angled tree branch or from a thin trunk from which a branch springs at an internal angle of about 45°. The blade is usually no more than about 5 cm wide at the tip and about 10 cm long with the rear curved into a tube to fit around the haft and abut on to a shoulder in the wood. A carver may have several adzes of different sizes, although there does not seem to be any clear nomenclature based on size. According to Rattray, a small adze with a blade of 2.5–5 cm wide was called an *asene sosowa* (literally, 'small' or 'lesser chipping or carving hoe'), while a larger one for splitting was referred to as a *soso paye*. A larger adze is sometimes called *adere*. The other tools used by carvers are knives (*asekan*), often European-made, and small knives (*sekamma*) for finishing off a piece and for cutting out detailed work. A few carvers, especially those who make stools, also use a thin, flexible blade, sharpened along one edge and with a handle at each end. This is called *akuntuma* or *mranee* and is much used as a spokeshave, being looped around the pillars of stools and pulled against the wood to remove long shavings. For the rest, simple chisels or planes (*pewa*) are sometimes owned and used in conjunction with a flat-headed hammer (*osae*). In carving drums or stools, awls (*fifiye*, *titiee*) are also used, along with a gouge (*tiye*, *bowere*) which is used to cut the close-packed narrow grooves which run vertically down the outer surfaces of the large *antumpam* and other drums. Besides imported knives, which are generally acknowledged to keep their edges better than those made from locally reworked metal, the main foreign-produced items used are coarse rasps (*twitwae*), for finishing off carvings, and whet-stones (*serebo*).

It is with such a limited range of tools, and often with only an adze, a knife and a file, that the Asante carver works. He starts by using an adze, or perhaps a saw (*owan*), to cut off a length of wood from a log. This is split into a number of billets with a wedge (*naame*) hammered into the top of the log near its outer edge. Once a split has been made, further wedges are inserted along the outer (vertical) face of the log. Alternatively, the log may be split (*pae*) by driving a large adze (Rattray's *soso paye*) so that it jams in the wood. Adze and wood are then lifted together and brought down with great force against the ground or against another log, driving the adze further into the log until it splits down its length. Wedges are nowadays made from iron or from hard wood such as *odum*. There is a faint possibility that formerly stone axes, '*Nyame akuma*, washed from the ground, were used for this purpose.

The primary billet detached in this way is split to produce a number of lengths of timber of triangular section. These are next split crossways (in a way which roughly coincides with their growth rings) to produce a fairly flat piece from the outer, broader end of the wedge and one or more narrower pieces from nearer the centre. The innermost piece of roughly triangular section is discarded or reserved for making smaller carvings.

The next stage in a carver's work is to adze the billet to make the faces roughly parallel. Here the advantages of using *oṣẹṣẹ* become noticeable, for the wood cuts easily and comes away in neat, even flakes. The base of the billet is rested against the ground or on a log. The carver swings the adze with a sharp, chopping movement and holds the timber so it is almost parallel to the outer face of the descending blade. In this way the amount of wood removed at each blow can be controlled almost exactly. Some carvers sketch or incise an outline of the finished carving on the block; others prefer to shape by eye as they adze.

The wood is rested on a block and adzed to its preliminary shape. The head

An umbrella top respresenting a saying about the snake which, even though it could not fly, finally caught the hornbill which owed it money. Ht 42.45 cm.

disc, the most difficult and delicate section, is now thinned: mistakes or faults here are best discovered early. Smaller and more delicate tools are used to shape the body, breasts and arms. The neck and arms, weak areas, are usually left until the end. The facial features and the characteristic neck rings (see illustration, p.167) are cut away with small blades, and then the whole carving is smoothed and later dyed black.

European tools have had little effect on Asante carving for most are designed for aligning, making true and smoothing planks or blocks for joining in multipart constructions, and require clamps or vices for use. Single-block carving, on the contrary, is a subtractive process, and the adze and knife are hard to better for removing small pieces of wood evenly and quickly. There are good reasons for believing that the distinctive oft-repeated form of *akua'mma* is not determined by the materials and techniques used. Firstly, the same tools

An umbrella top of a hen and chicks, carved by Osei Bonsu of Kumase, *c.*1920. This represents the saying that a hen may step on her chicks but never so heavily as to kill them. `Ht 30 cm.

and timber are used to produce figure carvings which have a distinctly different shape (for umbrella or staff tops, heddle pulleys, medicine snuffers, etc.). Secondly, there are strong technical factors which militate against fertility dolls being given their extreme form.

A good carver can adze, trim and smooth a doll in an hour or so. Carvers accept, however, that the neck, head and arms need the greatest care in carving. Ideally the head should be less than a centimetre deep at the centre and taper to almost paper thinness at the edges. It joins the neck at a point only a centimetre across. These areas are easily damaged in carving and become weaker as the doll becomes older, for as the timber dries it may warp and split along the grain. An old carving is both light and fragile. If the neck or arms are knocked, they may split or become detached. The fine edges of the head often show splitting or chipping within a few years of carving. Valued dolls are sometimes mended: holes are drilled each side of the split and thread used to bind together the sundered parts. The weakness where the head joins the neck arises from the change from the vertical run of the grain in the neck to the cross-grain line of the tilted head. If the large, flat head is knocked, pressure is concentrated here and the head often becomes detached. Similar damage can detach the unsupported arms or protruding breasts. Experienced carvers fully understand this could be avoided by making a different form of carving or by using tougher timber. Their reason for carving persistently in this form therefore is not primarily technological.

Is form determined by use? The dolls were often carried, as a real child would be, face forward on girls' or women's backs, tucked under a length of cloth wrapped round the body and with only the top of the back of the head showing. Undoubtedly a small, flat image is convenient to carry in this way, but other groups carry far more three-dimensional carvings in this position. Asante women also carry other awkward items: coconuts, medium-sized pots, bundles of cloth, shoes, etc. – in fact, anything which for some reason cannot be carried on the head. Mere flatness and lightness, therefore, do not seem to be determined by the method of carrying. The form of these *akua'mma* must be explained by other factors.

The most immediately striking feature of the doll is the head, and on the delicacy, shape and balance of this a carver is judged. In all Asante media modelling of the head exaggerates its height and reduces its depth; its proportion in relation to the body may be 1:3 or 1:4 as opposed to 1:6 or more in an actual person. In producing this form the craftsman is exaggerating the shape most esteemed in Asante society.

The Asante believe that the forehead is most attractive when it slopes backwards from the eyebrows, rising smoothly to the top of the head (*mpampam, atifi*) and giving the whole face, when seen from front or side, an egg or oval shape, broadest part uppermost. Those with high foreheads were considered to be especially beautiful. Formerly, elderly people state, attempts were made to give children's heads this ideal shape. Soon after birth a cloth pad was dipped in warm water and gently pressed against the infant's forehead, and this was repeated for several days. The practice seems now to have died out. Attempts

172

were also made to exaggerate the forehead by brushing, trimming or braiding the hair so that it stood radiated outwards and backwards from it. The ringed necks on *akua'mma* are also a stylisation of the most admired form of neck. The Asante believe that by the time of puberty men and women, but especially the latter, should ideally develop a neck with a series of rings or folds running around it. These are a mark of beauty and sexually exciting.

The heads and necks of *akua'mma* are, therefore, shaped after an ideal of human beauty. While people attempt to develop their bodies to that ideal, the ideal is also emphasised in these carvings. The carvings are in no sense naturalistic; they are not based on actual humans but emphasise the desired form for humans. But does the form have any other significance, especially in view of the fact that the Asante seem unable or unwilling to explain how these dolls can help women become fertile or why they have such a constant form?

In nearly all of these dolls the body is a simple column from which protrude stumpy arms, feminine breasts and the navel. Sexual organs are rarely, if ever, shown. A few dolls are carved with legs, and on these dolls female sexual organs are sometimes depicted. These, and the breasts, may be taken to indicate that if anything these are female dolls.

The vast majority of these dolls are coloured black which seems essential to their functioning. Asante colour classification is basically tripartite. The three basic colours, or ranges of colour, are *tuntum*, *fufuo* and *kokoo*. *Tuntum* designates all very dark shades which approach absolute blackness, *fufuo* covers pale, whitish, grey and cream colours, and *kokoo* all red, brown and yellow shades. Each colour has symbolic importance. White is generally associated with coolness, innocence and rejoicing, while red is associated with heat, anger, grief, witchcraft and warfare. The broad connotations of black are less precise, but it is associated with night and the ancestors, especially through their blackened stools and perhaps because there is a vague belief that daytime in the world of the spirits is night-time for ordinary people.

The declared purpose of these carvings is to help bring children into the world. The Akan believe in a rather vague way in reincarnation and claim that some children born into a lineage may be in some way a reincarnation of matrilineal forebears or possess some of their characteristics. There is a related belief that some children are merely deposited for a while in the human world by their 'ghost mothers', who then claim them back, the human incarnation of this child then dying.[11] The souls or personalities of children are thus believed to circulate between this world and the world of the spirits. The blackness of *akua'mma* is therefore consonant with their function as a bridge or channel between the realm of the dead and the yet unborn and the living, in much the same way as the ancestral stools perform this function.

The lack of sexual organs in these carvings may be explained in relation to the doll's function of bringing children into the world. To the Asante children are only potential human beings. Female, beautiful children are desired and their birth encouraged by all possible means, but in Asante eyes they can be considered fully human only after adolescence when their potential fertility and sexuality have been achieved. The dolls thus represent idealised forms of beauty and femininity, but potential rather than complete femininity. They give a physical expression to deeply held desires about fertility and the need for female children to carry on the lineage. The colour and form of the dolls summarise basic Asante ideas: the dolls represent, as it were, a potential person and do so in a way which cannot be simplified or reduced very much further, nor expressed in speech, particularly the allusive, indirect form of speech favoured by the Asante.

It is apparent that the fertility dolls have a rigid, abstract pose: they exist without doing anything, as it were. This total absence of activity fits in with their role as images of potential beings, children who cannot assume their own characters and roles until later in life. The vast majority of other Asante wood-carvings of people show them in a more active manner or, if not engaged on some particular activity, depict them expressing their intention by some

An executioner with a
victim's head.
Ht 30.3 cm.

stereotyped gesture, for example, with one hand cupped in the other in front of the body in request and supplication, or holding a breast as a sign of nurture.

Although many different sorts of wood-carving are known which fall outside the rigid limitations of the fertility dolls, it is difficult to establish where and how these were made and used. One definite class are those which were placed near the shrines of some gods and certain major witch-finding fetishes. The majority of these seem to represent named 'helpers' (*boafo*) of the shrine power, serving as messengers and aides to seek out those who offended the power and defend those under its protection. Such carvings may have been carried from area to area by those who travelled about promoting witch-finding powers. Carvings of priests and executioners are also known, the former usually covered with white clay, as they are in life, and holding an egg in one hand and a small sword in the other, as if dancing for the god. Executioners are usually

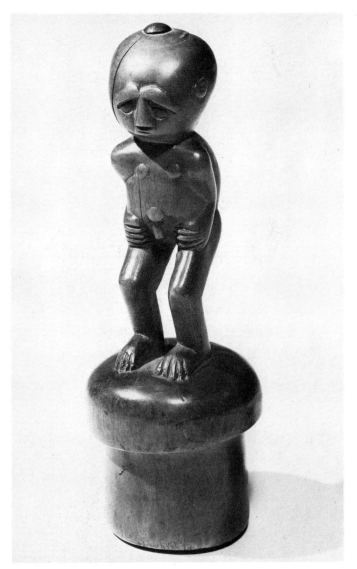

A stopper in the form of a hunchback for an imported stoneware flagon. Hunchbacks served the King as court criers.
Ht 22.5 cm.

depicted holding the head of a severed victim; one collected before about 1925 depicts a circumcised executioner – an oddity, for circumcision was traditionally forbidden in Asante and did not become widespread until very recently.

More tender themes are depicted: a large number of carvings are known of women suckling children, a few of women with twins. None of these shows any traces of sacrificial blood or eggs which would indicate they were kept near stools or in the rooms of gods, and it is unclear why they were made or where they were kept, although the general emphasis on fertility obviously reflects basic Asante values. One carving of a woman with twins is said to have been made by a carver to mark the birth of twins to his wife: it was kept in her room and shown to interested people as an example of her husband's skill and imagination. Another carver recalled that he had carved a wooden spoon topped with a female figure to commemorate the nubility rituals of a particularly charming and beautiful girl in his village.

A further set of wooden figures seems to have been used in play by young girls. The carvings placed in this class show a wide range of forms but nearly all have a more naturalistic appearance than the highly stylised flat-headed black dolls. Almost all of them depict humans standing with their arms slightly away from their bodies and with fully carved legs and feet. Most will stand up on flat surfaces but, the line of the grain running vertically through the figure, the feet have often become broken off in use. In many of these figures some attempt is made to indicate a particular style of hair-dressing, and the facial features are represented in some detail. Most show signs of heavy handling and wear and most are female and have beads about their waists and necks. Some have been dressed with odd lengths of cloth. A few such carvings are still used by young girls who play with them or carry them on their backs, held on by a length of cloth, as real children would be. It is probable that many of these were made by local carvers, even the fathers or uncles of the little girls to whom they were given; a large number are rather crudely made. It is difficult to trace them back to their particular places of origin, since many have been passed from hand to hand before they are finally sold to local dealers.

The personal, innovative side of carving is especially shown by wooden combs. These were made by men for sale locally or, more often, as gifts to their wives or girl-friends. They show a number of different forms but in many cases incorporate traditional motifs, such as the backward-facing *sankofa* bird with more modern or unusual elements: ships, lorries, cocoa beans and flags. Many are also personalised by having cut into them the name of the carver or recipient, the date and part of a saying, prayer or aphorism.

Local carvers also produced elaborately carved spoons, some with intricate handles in the form of knots or rope work, often ending in a grinding surface. These were used principally to serve out mashed yam which was offered as a food to gods and later shared by the priest and congregation. Such spoons were proudly hung in the shrines or in the open rooms (*pato*) of temples and they were also used as display items and for the same purpose in girls' nubility rites.

Carvers also produced a number of other items. Chief amongst these were chewing-sticks (*asakyimannua*). It was usual for men and women to chew roughly split lengths of wood from a particular tree: the stick had a distinctive flavour, and the chewed end formed a 'brush' of fibres which from time to time was spat out. Elaborately carved, non-functional chewing-sticks, about 15 cm long, decorated with small figures or flat heads like those found on fertility dolls, were carried in the mouth by senior women, royal daughters and by some adolescent girls at their nubility rites, the ends away from the mouth coloured blue. A few gold chewing-stick tips are known. Elaborate chewing-sticks seem to have been used only by women who also used circular wooden fans (*papa*) with rod-like handles. Senior chiefs were fanned with large fans made of basketwork, ostrich feathers or by lozenge-shaped fabric-covered fans, but queen mothers used these smaller wooden fans; they may also have been used as an adjunct in dancing in the same way as handkerchiefs are now used by women to increase the range and subtleties of their hand gestures.

A large ladle or scoop, possibly used to place food offerings before a god. Ht 46.75 cm.

13 The role of the image

It is clear that the material culture of the Asante people became increasingly diversified and elaborate over the centuries. Old forms, such as swords or elephant-tail whisks, were modified to carry new meanings necessitated by the growing specialisation of roles within Asante society. Exotic items, such as staffs or metal vessels, were absorbed into Asante culture and their forms gradually modified. The use of gold-dust as currency encouraged the creation of large numbers of brass castings to serve as weights and, within limits, led to these being given a wide range of forms.

The concentration of wealth and power was signalled by the types of items used and their degree of elaboration. As power shifted, so regalia were redistributed. The developing political system was able to use and absorb exotic items because these came to it as rare and valuable things, initially obtained by those in the most senior and wealthy positions. These items were used to show wealth and power had been achieved and to give a superficial order to the underlying complexities of the political struggle.

Clearly, not all types of image had the same function or conveyed their meaning in the same way. A broad distinction can be drawn between those images and regalia used to show or indicate status, or rather to suggest types of relationship between one status and another, and those images, especially fertility dolls, which were created to express an ideal form, even to help bring that form into existence.

In considering artefacts the Asante have an extensive critical vocabulary. A fine smooth finish, without fault or blemish (*efi*, literally, 'dirt' or 'muck') is important, as is balance and symmetry and a general lightness or fineness of line in wood-carvings. Skill in creation, the quality of materials used and their control by the maker are all appreciated.[1]

By the nineteenth century, possibly earlier, craft production was becoming concentrated in particular villages probably because of the availability of resources and a location near major roads and centres of population. Some villages had a single speciality: '. . . almost all the inhabitants were engaged in weaving'; while others had produced several goods: '. . . cloth, beads and pottery were manufacturing in all directions and the blacksmiths forges were always at work.'[2] Crafts especially tied to the needs of the political hierarchy were produced in places close to the capital where craftsmen were under court surveillance.

Most individual cases of craft production remained a matter of direct contact between user and maker: few important goods were produced for sale, and there existed no straightforward mechanism by which their monetary value was calculated. Most items of regalia were produced on commission. The craftsman brought his particular skill and experience to the transaction, but the final form was also affected by the needs of the user and his or her status within Asante society. Traditions suggest that payment was negotiated between the two parties and might be spread over a considerable period with, perhaps, advances being given for the purchase of necessary raw materials and an *aseda*, a counter-gift or thanks-offering, on receipt of the finished item. It is also said that those working for a senior chief as metalworkers, carvers, weavers, sandal-makers, etc. would do the work in the chief's palace, housed and fed at his expense until the work was completed, and then rely on his generosity for the gift of an appropriate sum in gold-dust.

Status and social roles are indicated by many Asante images. Gold-weights depict the tools of particular groups or show people engaged in activities characteristic of certain occupations or offices. Hair-styles showing particular social roles (for example, priests' uncut tresses, warriors' small moustaches, *fam-fam*, and beards) are shown on weights and funerary terracottas, and weights show items of dress or adornment (fibre skirts, *kra* discs) indicating distinct occupations. Size also served to indicate status, and the form, size and elaborateness of regalia and the materials used are related to the standing and history of the office or stool to which they belong. Certain types of stools, sandals, staffs, umbrella tops and metal castings were formerly restricted to particular ranks within society, those used by the Asantehene being the largest, most splendid and most expensive in terms of time and material. In some cases, therefore, status is indicated by what the image depicts; in others by its size and the substance used to create the image.

At one level the art of the court was intended to impress the populace and to signal differences of rank and function among its users. It was an art which was intended to be bright, colourful and also, in many cases, effective when seen from a distance. Much of it is classed by the Asante as shining or bright (*fitaa*, *hyiren*). It was a public art, or rather an art which was periodically presented in public though for much of the time securely locked away within palaces and their stool rooms. Swords, umbrellas, gold pipes, sandals, cloths, headbands and so on were elements in the public presentation of the chief. This presentation was also created by the activities of his officials: drummers and ivory-horn blowers, who made their instruments 'speak' his praises or snatches of stool history by imitating the tones of speech, those sweeping before him with elephant-tail switches (the *ahoprafo*), umbrella-bearers (*kyiniefo*), fan-bearers, hunchbacked court criers with their shaggy black monkey-skin caps, and all the other personnel who surrounded chiefs on their public appearances.

In these circumstances these items served to declare the richness and standing of those bearing them and, because the right to have particular forms was won by defeating other chiefs, or granted or confirmed by the Asantehene, to express crucial events in the history of that stool. Some of these images – for example, umbrella tops or gold effigies attached to swords – might depict those defeated and slain in war, in the same way as the jaw-bones attached to horns or the skulls and leg bones tied to drums showed past victories and continued to humiliate the defeated chiefdom and its people.

But it is probable that the significance of particular types of image differed from level to level. To those with knowledge of the history of particular chiefdoms and offices the regalia worn or carried and the images displayed might call to mind distinctions which would not be apparent to the mass of population. To the latter the sheer mass of golden regalia and its apparently infinite variety were the most significant features. In some cases a form of visual hyperbole was used to show the power and wealth of the possessor: vast masses of imported keys were carried in bunches or large silver copies made and tied together, or gold-topped staffs were carried in large bundles.

Cutting across this distinction between the esoteric knowledge of the court and the impression regalia made on the less well-informed was the fact that many artefacts possessed a verbal dimension, or rather entered into a elaborate and flexible form of verbal discourse. Each artefact or element in an artefact, its form or decoration, could serve as the point from which verbal elaboration could proceed. The vast majority of representational forms were perceived as having this verbal dimension, and this was also the case in some apparently non-representational forms.

The richness and wit of Asante speech and poetry cannot be over-emphasised. Proverbs and aphorisms (*mmebusɛm*) were a crucial element in everyday life and were continually being invented or modified. Several thousand have been recorded over the last hundred years or so.[3] Knowledge of such sayings was essential for a person to advance in Asante society. They were thought to represent traditional wisdom and served to sway debates and clinch arguments. Senior men and women, and especially chiefs and officials, were expected to know dozens, even hundreds, of these sayings, and in the old days friendly competitions were held to see who knew the most, each person trying to cap the saying offered by the preceding person. With the Asante delight in such sayings went an associated reluctance or unwillingness to refer directly to important matters. Many elegant phrases existed to refer to embarrassing or important matters and were often used to avoid punishment or, at best, ostracism. If a king died, for example, the matter would never be mentioned except through such phrases as 'the great tree has fallen', or 'the King has gone to his village', or 'he has gone behind his *kra*'. Similarly, a girl's first menstruation was indicated by phrases like 'she's done something' or 'she's shot an elephant'. Knowledge of proverbs and aphorisms allowed, even encouraged, an indirect, subtle and allusive form of discussion for, by speaking in proverbs, even the most serious matters could be referred to and explored without having to be mentioned by name.

Each proverb poses some sort of parallelism between an existing situation and the situation encapsulated in it. Although the saying may appear simply to make a straightforward observation – for example, 'no one sells his hen without a good reason' (*Obi ntɔn ne kokobere kwa*)[4] or 'the tortoise goes off in a laughable manner but he can escape all the same' (*Akyekyere kɔ serew serew na oguang ara neng*)[5] – it is produced with a consciousness that it parallels elements in the existing situation. The proverb provides a structured model or summary of what is happening, may happen or could happen. Its function in Asante discourse is to suggest the true pattern and significance of existing or impending events in human society and to point to how these can turn out.

The proverb essentially poses a relationship between one creature or thing and another, expressed in concrete terms but having a more abstract significance – for example, 'When a dog picks up an egg, it will break in its mouth' (ǫkraman fa kesua a, ebeboẉo n'anam'),[6] or 'An old man was in the world before a chief was born' (Akwakora te ho ansansa wǫwoo paynin).[7] It is then the practice of the user of the proverb and those who hear it to draw parallels between one or other of the protagonists who acts in the proverb and those in the still unfolding situation they face.

By quoting one proverb after another, by offering proverbs with contrary or different meanings and by changing the relationships posed by the proverbs, a matter can be discussed and explored in a wide number of ways and a number of possible solutions, or strings of possible relationships, can be considered without being referred to directly. There is also, of course, an essential ambiguity in this process, for it is the individual's responsibility to perceive which party or which event in the social situation is to be seen as paralleling one or other element in the proverbial relationship.

An account of a meeting between the British governor Rowe and an Asante embassy in 1881 gives a slight indication of the Asante use of such indirect and allusive speech in diplomatic negotiation. The senior Asante stated his intention by declaring 'I have come down to stop all those small leaks in the roof which have been giving trouble of late. If I cannot do this, we must have a new roof'. (This was interpreted as 'I have come for peace'.) Rowe replied in the same way and ended by declaring 'I am not a mudfish'. Native informants of Ellis,[8] who recorded this exchange, glossed the last remark in several ways. One said the governor was declaring he was not a mudfish which buries itself and so was not easily caught, that is, he was not a fool; another said that as the mudfish stirs up mud and cannot be seen the governor was declaring his openness; a third said the fish had venomous spines which wound those who touch it and so the governor was saying he did not wish harm to the Asante. Finally, a colonial official said the mudfish was worthless and the governor was stressing he was not. Clearly, such high allusive speech opened up a vast range of possibilities for fruitful ambiguity and misunderstanding.

The use of such sayings was not restricted to debate or discussion. Slaves were given names which were parts of proverbs, or their masters called them by the first few words of a saying and they had to respond by completing it.[9] Nowadays dogs are sometimes called by such expressions; by shouting at them in this way their owner is given the opportunity to broadcast a warning or a general observation which he feels suitable to his situation with those around him. In the same way such sayings are today also painted on lorries or houses: a statement of a personal position, a caution to those who can see the applicability of the saying to themselves, and a general expression of an accepted truism about human life in society.

In this system it will be apparent there is no single, fixed meaning to many images; they merely provide a starting-point for a mental or spoken chain of sayings. An image of a single creature, such as a crocodile, may serve to suggest several proverbs about crocodiles which propound several different types of relationships or metaphorical structures concerning, for example, the relation of the strong to the weak, or the nature of water-dwellers who can also move on land. The same relationships can also, of course, be derived from images of other creatures; so in certain circumstances two different images may serve to express parallel or closely similar meanings, or, conversely, images of the same creature can produce opposed meanings. Meaning in Asante, therefore, is not determined solely by the object, for this is never perceived or understood isolated from verbal chains which can be developed to suit situations.

The actual images chosen, however, seem to have been selected on a variety of principles. Some are drawn from natural objects which the Asante find attractive because of their symmetrical or balanced form: the fern-like *aya* leaf or the rosette-like leaf of the ground-nut plant (a casting of which adorns the hilt of the *Bosommuru* sword of the Takyimanhene, for example). Some are chosen because of distinctive physical properties: the resilient *babadua* reed, the elephant for its size, the pineapple for its yellow richness and sweetness; while others – cannons, swords or shields – are chosen for their function. Some, like the stars and moons which adorn chiefs' headbands, are selected because they appear to have a natural complementary association as well as being regarded as beautiful in themselves. Nevertheless, although the number of images used is limited, and although a particular form may have been copied and recopied according to shifts in political power, the significance of any image easily escapes from this limitation: the form depicted is only the starting-point of a chain of metaphorical or analogical statements which can be developed or modified as required. It is these which allow those who see or use the image to oscillate between their perception of the social situation and sayings which suggest certain basic patterns or relationships which could exist within it.

In some cases, however, human images have a far more fixed meaning and do not always serve to communicate proverbs. Many express their primary significance by means of their stance, posture and the hand movements they are depicted as making, drawing upon a widely understood set of gestures used in Asante society. A person bending slightly forward, for example, one hand cupped in the other in front of the body is begging or pleading; a man with a finger to one eye indicates a knowing watchfulness; while one with both hands on his stomach is interpreted as expressing humiliation at having to take food from his enemies. The most extreme case is that of the fertility *akua'mma* where there is little verbalisation at all. The shape and colour of these carvings, it has been argued, represent in minimal significant form certain desires and ideals connected with women's prime role, that of child-bearing. They do not become part of any verbal chain, for unlike other images which suggest relationships these are more of the order of statements or definitions: they represent the minimal required human features.

Clearly it is important for many Asante artefacts and images to be witty: to express certain truisms concisely and pleasingly. Many of these images are thus absorbed into a wider system of debate and discourse: they suggest ideas about ideal forms of relationship and, by their public appearance, serve to keep these to the forefront of Asante consciousness.

Notes

Chapter 1
Introduction: the Asante background

1 T.E. Bowdich, *Mission from Cape Coast Castle to Ashantee*, London, 1819, pp.34–5.

2 See, for example, Adu Boahen, 'The origins of the Akan', *Ghana Notes and Queries*, 9, Legon, 1966, and M. Posnansky, 'Archaeology and the origins of Akan society', *History of Ghana*, ed. M. Dodds, Accra, 1974. For the earliest eye-witness accounts located see W. Huydecoper, *Diary*, trans. G. Irwin, Legon, 1962.

3 See, for example, A.A.Y. Kyerematen, 'Ashanti Royal Regalia: their History and Function', D.Phil. dissertation, Oxford, 1966, pp.101–4, and R.S. Rattray, *Ashanti Law and Constitution*, Oxford, 1929, pp.131,236.

4 See I. Wilks, 'Land, labour, capital, and the forest kingdom of Asante: a model of early change', *The Evolution of Social Systems*, eds. M.J. Rowlands and J. Friedman, London, 1977.

5 See I. Wilks, *Asante in the Nineteenth century*, Cambridge, 1975, *passim*, for the political evolution of Asante.

6 See M.D. McLeod, 'Akan gold-weights and imports: a note on carriages', *Akan-Asante Studies*, British Museum Occasional Papers No.3, London, 1979, and M.A. Priestley and I. Wilks, 'English gifts to the King of Ashanti in the eighteenth century', *Ghana Notes and Queries*, 2, Legon, 1961.

Chapter 2
Forest and settlement

1 See I. Wilks, 'Land, labour, capital and the forest kingdom of Asante: a model of early change', *The Evolution of Social Systems*, eds. M.J. Rowlands and J. Friedman, London, 1977, pp.1–42.

2 A.E. Ellis, *The Land of Fetish*, London, 1883, p.272.

3 T.E. Bowdich, *Mission from Cape Coast Castle to Ashantee*, London, 1819, pp.20,22.

4 R. Austin Freeman, *Travels and Life in Ashanti and Jaman*, London, 1898, pp.40,41.

5 Frederick Boyle, *Through Fanteeland to Coomassie*, London, 1874, p.87.

6 Joseph Dupuis, *Journal of a Residence in Ashantee*, London, 1824, pp.48,66.

7 ibid., p.35.

8 F. Ramseyer and J. Kuhne, *Four Years in Ashantee*, New York, 1875, p.54.

9 Winwood Reade, *The Story of the Ashantee Campaign*, London, 1874, p.309.

10 R.S. Rattray, *Religion and Art in Ashanti*, Oxford, 1927, p.4.

11 R.S. Rattray, *Ashanti Law and Constitution*, Oxford, 1929, p.213.

12 J.G. Christaller, *A Dictionary of the Asante and Fante Language called Tschi*, 2nd edn, Basle, 1933, p.158.

13 T.B. Freeman, *Journal of Two Visits to the Kingdom of Ashanti*, London, 1843, p.57.

14 Rattray, 1929, pp.114,213,214,304.

15 Ramseyer and Kuhne, p.39.

16 Dupuis, pp.58,61.

17 Ramseyer and Kuhne, p.54.

18 R.S. Rattray, *Ashanti*, Oxford, 1923, pp.82,95–6.

19 R.S. Rattray, 1927, p.67.

20 G.A. Henty, *The March to Coomassie*, 2nd edn, London, 1874, pp.357,359.

21 Dupuis, p.48.

Chapter 3
Kumase

1 W. Huydecoper, *Diary* (28 April 1816–18 May 1817), trans. G. Irwin, Legon, 1962, p.20.

2 T.E. Bowdich, *Mission from Cape Coast Castle to Ashantee*, London, 1819, p.322.

3 ibid., p.308.

4 ibid., p.308 and pl.8.

5 ibid., p.304.

6 ibid., p.305.

7 ibid., p.306.

8 T.B. Freeman, *Journal of Two Visits to the Kingdom of Ashanti*, London, 1843.

9 Huydecoper, p.15.

10 Joseph Dupuis, *Journal of a Residence in Ashantee*, London, 1824, p.111.

11 Winwood Reade, *The Story of the Ashantee Campaign*, London, 1874, p.357.

12 G. Loyer, 'Abstract of a voyage to Issini', *A New General Collection of Voyages and Travels*, Thomas Astley, London, 1745–7, p.436.

13 Bowdich, p.306.

14 Huydecoper, p.20.

15 W. Winniet's Journal, Ghana National Archives, Accra, entry for 19 October 1848.

16 Garnet Wolseley, *The Story of a Soldier's Life*, London, 1903, p.360.

17 Bowdich, p.306.

18 Dupuis, p.61.

19 W. Winniet's Journal, entry for 9 October 1848.

20 F.A. Ramseyer and J. Kuhne, *Four Years in Ashante*, New York, 1875, p.147.

21 H. Brackenbury, *The Ashanti War*, Edinburgh and London, 1874, vol. 2, pp.326–7.

22 For pictures and descriptions of such buildings see M. Swithebank, *Ashanti Fetish Houses*, Accra, 1969.

23 Bowdich, p.309.

24 ibid., p.309.

25 Dupuis, p.137.

26 Frederick Boyle, *Through Fanteeland to Coomassie*, London, 1874, p.355.

27 ibid., pp.384–5.

28 Ramseyer and Kuhne, pp.225–7.

29 ibid., pp.141,267.

30 Bowdich, p.300.

31 Freeman, 1844, p.159.

32 Ramseyer and Kuhne, p.103.

33 J. Gros, *Voyages, aventures et captivité de J. Bonnat chez les Achantis*, Paris, 1884, pp.184–5, and T.B. Freeman, *Journal of Two Visits to the Kingdom of Ashanti*, London, 1843, p.129.

34 Bowdich, p.76.

35 Ramseyer and Kuhne, pp.106,164,172.

36 Gros, pp.168,196.

Chapter 4
Gods and lesser powers

1 R.S. Rattray, *Ashanti*, Oxford, frontispiece and pp.94,142,144,175.

2 T.B. Freeman, *Journal of Two Visits to the Kingdom of Ashanti*, London, 1843, p.31.

3 R.S. Rattray, *Ashanti Proverbs*, Oxford, 1916, nos.9 and 11.

4 See M.J. Field, *Search for Security: An Ethno-psychiatric Study of Rural Ghana*, London, 1960, *passim*, for gods and new cults.

5 R.S. Rattray, *Religion and Art in Ashanti*, Oxford, 1927, p.45.

6 William Bosman, *A New and Accurate Description of the Coast of Guinea*, London, 1705, p.150.

7 J. Gros, *Voyages, aventures et captivité de J. Bonnat chez les Achantis*, Paris, 1884, p.199.

8 Rattray, 1916, nos.18 and 24.

9 F.A. Ramseyer and J. Kuhne, *Four Years in Ashantee*, New York, 1875, p.35.

10 Gros, p.232.

11 Ramseyer and Kuhne, p.207.

12 A.E. Ellis, *The Land of Fetish*, London, 1883, p.232.

13 Ramseyer and Kuhne, p.207.

14 See I. Wilks, *Asante in the Nineteenth Century*, Cambridge, 1975, and 'The position of Muslims in Metropolitan Ashanti in the early nineteenth century', *Islam in Tropical Africa*, ed. I.M. Lewis, London, 1966.

15 See Rattray, 1927, p.29.

16 T.E. Bowdich, *Mission from Cape Coast Castle to Ashantee*, London, 1819, pp.232–3.

17 See Rene Bravmann, *Islam and Tribal Art in West Africa*, Cambridge, 1974, *passim*.

18 The Prince of Wales was photographed with one such mask in Akwamu during his visit to the Gold Coast.

19 M.D. McLeod, 'On the spread of anti-witchcraft cults in modern Asante', *Changing social structure in Ghana*, ed. J. Goody, London, 1975.

20 Rattray, 1927, pp.9–24.

21 See McLeod, 1975.

Chapter 5
Gold and gold-working

1 Many aspects of nineteenth-century political history are discussed in I. Wilks, *Asante in the Nineteenth Century*, Cambridge, 1975, and Thomas J. Lewin, *Asante before the British*, Lawrence, Kansas, 1979.

2 John William Blake, *Europeans in West Africa 1450–1560*, Hakluyt Society, vol.2, London, 1942, p.73.

3 ibid., p.93.

4 ibid., p.343.

5 ibid., pp.379–426, for general trading conditions between Europeans and Africans.

6 Thomas Astley, *A New General Collection of Voyages and Travels*, London, 1745–7, p.343.

7 William Bosman, *A New and Accurate Description of the Coast of Guinea*, London, 1705, p.73.

8 ibid., pp.81–2.

9 ibid., p.82.

10 ibid., p.182.

11 J. Barbot, *A Description of the Coasts of North and South Guinea*, London, 1732, pp.231–2,259.

12 ibid., p.259.

13 ibid., pl.22.

14 J.J. Crooks, *Records Relating to the Gold Coast Settlements from 1750–1874*, Dublin, 1923, p.4.

15 Wellcome Coll. no.z.12174.

16 R. Lee, *The African Wanderers: or, the Adventures of Carlos and Antonio*, London, 1874, p.72.

17 E.W. Smith, *Aggrey of Africa*, London, 1929, p.21.

18 See Timothy F. Garrard, 'Akan metal arts', *African Arts*, XIII, 1, Los Angeles, 1979.

19 T.E. Bowdich, *Mission from Cape Coast Castle to Ashantee*, London, 1819, pp.31–41.

20 R.S. Rattray, *Ashanti Law and Constitution*, Oxford, 1929, p.114.

21 J. Gros, *Voyages, aventures et captivité de J. Bonnat chez les Achantis*, Paris, 1884, p.197.

22 Wilks, 1975, p.419.

23 R.S. Rattray, *Religion and Art in Ashanti*, Oxford, 1927, p.117.

24 F.A. Ramseyer and J. Kuhne, *Four Years in Ashantee*, New York, 1875, p.171.

25 Wilks, 1975, p.439.

26 Bowdich, p.115.

27 T.B. Freeman, *Journal of Two Visits to the Kingdom of Ashanti*, London, 1843, p.126.

28 Joseph Depuis, p.167.

29 Bowdich, pp.64,71,72.

30 Freeman, 1843, p.157.

31 H. Brackenbury, *The Ashanti War*, London, 1874, p.267.

32 Bowdich, p.311.

33 File 2960, National Archives, Kumase.

34 See B. Menzel, *Goldgewichte aus Ghana*, Berlin, 1968, and Timothy F. Garrard, *Akan Weights and the Gold Trade*, London, 1980, for general accounts of Asante metal casting.

35 Bowdich, p.312.

Chapter 6
The court and regalia

1 T.E. Bowdich, *Mission from Cape Coast Castle to Ashante*, London, 1819, p.279.

2 Winwood Reade, *The Story of the Ashantee Campaign*, London, 1874, p.270.

3 For details see I. Wilks, *Ashante in the Nineteenth Century*, Cambridge, 1975, p.202.

4 See W.E.F. Ward's introduction to the reprint of Bowdich, London, 1966.

5 See Wilks, 1975, pp.202–4.

6 *Asante Seminar*, 4, Evanston, Illinois, 1976, pp.42–3.

7 John William Blake, *Europeans in West Africa 1450–1560*, Hakluyt Society, vol.2, London, 1942, p.379.

8 Purchas, *His Pilgrimes*, Hakluyt Society, VI, Glasgow, 1895, p.307.

9 Thomas Astley, *A New General Collection of Voyages and Travels*, London, 1745–7, p.398.

10 Blake, 1942, p.379, and William Bosman, *A New and Accurate Description of the Coast of Guinea*, London, 1705, p.128.

11 Bosman, p.185.

12 ibid., pp.188,194.

13 Astley, p.423.

14 See Rene A. Bravmann, 'The state sword – a pre-Ashanti tradition', *Ghana Notes and Queries*, 10, Legon, 1968, and A. Van Dantzig, 'A note on "The state sword – a pre-Ashanti tradition"', *Ghana Notes and Queries*, 11, Legon, 1970.

15 Bowdich, p.35.

16 Joseph Dupuis, *Journal of a Residence in Ashantee*, London, 1824, p.74.

17 W. Huydecoper, *Diary*, trans. G. Irwin, Legon, 1962, pp.2,15,19,23.

18 Dupuis, p.59.

19 Governor Winniet, 'Journey to Kumasi', National Archives, Accra, vol.ADM 1/2/4, 1848.

20 F.A. Ramseyer and J. Kuhne, *Four Years in Ashante*, New York, 1875, p.53.

21 Kumasi Mss, p.210.

22 Francis Agbodeka, *African Politics and British Policy in the Gold Coast 1868–1900*, London, 1971, p.87.

23 A.A.Y. Kyerematen, *Panoply of Ghana*, London, 1964, p.36.

24 Bowdich, p.298.

25 Bowdich, p.59.

26 A.A.Y. Kyerematen, 'Ashanti Royal Regalia: Their History and Function', D.Phil. dissertation, Oxford, 1966, p.380.

27 Bowdich, p.312.

28 See D. Ross, 'The iconography of Asante sword ornaments', *African Arts*, XI, 1, Los Angeles, 1977.

29 T.B. Freeman, *Journal of Various Visits to the Kingdom of Ashanti, Aku and Dahomi in Western Africa*, London, 1844, pp.53,122.

30 W. Tordoff, *Ashanti under the Prempehs 1888–1935*, London, 1965, p.223.

31 Kyerematen, 1966, pp.130,211,260.

32 Joseph Ageyman-Duah, 'Asante stool histories', Institute of African Studies, Legon, n.d., nos.23,59,66,75,125.

33 Astley, p.451.

34 J. Atkins, *A Voyage to Guinea, Brasil and the West Indies*, London, 1735, p.100.

35 W. J. Mueller, *Die Africanische auf der Guineischen Gold-Cust gelegene Landschafft Fetu*, Hamburg, 1673, p.103.

36 Dennis Kemp, *Nine Years at the Gold Coast*, London, 1898, p.72.

37 W.W. Claridge, *A History of the Gold Coast and Ashanti*, London, 1915, vol.1, p.205.

38 H.W. Daendels, *Journal and Correspondence*, Pt 1, ed. E. Collins, Legon, 1964, p.61.

39 Huydecoper, p.22.

40 Daendels, pp.140,160.

41 ibid., pp.105,106.

42 ibid., p.264.

43 Bowdich, p.104.

44 See Bowdich, pl.2.

45 R. Lee, *The African Wanderers: or, the Adventures of Carlos and Antonio*, London, 1847, p.333.

46 Brodie Cruickshank, *Eighteen Years on the Gold Coast of Africa*, London, 1853, vol.1, p.256, and John Beecham, *Ashantee and the Gold Coast*, London, 1841, p.113.

47 Frederick Boyle, *Through Fanteeland to Coomassie*, London, 1874, p.139

48 Ramseyer and Kuhne, p.85.

49 Marcus Allen, *The Gold Coast*, London, 1874, p.73, and R.F. Burton and V.L. Cameron, *To the Gold Coast for Gold*, London, 1883, vol.2, pp.99–100.

50 Prints of these pictures are now lodged in several places including the Foreign and Commonwealth Office Library, London, and Rhodes House Library, Oxford.

51 See, for example, photographs in F.C. Fuller, *A Vanished Dynasty Ashanti*, London, 1921, and R.S. Rattray, *Religion and Art in Ashanti*, Oxford, 1927, fig.48.

52 Rattray, 1927, p.279.

53 Bowdich, pp.36,39.

54 H.M. Cole and D. Ross, *The Arts of Ghana*, Los Angeles, 1978, p.153.

55 Bosman, p.185.

56 Purchas, p.307.

57 Astley, p.423.

58 Duarte Pacheo Pereira, *Esmeraldo de Situ Orbis*, trans. and ed. G.H.T. Kimble, Hakluyt Society, London, 1937, p.120.

59 Roger Barlow, *A Brief Summe of Geographie*, ed. E.G.R. Taylor, London, 1932, p.106.

60 Blake, p.206.

61 Bosman, p.136.

62 Marion Johnson, 'Ekyem, the state shield', *Akan-Asante Studies*, British Museum Occasional Papers, No 3, London, 1979.

63 Cruickshank, p.64.

64 *Asantesem*, 9, Evanston, Illinois, 1978, p.45.

65 *Asantesem*, 5, 1976, pp. 26–8, illuminates the Asante view.

66 R.F. Burton and V.L. Cameron, *To the Gold Coast for Gold*, London, 1883, pp.319–20.

67 Public Record Office, file no.879/18, 232, 29 Jan–21 July, 1881.

68 Rattray, 1927, figs.154,155,157.

69 Bowdich, p.34.

70 Photographs now in the Foreign and Commonwealth Office Library, London.

71 Rattray, 1927, p.130.

72 J.G. Christaller, *A Collection of three thousand six hundred Tshi Proverbs*, Basle, 1879, no.956.

73 Bowdich, p.237.

74 Rattray, 1927, p.130.

Chapter 7
Stools and chairs

1 John William Blake, *Europeans in West Africa 1450–1560*, Hakluyt Society, vol.1, London, 1942, p.73.

2 R.S. Rattray, *Religion and Art in Ashanti*, Oxford, 1927, pp.272–3.

3 T.E. Bowdich, *Mission from Cape Coast Castle to Ashantee*, London, 1819, p.313.

4 Bowdich, p.36.

5 A.A.Y. Kyerematen, *Panoply of Ghana*, London, 1964, p.24.

6 For the religious aspect of stools see P.K. Sarpong, *The Sacred Stools of the Akan*, Tema, 1971. For other aspects see Sharon Patton, 'The stool and Asante chieftaincy', *African Arts*, XIII, 1, Los Angeles, 1979.

7 Bowdich, p.39.

8 See I. Wilks, *Asante in the Nineteenth Century*, Cambridge, 1975, ch.12, *passim*, for this period.

9 John Beecham, *Ashantee and the Gold Coast*, London, 1841, p.146.

10 Kyerematen, 1964, p.22.

11 M.D. McLeod, 'A note on an Asante royal chair of Iberian origin', *Akan-Asante Studies*, British Museum Occasional Papers No. 3, London, 1979.

Chapter 8
Gold-weights

1 For the possible evolution of weight forms see Timothy F. Garrard, *Akan Weights and the Gold Trade*, London, 1980, *passim*.

2 ibid., pp.24–6.

3 Bowdich, p.228.

4 See Garrard, 1980, *passim*, for possible chronologies of weights.

5 ibid., chs.7,8.

6 A.D. Hewson, 'New Developments in Statistical Quantum Theory', British Museum Research Laboratory, London, 1978.

7 M.D. McLeod, 'Akan gold-weights and imports: a note on carriages', *Akan-Asante Studies*, British Museum Occasional Papers No 3, London, 1979.

Chapter 9
Brass vessels

1 R.S. Rattray, *Ashanti*, Oxford, 1923, p.9.

2 Rattray, 1923, pp.313–15, and Roy Sieber, 'African Art and Culture History', *Reconstructing African Culture History*, eds. C. Gabel and N. Bennett, Boston, 1967.

3 William Bosman, *A New and Accurate Description of the Coast of Guinea*, London, 1705, p.128.

4 R.S. Rattray, *Religion and Art in Ashanti*, Oxford, 1927, p.53.

5 M.D. McLeod, 'Three important royal kuduo', *Akan-Asante Studies*, British Museum Occasional Papers No 3, London, 1979.

Chapter 10
Clothing and cloth

1 F.A. Ramseyer and J. Kuhne, *Four Years in Ashantee*, New York, 1875, p.163.

2 T.E. Bowdich, *Mission from Cape Coast Castle to Ashantee*, London, 1819, p.32.

3 ibid., p.272.

4 ibid., p.97.

5 ibid., p.272.

6 Information in papers left by Sir Cecil Armitage, now in the Museum of Mankind.

7 R.S. Rattray, *Religion and Art in Ashanti*, Oxford, 1927, pp.134,220.

8 Bowdich, p.310.

9 Kumasi MSS, p.151.

10 Rattray, 1927, pp.264–8.

11 H.W. Daendels, *Journal and Correspondence*, Pt 1, ed. E. Collins, Legon, 1964, p.64; and W. Huydecoper, *Diary*, trans. G. Irwin, Legon, 1962, p.53.

12 Bowditch, pp.122–3.

13 ibid., p.85.

14 ibid, p.124.

15 Joseph Dupuis, *Journal of a Residence in Ashantee*, London, 1824, p.93.

16 Bowdich, p.122.

17 Shown in a photograph taken in 1885.

18 For general discussions of Asante weaving see B. Menzel, *Textilien aus Westafrika*, Berlin, 1972–3, and Venice Lamb, *West African Weaving*, London, 1975.

19 Rattray, 1927, pp.236–50.

20 Bowdich, p.259 (footnote).

Chaper 11
Pottery

1 See R.S. Rattray, *Religion and Art in Ashanti*, Oxford, 1927, pp.295–308 for a general account of pottery making.

2 William Bosman, *A New and Accurate Description of the Coast of Guinea*, London, 1705, p.232; Purchas, *His Pilgrimes*, Hakluyt Society, VI, Glasgow, 1895, pp.346–7.

3 Brodie Cruickshank, *Eighteen Years on the Gold Coast of Africa*, London, 1853, vol.2, pp.270–1.

4 See Roy Sieber, 'Kwahu terracottas, oral traditions and Ghanaian history', *African Art and Leadership*, eds. D. Fraser and H.M. Cole, Madison, 1972, and 'Art and history in Ghana', *Primitive Art and Society*, ed. A. Forge, London, 1973.

Chapter 12
Wood-carvings

1 See R.S. Rattray, *Religion and Art in Ashanti*, Oxford, 1927, figs.194,195, p.281.

2 Based on the author's field inquiries in 1967 and 1972.

3 See K. Ameyaw, 'Funerary effigies from Kwahu', 'A wooden doll from Kwahu', *Ghana Notes and Queries*, 8, Legon, 1966.

4 Author's field research 1965–7.

5 See J.G. Christaller, *A Dictionary of the Asante and Fante Language called Tschi*, 2nd edn, Basle, 1933, entry for *akua*, p.267.

6 ibid., p.267.

7 ibid., p.447.

8 Rattray, 1927, p.6.

9 T.E. Bowdich, *Mission from Cape Coast Castle to Ashantee*, London, 1819, p.312.

10 See Rattray, 1927, p.270–1.

11 Rattray, 1927, p.60.

Chapter 13
The role of the image

1 See Dennis M. Warren and J. Kweku Andrews, *An Ethno-Scientific Approach to Akan Art and Aesthetics*, Philadelphia, 1977, *passim*.

2 T.E. Bowdich, *Mission from Cape Coast Castle to Ashantee*, London, 1819, pp.30,32.

3 See, for example, J.G. Christaller's collection, *A Collection of three thousand six hundred Tshi Proverbs*, Basle, 1879.

4 R.S. Rattray, *Ashanti Proverbs*, Oxford, 1916, no.199.

5 ibid., no.152.

6 ibid., no.257.

7 ibid, no.402.

8 A.E. Ellis, *The Land of Fetish*, London, 1883, pp.289–90.

9 *Asante Seminar*, 3, Evanston, Illinois, 1975, pp.19–20.

Bibliography

Agbodeka, Francis *African Politics and British Policy in the Gold Coast 1868–1900*, London, 1971

Ageyman-Duah, Joseph 'The Ceremony of Enstoolment of the Asantehene', *Ghana Notes and Queries*, 7, Legon, 1965

Akrofi, C.A. *Twi Mmebusem/Twi Proverbs*, Accra, n.d.

Allen, Marcus *The Gold Coast*, London, 1874

Ameyaw, K. 'Funerary effigies from Kwahu', 'A wooden doll from Kwahu', *Ghana Notes and Queries*, 8, Legon, 1966

Anti, A.A. *The Ancient Asante King*, Accra, n.d.

Antubam, Kofi *Ghana's Heritage of Culture*, Leipzig, 1963

Appiah, P. 'Akan symbolism', *African Arts*, XIII, 1, Los Angeles, 1979

Arhin, Kwame
'The modern craftsman', *Ghana Notes and Queries*, 8, Legon, 1966
'The financing of the Ashanti expansion (1700–1820)', *Africa*, XXXVII, 3, London, 1967
'The structure of greater Ashanti (1700–1824)', *Journal of African History*, VIII, 1, London, 1967

Arkell, J. 'Gold Coast copies of fifth–sixth century bronze lamps', *Antiquity*, 24, London, 1950

Armitage, C.H. and Montanaro, A.F. *The Ashanti Campaign of 1900*, London, 1901

Asante Seminar, 1–6, *Asantesɛm* 7–11, Evanston, Illinois, 1975–1980

Assimeng, Max J. (ed.) *Traditional Life, Culture and Literature in Ghana*, Buffalo, 1976

Astley, Thomas *A New General Collection of Voyages and Travels*, London, 1745–7

Atkins, J. *A Voyage to Guinea, Brasil and the East Indies*, London, 1735

Barbot, J. *A Description of the Coasts of North and South Guinea*, London, 1732

Barlow, Roger *A Brief Summe of Geographie*, ed. E.G.R. Taylor, London, 1932

Bassing, A. *European-Inspired Akan Goldweights*, Occasional Papers, National Museum, Accra, 1970

Bassing, A. and Kyerematen, A.A.Y. 'The enstoolment of an Asantehene', *African Arts*, V, 3, Los Angeles, 1972

Beecham, John *Ashantee and the Gold Coast*, London, 1841

Blake, John William *Europeans in West Africa 1450–1560*, Hakluyt Society, 2 vols, London, 1941–2

Boahen, Adu 'The origins of the Akan', *Ghana Notes and Queries*, 9, Legon, 1966

Boser-Sarivaxevanis, R. *Textilhandwerk in West Africa*, Basle, 1973

Bosman, William *A New and Accurate Description of the Coast of Guinea*, London, 1705

Bowdich, T.E.
Mission from Cape Coast Castle to Ashantee, London, 1819
An Essay on the superstitions, customs and arts, common to the ancient Egyptians, Abyssinians and Ashantees, Paris, 1821

Boyle, Frederick *Through Fanteeland to Coomassie*, London, 1874

Brackenbury, H. *The Ashanti War*, 2 vols, Edinburgh and London, 1874

Braunholtz, H.J. and Wild, R.P. 'Notes on two pottery heads from near Fomena, Ashanti', *Man*, XXXIV, 2, London, 1934

Bravmann, Rene A.
'The state sword – a pre-Ashanti tradition', *Ghana Notes and Queries*, 10, Legon, 198
'The diffusion of Ashanti political art', *African Art and Leadership*, eds. D. Fraser and H.M. Cole, Madison, 1972
Islam and Tribal Art in West Africa, Cambridge, 1974

Brinkworth, I. 'Ashanti art in London: the Wallace Collection', *West African Review*, London, 1960

Burton, R.F. and Cameron, V.L. *To the Gold Coast for Gold*, 2 vols., London, 1883

Busia, Kofi A.
The Position of the Chief in the Modern Political System of Ashanti, London, 1951
'The Ashanti', *African Worlds*, ed. D. Forde, London, 1954

Butler, W. *Akim Foo*, London, 1875

Calvocoressi, D. 'European trade pipes in Ghana', *West African Journal of Archaeology*, Legon, 1975

Christaller, J.G.
A Collection of three thousand and six hundred Tshi Proverbs, Basle, 1879
A Dictionary of the Asante and Fante Language called Tschi, 2nd edn, Basle, 1933

Churchill, A. *A Collection of Voyages and Travels*, London, 1704

Claridge, W.W. *A History of the Gold Coast and Ashanti*, 2 vols., London, 1915

Cole, H.M.
'The art and festival in Ghana', *African Arts*, VIII, 3, Los Angeles, 1975
'Artistic and communicative values of beads in Kenya and Ghana', *The Bead Journal*, 1, 3, Los Angeles, 1975
'Art studies in Ghana', *African Arts*, XIII, 1, Los Angeles, 1979

Cole, H.M. and Ross, D. *The Arts of Ghana*, Los Angeles, 1978

Coronel, P.C. 'Aowin terracotta sculpture', *African Arts*, XIII, 1, Los Angeles, 1979

Crane, C.R. *The Voyages of Cadamosto*, Hakluyt Society, London, 1937

Crooks, J.J. *Records Relating to the Gold Coast Settlements from 1750–1874*, Dublin, 1923

Cruickshank, Brodie *Eighteen Years on the Gold Coast of Africa*, 2 vols., London, 1853

Daaku, K.Y. *Trade and Politics on the Gold Coast 1600–1720*, London, 1970

Daendels, H.W. *Journal and Correspondence*, Pt 1, ed. E. Collins, Legon, 1964

Dapper, D.O. *Description de l'Afrique*, Amsterdam, 1686

Davies, O.
'A West African stool with gold overlay', *Annals of the Natal Museum*, 20, 3, Natal, 1971
Archaeology in Ghana, London, 1961

Delange, J. 'Un kuduo exceptional', *Objets et Mondes*, 5, Paris, 1965

Dickson, K.B. *A Historical Geography of Ghana*, Cambridge, 1969

Donne, J.B. 'The Celia Barclay Collection of African art', *The Connoisseur*, 180, London, 1972

Duncan, John   *Travels in Western Africa in 1845 and 1846*, 2 vols., London, 1847

Dupuis, Joseph   *Journal of a Residence in Ashantee*, London, 1824

Ellis, A.E.   *The Land of Fetish*, London, 1883

Fagg, W.   'A golden ram head from Ashanti', *Man*, LIV, 20, London, 1954

Field, M.J.   *Search for Security: An Ethno-psychiatric Study of Rural Ghana*, London, 1960

Fischer, E. and Himmelheber, H.   *Das Gold in der Kunst West-afrikas*, Zurich, 1975

Fortes, Meyer   *Kinship and the Social Order*, Chicago, 1969

Fraser, Douglas   'The symbols of Ashanti kingship', *African Art and Leadership*, eds. D. Fraser and H.M. Cole, Madison, 1972

Freeman, R. Austin   *Travels and Life in Ashanti and Jaman*, London, 1898

Freeman, T.B.
Journal of Two Visits to the Kingdom of Ashanti, London, 1843
Journal of Various Visits to the Kingdoms of Ashanti, Aku and Dahomi in Western Africa, London, 1844

Fuller, F.C.   *A Vanished Dynasty Ashanti*, London, 1921

Fynn, J.K.   *Asante and Its Neighbours 1700–1807*, London, 1971

Garrard, Timothy F.
'Studies in Akan goldweights, pts 1–4', *Transactions of the Historical Society of Ghana*, XIII–XIV, Legon, 1972–3
'Akan metal arts', *African Arts*, XIII, 1, Los Angeles, 1979
Akan Weights and the Gold Trade, London, 1980

Ghana Museum and Monuments Board   *Clay Figures used in Funeral Ceremonies*, Accra, n.d.

Goody, J.   'The Mande and the Akan Hinterland', *The Historian in Tropical Africa*, eds. J. Vansina, R. Mauny and L.V. Thomas, London, 1964

Gordon, Charles Alexander   *Life on the Gold Coast*, London, 1874

Gros, J.   *Voyages, aventures et captivité de J. Bonnat chez les Achantis*, Paris, 1884

Hinderling, P.   'Three human figures from near Kumasi, Ghana', *Man*, LXI, 425, London, 1961

Hugot, H.J.   'Un vase en bronze d'origine inconnue', *Notes africaines*, 87, Dakar, 1960

Hutchison, T.J.   *Impressions of West Africa*, Plymouth, 1858

Huydecoper, W.   *Diary*, trans. G. Irwin, Legon, 1962

Isert, P.E.   *Voyages en Guinée et dans les Iles Caraibes en Amérique*, Paris, 1973

Johnson, Marion
'M. Bonnat on the Volta', *Ghana Notes and Queries*, 10, Legon, 1968
'Ashanti, Juaben and M. Bonnat', *Transactions of the Historical Society of Ghana*, XII, Legon, 1971
'Ashanti craft organisation', *African Arts*, XIII, 1, Los Angeles, 1979
'Ekyem, the state shield', *Akan-Asante Studies*, British Museum Occasional Papers No. 3, London, 1979

de Joinville, Prince   *Memoirs*, London, 1895

Kemp, Dennis   *Nine years at the Gold Coast*, London, 1898

Kjersmeier, C.
Ashanti Goldweights in the National Museum, Copenhagen, 1941
Ashanti-Vaegtlodder, Copenhagen, 1948

Kyerematen, A.A.Y.
Daasebre Osei Tutu Ageyman Prempeh II, Kumase, n.d.
Kingship and Ceremony in Ashanti, Kumase, n.d.
Panoply of Ghana, London, 1964
'Ashanti Royal Regalia: Their History and Function', D.Phil dissertation, Oxford, 1966
'The royal stools of Ashanti', *Africa*, XXXIX, 1, London, 1969

Lamb, Venice   *West African Weaving*, London, 1975

Lee, R.   *The African Wanderers: or, the Adventures of Carlos and Antonio*, London, 1847

Lewin, Thomas J.   *Asante before the British*, Lawrence, Kansas, 1979

Lystad, R.A.   *The Ashanti – A Proud People*, New Brunswick, 1958

McCaskie, T.C.   'Innovational eclecticism: the Asante empire and Europe in the nineteenth century', *Comparative Studies in Society and History*, XIV, 1, London, 1972

McLeod, M.D.
'Aspects of African art', *Poro '75*, Milan, 1975
'Verbal elements in West African art', *Quaderni Poro*, Milan, 1976
'T.E. Bowdich: an early collector in West Africa', *Collectors and Collections, The British Museum Yearbook 2*, ed. R. Camber, London, 1977
'Aspects of Asante images', *Art in Society*, eds. M. Greenhalgh and V. Megaw, London, 1978
'Asante spokesmen's staffs: their probable origin and development', 'A note on an Asante royal chair of Iberian origin', 'Akan gold-weights and imports: a note on carriages', 'Three important royal kuduo', *Akan-Asante Studies*, British Museum Occasional Papers No. 3, London, 1979
'Music and gold-weights in Asante', *Music and Civilization, The British Museum Yearbook 4*, ed. T.C. Mitchell, London, 1980

de Marees, P.   'A description and historical declaration of the golden kingdom of Guinea', Purchas, *His Pilgrimes*, Hakluyt Society, VI, Glasgow, 1895

Menzel, B.
Goldgewichte aus Ghana, Berlin, 1968
Textilien aus Westafrika, Berlin, 1972–3

Metcalfe, G.E.   *MacLean of the Gold Coast*, London, 1962

Meyerowitz, E.L.R.
The Sacred State of the Akan, London, 1951
Akan Traditions of Origin, London, 1952
The Divine Kingship and Ghana and Ancient Egypt, London, 1960
The Early History of the Akan States of Ghana, London, 1974

Mueller, W.J.   *Die Africanische auf der Guineischen Gold-Cust gelegene Landschafft Fetu*, Hamburg, 1673

Nketia, J.H.K.
Funeral Dirges of the Akan People, London, 1955
Drumming in Akan Communities of Ghana, London, 1963

Opoku, A.A.   *Festivals of Ghana*, Accra, 1970

Ott, A.   'Akan gold weights', *Transactions of the Historical Society of Ghana*, IX, Legon, 1968

Ozanne, P.C.   Review article of the book *Excavation at Dawu*, *Transactions of the Historical Society of Ghana*, VI, Legon, 1962

Patton, S.F.   'The stool and Asante chieftaincy', *African Arts*, XIII, 1, Los Angeles, 1979

Paulme, D.
'Les poids – proverbes de la Côte d'Ivoire au Museé de l'Homme', *Journal de la Societé des Africanistes*, 11, 5, Paris, 1941
'Apropos des Kuduo Ashanti' *Presence Africaine*, 10, 11, Paris, 1951

Pereira, Duarte Pacheco   *Esmeraldo de Situ Orbis*, trans. and ed. G.H.T. Kimble, Hakluyt Society, London, 1937

Perregaux, E.   'Chez les Achanti', *Bulletin de la Société neuch-ateloise de Geographie*, XVII, Neuchatel, 1906

Posnansky, M.
'Archaeology and the origins of Akan society', *History of Ghana*, ed. M. Dodds, Accra, 1974
'Dating Ghana's earliest art', *African Arts*, XIII, 1, Los Angeles, 1979

Priddy, B.   'Some terracotta figures in the Ghana National Museum', *Figurative Art in Ghana*, Occasional Papers, Accra, 1970

Priestley, M.A. and Wilks, I.
'English gifts for the king of Ashanti in the eighteenth century', *Ghana Notes and Queries*, 2, Legon, 1961
'The Ashanti kings in the eighteenth century: a revise chronology', *The Journal of African History*, I, 1, London, 1960

Prussin, Labelle 'Traditional Asante architecture', *African Arts*, XIII, 2, Los Angeles, 1980

Purchas, *His Pilgrimes*, Hakluyt Society, VI, Glasgow, 1895

Quarcoo, A.K.
The Language of Adinkra Patterns, Legon, 1972
Leadership Art, Legon, 1975

Ramseyer, F.A. and Kuhne, J. *Four Years in Ashantee*, New York, 1875

Rattray, R.S.
Ashanti Proverbs, Oxford, 1916
Ashanti, Oxford, 1923
Religion and Art in Ashanti, Oxford, 1927
Ashanti Law and Constitution, Oxford, 1929
A Short Manual of the Gold Coast, London, 1924

Reade, Winwood *The Story of the Ashantee Campaign*, London, 1874

Reindorf, C.C. *The History of the Gold Coast and Asante*, 2nd edn, Basle, n.d.

Ricketts, H.J. *Narrative of the Ashantee War*, London, 1831

Romer, L.F. *The Coast of Guinea*, trans. K. Bertelsen, Legon, 1965

Ross, D.
'Ghanaian forowa', *African Arts*, VIII, 1, Los Angeles, 1974
'The iconography of Asante sword ornaments', *African Arts*, XI, 1, Los Angeles, 1977

Sarpong, P.K.
'The sacred stools of the Ashanti', *Anthropos*, 26, 1–2, Salzburg, 1967
The Sacred Stools of the Akan, Tema, 1971
Ghana in Retrospect: Some Aspects of Ghanaian Culture, Accra, 1974

Shaw, C.T. *Excavation at Dawu*, London, 1961

Sieber, Roy
'African art and culture history', *Reconstructing African Culture History*, eds. C. Gabel and N. Bennett, Boston, 1967
'Kwahu terracottas, oral traditions and Ghanaian history', *African Art and Leadership*, eds. D. Fraser and H.M. Cole, Madison, 1972
'Art and history in Ghana', *Primitive Art and Society*, ed. A. Forge, London, 1973

Smith, E.W. *Aggrey of Africa*, London, 1929

Smith, S.C. 'Kente cloth motifs', *African Arts*, IX, 1, Los Angeles, 1975

Stanley, Henry M. *Coomassie and Magdala, The Story of Two Campaigns*, London, n.d.

Swithebank, M. *Ashanti Fetish Houses*, Accra, 1969

Tenkorang, S. 'The importance of firearms in the struggle between Ashanti and the coastal states', *Transactions of the Historical Society of Ghana*, IX, Legon, 1968

Thomas, N.W. 'Ashanti and Baule gold-weights', *Journal of the Royal Anthropological Institute*, 50, London, 1920

Thomassey, P. *Autour des poids d'or Ashanti-Baoule*, Première Conférence Internationale des Africanistes de l'Ouest, Abijan, 1951

Tordoff, W. *Ashanti under the Prempehs 1888–1935*, London, 1965

Valentin, P. 'Les Pipes en Terre des Ashanti', *Arts d'Afrique Noire*, 19, Villiers-les-Bel, 1976

Van Dantzig, A. 'A note on "The state sword – a pre-Ashanti tradition"', *Ghana Notes and Queries*, 11, Legon, 1970

Ward, W.E.F. *A History of Ghana*, 2nd edn, London, 1958

Warren, Dennis M.
'Bono royal regalia', *African Arts*, VIII, 2, Los Angeles, 1975
'Bono state art', *African Arts*, IX, 2, Los Angeles, 1976

Warren, Dennis M. and Andrews, J. Kweku *An Ethno-Scientific Approach to Akan Art and Aesthetics*, Philadelphia, 1977

Wild, R.P.
'Funerary equipment from Agona-Swedru, Winnebah district, Gold Coast', *Journal of the Royal Anthropological Institute*, 67, London, 1937
'A method of bead-making practised on the Gold Coast', *Man*, XXXIX, 17, London, 1937

Wilks, I.
The Northern Factor in Ashanti History, Legon, 1961
Asante in the Nineteenth Century, Cambridge, 1975
'Land, labour, capital, and the forest kingdom of Asante: a model of early change', *The Evolution of Social Systems*, ed. M.J. Rowlands and J. Friedman, London, 1977

Wolseley, Garnet *The Story of a Soldier's life*, London, 1903

Zeller, R. 'Die Goldgewichte von Asante', *Baessler-Archiv*, 3, Basle, 1972

Bibliographies

Amedekay, E.Y. *The Culture of Ghana: A Bibliography*, Accra, 1970

Cardinall, A.W. *A Bibliography of the Gold Coast*, Accra, 1932

Johnson, A.F. *A Bibliography of Ghana 1930–1961*, Evanston, Illinois, 1964

Sampson, A. Andrews *Ashanti and Brong-Ahafo: An Annotated Bibliography*, Michigan, 1967

Glossary

The Asante words in this glossary are arranged alphabetically according to the initial letter of their root; prefixes such as o, e and a are ignored. Thus, for example, the word *ǫbosom* is listed under B and not O, and the word *ohene* is listed under H and not O.

abampuruwa: small metal box for holding gold-dust.

batakari: cotton smock from northern Ghana.

Bakakari Kęse: the Great Batakari, a protective talismanic smock worn by senior chiefs.

ǫbayifo (pl. *abayifo*): 'witch', someone with the power to harm mystically.

ębę: proverb.

mmębusęm (pl.): witty sayings, proverbs, aphorisms.

obosom (pl. *abosom*): god, power, divinity.

bradan: simple hut at edge of a village, occupied by menstruating women.

bragoro: (lit. 'the menstruation play'), nubility rite performed for girls after their first menstruation.

abrono: quarter or division in a town.

abusua: matrilineal descent group.

abusua kęse: great matrilineal clan.

abusua kuruwa: family cup or pot.

dabone (pl. *nnabone*): a 'bad' day in the forty-two-day cycle of days, on which rites are performed for ancestors and gods.

adae: the two main 'bad' days on which rites to gods and ancestors are performed. These two *adae* are *Wukudae*, Wednesday *adae*, and *Kwessidae*, Sunday *adae*.

odekuro: village headman or chief.

adaka: box or chest.

Adaka Kęse: the Asantehene's Great Chest, used for storing reserves of gold-dust.

aduro: medicine, herbal or otherwise, eaten, injected or applied to the skin.

dwa: stool.

famfa: scoop used in removing impurities from gold-dust.

afena: large sword.

efie: house, dwelling-place.

fotoǫ: bundle containing gold-weighing equipment.

forowa (pl. *mforowa*): vessel constructed from sheet brass, usually used for keeping vegetable oil pomade.

gyadua (pl. *gyannua*): tree grown in towns to provide shade and to express the place's firm foundation.

hwędǫm: large chair copied from a European prototype.

hyire: white clay used for decorating buildings and applied to the body to show innocence and purity.

akoṇṇua (pl. *nkoṇṇua*): stool, synonym for office.

kente: woven cloth distinguished by its complex patterns and, generally, many colours.

okǫmfoǫ (pl. *akǫmfo*): priest possessed by a god (*ǫbosom*).

okra: soul, also used for junior royal servants, 'the King's creatures'.

akua'ba (pl. *akua'mma*): small human figure in wood, metal or clay.

kuduo: cast-brass vessel.

akuraa: temporary encampment in the bush.

okrom: village, town.

okyeame (pl. *akyeame*): chief's spokesman or 'linguist'.

oman: state, large political unit.

mmramoǫ (pl. *abramoǫ*): gold-weight.

'Nyame: the supreme god, also known by other names, for example, Nyankupon, Otweaduampon.

'Nyame'dua: God's tree, a small altar made of a bowl in the branches of a tree.

saawa: spoon, especially for use with gold-dust.

Asantehene: King of all Asante.

nsania (pl.): scales for weighing gold-dust.

ǫsese: small, temporary hut.

asipim: brass nail-decorated chair, copied from a European prototype.

sumaṇ (pl. *asumaṇ*): 'fetish', combinations of objects and substance believed to have particular powers to affect events.

sunsuṃ: spirit, soul, essence.

tano (pl. *atano*): a major god, after the river Tano.

ntwuma: deep red clay used to decorate buildings, applied to the body to show grief and anger.

wura'm: forest or bush.

Index